God and People:

The Social Laws and Social System Underlying Judaism, Christianity, Islam and Democracy

God and People:

The Social Laws and Social System Underlying Judaism, Christianity, Islam and Democracy

Manfred Davidmann

Dear Carmela and Karim

We are grateful for all your help and support in what we are trying to achieve — thank you very much. With best wishes from Manfred and Angelika

7. 8. 2011

Social Organisation Limited

Published by Social Organisation Limited
PO Box 61
Stanmore, Middlesex
HA7 4PU
Great Britain

ISBN 978-0-85192-054-2

This book is a collection of works by Manfred Davidmann about the God-given human rights, social laws and social system, and about the worldwide struggle to achieve them, to achieve freedom, liberty, independence and a good and secure life, here and now in this life.

Manfred Davidmann not only proves the meaning and intent of Genesis, the first volume of the Pentateuch, but also exposes the mistranslations and political misrepresentations of the past. For example he establishes the meaning of the names of God which 'had been lost'. Clearly described and defined is the role of the family under modern conditions, and the differences between the behaviour of human beings and that of the primitive animals from which human beings evolved.

Printed and bound in Germany: Druckerei C. H. Beck, Nördlingen

CONTENTS

I am glad to have this opportunity of expressing my sincere thanks to Dr. Angelika Schaumberg. Without her continuing support, encouragement and help, this book might never have been compiled.

Chapter 1

Overview

This book consists of consecutive free-standing chapters, is a collection of works by Manfred Davidmann which state and describe the God-given human rights, social laws and social system. It defines and illustrates the worldwide struggle to achieve them, to achieve freedom, liberty, independence and a good and secure life, here and now in this life.

The chapters and their sections follow each other in an intended sequence in which each is aiding and contributing to understanding the other chapters.

Manfred Davidmann, for example, not only proves the meaning and intent of Genesis, the first volume of the Pentateuch, but also exposes the mistranslations and political misrepresentations of the past. For example he establishes the meaning of the names of God which 'had been lost'. Clearly described and defined is the role of the family under modern conditions, and the differences between the behaviour of human beings and that of the primitive animals from which human beings evolved.

The main chapters are:

1. Overview
2. The Real World in which We Live
3. The God-given Human Rights, Social Laws and Social System
4. Struggle for Freedom, Liberty and Independence: The Social Cause-and-Effect Relationship
5. Family and Community: Family, Sex and the Individual
6. The Meaning of Genesis
7. About the Author

2 The Real World in which We Live

The life we lead, the real world in which we live, is changing at an accelerating pace. And the quality of our lives is changing accordingly, for better or worse depending on how we behave towards each other.

At this point of time we still have not learned the lessons of the past. Too often do we still behave like pre-human apes instead of behaving like human beings, ignoring the resulting suffering and pain being caused.

So we start by looking at the way in which we live and have organized our lives, looking at the reality behind smokescreens, white-washing euphemisms and empty vague and meaningless excuses and phrases.

2.1   The Social Costs of Unemployment

The effects of uncontrolled trade between low-wage and high-wage countries ('outsourcing' or 'globalisation'), are the increasing unemployment and falling living standards in high-wage countries.

Unemployment has reached an unacceptable level. It is a principle of economics that social costs have to be paid by those causing them. And this applies equally well to the social costs of redundancy and unemployment when transferring operations to countries with lower wages or fewer environmental safeguards.

But manufacturers and suppliers tend to increase their profits by passing on to the community the social costs of their operations, costs such as disposal of packaging and waste, or of polluting, or of redundancy and unemployment caused by them.

2.2   Bureaucracy and The Meaning of Democracy

What needs to be stressed is that in a participative (democratic) organisation policies are decided by a well-informed population at the level of the population and that policies then become binding on management or government.

In an authoritarian organisation, the policy decisions are taken at the top or near the top by the hierarchy (establishment) and are binding on the organisation's members. Decision-taking at the top is sometimes referred to as 'deciding centrally'. Authoritarian organisation is the opposite of democracy and underlies dictatorship.

So what we see is conflict between authoritarian minds wishing to dominate, control and exploit on the one hand and, on the other hand, citizens wishing to maintain and improve the standard of living and quality of life for the population as a whole.

2.3   Multinational (Global) Operations, and Government Of, By, and For the People

How individuals in responsible positions or authority, in local and national government, are managing our affairs on our behalf and for us, is of crucial importance to every citizen.

Government has to make ends meet, has to bring about a rising standard of secure living, social security and an increasing quality of life for its citizens. There can be ups and downs but, says Manfred Davidmann, "failure to make ends meet is just as directly and surely the result of bad leadership and management as it is in any commercial enterprise."

This is a severe criticism also of the kind of experts and consultants used, and of the way they are used. "The quality of one's experts and whether and how their expertise is used, and applied, are of decisive importance."

In 1996, for example, Manfred Davidmann pointed out that imports were now being priced at what the market will bear, or just under. The enormous profit margins then cause production to move from high-wage to low-wage countries. The consequence is a lowering of standard of living in high-wage countries to that in low-wage countries, instead of raising the standard of living in low-wage countries to that in high wage countries. {1}

It is an accepted principle of economics, that the social costs of an enterprise's operations have to be paid by the enterprise, expressed by the maxim 'The polluter pays'. In other words, the social costs of unemployment have to be paid by the enterprise which caused the unemployment. {2}

However, multinationals tend to regard profit as the sole consideration, regardless of the consequences to the community, regardless of the cost to people. Instead of producing more effectively and competitively at home, owners and directors find it easier and more profitable to import from low-wage countries. Unemployment increases at home, and increasing unemployment and social need is used to force down wages and living standards. {4}

Owners and directors in this way profit from the unemployment and the lower standard of living their operations cause in the home-country. They will continue to profit from increasing unemployment and its consequences as long as they do not have to pay the social costs of their operations. In other words, as long as they are allowed to pass this part of their operating costs to the community.

Employers should pay wages which will provide a good life for employees and their families. But the lower the wage paid, the higher the profit. And there will be employers who are more interested in their own profits than in the welfare of their employees.

Some employers may then pay wages which are so low that employees are forced to work long hours merely to survive. A government may then make up such wages with income-support benefits to a poverty-existence level. Which is apparently what happened in the UK while minimum-wage requirements ceased to be applied. And which is also being done in Germany.

In such ways taxpayers' moneys are used to subsidise the profits of companies (corporations), of their owners. {5}

2.4   Men and Women, Family and Children; Dominance, Oppression and Exploitation

We are here dealing with the root causes of our major social problems, showing how to resolve the problems by dealing with their basic causes.

200 million years of evolution are behind us, from reptilian beast through mammalian animal to human being. Human beings are mammals and we are unique in that our children need protecting and bringing up in a humane, emotionally and mentally stimulating environment for between 18 and 25 years, to enable them to mature into socially responsible adults. Men and women co-operate with each other and look after each other and their children, within the family, to achieve this.

The family looks after the interests of all its members, as individuals as well as collectively. Members of a family stand by, support and help each other in times of need.

This gives great strength to each member of the family in the struggle for daily bread, security and happiness. Hence human beings work primarily for their family and the family is the basic unit of society.

When one member of a family dominates others, then competition, conflict and struggle replace co-operation and teamwork. Dominance weakens all the family's members, robbing them of emotional and economic support, and so makes it easier to exploit them through their needs. All the family's members suffer as a result.

In the working environment we see a world-wide struggle to achieve a humane way of life, each family, person or community struggling to advance at their own level of development, struggling against those who wish to dominate, exploit, oppress. A struggle whose successful outcome depends on trustful co-operation, companionship and teamwork.

We know that dominating does not work in normal circumstances. Authoritarian organisations are much less effective than participative ones. In authoritarian organisations morale is low, people cease to care and tend to work against each other instead of co-operating with each other for the benefit of the organisation. Which applies equally well to a family.

Strength to resist oppression and exploitation comes from men and women co-operating with each other and so men and women struggle together to achieve a better life, a humane way of living and of government, and social security.

Human rights are based on controlling primitive dominating behaviour, on concern, care and affection for our young and our families, for people and for our communities. Human rights express themselves in co-operation and teamwork between men and women to achieve a good life of high quality.

It is in democracies that a high standard of living has been achieved. In democracies people can struggle openly for a better life but we see that what has been gained has to be defended and extended.

2.5   Family's Role and Life in the Real World; Protecting, and Caring for, the Next Generation; Causes of Social Break-up

Society corrupts itself when human care, affection and concern for one's own family, and for other people, are weakened, are bypassed by self-interest at expense of others. People who behave in such ways become isolated and divided against each other.

Basic is that people behave in a way which enables them to trust and assist each other, that men and women co-operate with each other in a way which will protect and strengthen both, behaving in a way which ensures that all benefit from gains made.

Each member of the family gets strength from the others. Two heads are better than one, and work divided between two people in such a way that each can become expert in his or her own area is done much better than one person trying to do it all. The family gives people enormous emotional and economic strength to overcome life's problems. Husband and wife battle on together back-to-back and they do so successfully regardless of how tough the struggle may be. You cannot win all the battles but what cements the relationship is not just battles won but

17

battles fought together. The depth of such a relationship between husband and wife and the wealth of strength it gives regardless of the opposition, this you know as well as I do. The children follow the example of their parents, gain the same strength and pass it on. It all depends on deep and secure emotional involvement between two people, between husband and wife.

3 The God-given Human Rights, Social Laws and Social System

This chapter is a comprehensive statement of the God-given human rights and obligations which underlie freedom, liberty, independence and well-being. They underlie and determine a good life of high quality. People at all stages of development are struggling to achieve these rights and benefits, all over the planet.

Directly relevant to today's social and economic problems, these rights and obligations determine the quality of life in areas such as social and economic security, social responsibility and accountability, ownership and decision-making, government and management, humane behaviour, teamwork and trustful cooperation.

These human rights, these social rules and this social system, are the very foundation of the three main religions of Judaism, Christianity and Islam.

What these religions have in common is that in each case a ruling elite succeeded in bypassing or overturning the religion's essential God-given benevolent social provisions and human rights {1, 2, 14-15, 6-9}, in this way exposing their communities and whole populations to oppression and exploitation.

What Manfred Davidmann has done with his works on the Pentateuch and the Bible, on religion and church-state relations, is to expose and correct the misinterpretations and mistranslations of the past. His works are major breakthroughs, constituting essential information for understanding the meaning and significance of the Pentateuch and the Bible.

4   Struggle for Freedom, Liberty and Independence: The Social Cause-and-Effect Relationship

The Ten Commandments are so important and are so well known because it is behaviour in accordance with these laws which is the basis for people trusting each other and so for people co-operating and working well with each other. They are here listed both in biblical language and in plain English.

It is the Ten Commandments as a whole which underlie freedom, independence and strength to oppose and resist oppression. Wherever there is any spiritual and material freedom today it exists because people followed these laws (rules) of behaviour and it exists to the extent to which they do so. In other words, following the provisions of the law results in freedom and ensures it, ensures strength and security.

History shows that in the past the people have been betrayed again and again, by non-observant leaderships no matter whether right or left and by so-called orthodox or fundamentalist leaderships who weakened the application of the law so as to be able to oppress the people in order to exploit them. It was those who did not follow the law who in the past grasped power and then weakened and defeated the hope for achieving freedom and a good life for the people and thus in due course for all humanity.

It is equally certain that the same battle is being fought today and it is just as certain that on the one hand is the opportunity to gain freedom while on the other hand our defeat can only result in mankind rapidly destroying itself.

To free ourselves from mental conditioning and brainwashing we have to follow the Ten Commandments and apply the social laws and the social system of the Pentateuch.

And the Pentateuch records and details the Social Cause-and-Effect Relationship, a fundamental scientific law which is stated as such and which was discovered there by Manfred Davidmann. This states that the consequences of keeping or not keeping the social laws are inescapable, that what happens to one is in the end the inevitable result of one's own behavior. It is stated to enable people to benefit from knowing the effects of their behavior.

Ignorance of these rules of behavior is no excuse and the relationship applies to all. History and social science confirm it, the prophets knew and understood it and predicted accordingly. Jesus confirmed it; the Koran records Prophet Mohammed repeatedly confirming the Pentateuch, referring to it both as a guide and as a warning.

Whole communities prosper or suffer as a consequence of their collective behavior. Manfred Davidmann says, "The consequences of our behavior cannot be avoided but we can change the course of events by changing our behavior."

He states "A new factor has entered the equation. It is now possible for the first time in the history of human beings on this planet for just one or only a few socially irresponsible persons to do something or to introduce changes which could destroy us all or else make this planet uninhabitable for human beings."

5 Family, Community, Sex and the Individual

This work examines root causes of what are now major social problems and shows how to resolve the problems by dealing with their basic causes.

Human beings work primarily for their family and members of a family stand by, support and help each other in times of need. The family is the basic unit of society and it looks after the interests of all its members, as individuals as well as collectively. This gives great strength to each member of the family in the struggle for daily bread, security and happiness.

And in "Family, Community, Sex and the Individual", Manfred Davidmann exposes the causes of what seems to be progressive breaking down of family life and of social strength. This report is an unprecedented and comprehensive overview, states new insights, proves basic underlying causes.

For example, in a comprehensive review, Manfred Davidmann defines the role of the family as being:

> To struggle as a family to survive.
>
> To protect and support mother and children until children become mature and independent adults capable of providing for themselves.
>
> To provide a good standard of living and a life of high quality. Which includes struggling against oppression and exploitation - and sometimes one has to fight to preserve a good way of life.
>
> To serve the interests of, and to support, each member of the family. In turn, each member of the family supports the family.

Here he also covers and reports on the impact of casual sexual relations and its effects on individuals, family and community, on the social strength of individuals and communities.

Manfred Davidmann was the first to clearly describe and show, eight years ago, the effects of increasing life spans on the family, on its members and on their responsibilities. He also illustrated the underlying basis of teamwork within the family, stating the various roles and responsibilities and functional relationships of its members for effective teamwork within the family.

6   The Meaning of Genesis

What Manfred Davidmann has done with his works on the Pentateuch and the Bible, on religion and church-state relations, is to expose and correct the misinterpretations and mistranslations of the past. His works are major breakthroughs, constituting essential information for understanding the meaning and significance of the Pentateuch and of the Bible.

In his "Meaning and Significance of the Names of God in Genesis", for example, Manfred Davidmann proved the meaning and significance of the different names of God which had been lost. In "Meaning and Intent of Genesis: Essential Notes on Hebrew Grammar," he stated the fundamental rules which were ignored at time of translation because required background knowledge was not available, with consequent mistranslations. And in "Bible Translations, Versions, Codes and Hidden Information in Bible and Talmud", he showed how changes made in the past obscured the intended meaning.

The chapters on Genesis describe and illustrate the meaning and intent of Genesis. Each is self-contained but together they provide the knowledge needed for understanding Genesis, its allegories and their significance. These allegories illustrate and define the difference between good and evil, and the importance of behaviour on social strength, well-being and good life under modern conditions.

Manfred Davidmann's research and discoveries showed and proved that the source text of Genesis, written several thousand years ago, corresponds in the major steps to the order in which the earth and life are known to have been formed and developed.

Described is the formation of the earth and early plant life, and evolution by 'the survival of the fittest'. The evolution from reptilian to mammalian instincts, feelings and behaviour is clearly stated, as is the evolution and corresponding behaviour, feeling and thinking of human beings from humanoids (animals resembling humans) through Homo erectus (early man) to Homo sapiens (human beings, ourselves).

There is no conflict or contradiction between what is recorded in the source text of Genesis and our scientific knowledge about evolution of human beings and of our planet.

Manfred Davidmann also summarises corresponding present social problems and describe the Pentateuch's social laws and social system for overcoming them.

6.1 Creation, Evolution and the Origin of Evil

Genesis is the first volume of the Pentateuch. It begins by describing how the planet was created, in other words how it was formed, the changes which occurred as the planet aged, how plants and animals were formed, evolved and populated the planet. It describes how human beings evolved and also how the behaviour of life forms changed as human beings evolved.

When the Pentateuch (Five Books of Moses) was written, people had but little knowledge about science or evolution compared with what is known today. So concepts for which we now have precise terms were described rather than stated and were expressed in religious terms so that they could be appreciated and followed by the population.

Understanding this we see that there is no conflict, no contradiction, no divergence, only awe-inspiring agreement, between what was recorded in Genesis and what we now know about the evolution of human beings. And Genesis defines good and evil, pointing to the root of evil.

6.2 Pre-flood Evils and the Social Problems of Our Time

Genesis (in its chapters 5 and 6) describes the behaviour of human beings before the flood. There is no conscious knowledge of good and evil and of the difference between them and their behaviour is like that of their primitive ancestors. Their behaviour is stated and condemned as evil. These two chapters of Genesis outline evil behaviour.

Genesis (chapter 5) shows people amassing possessions and wealth and dominating others by brutal strength. It contains a hidden list of pre-flood evil behavior.

This chapter also summarises corresponding present social problems, and describes the Pentateuch's social laws and social system for overcoming them.

6.3 Morality, Sexual Behaviour and Depravity

Genesis chapter 6 adds unrestrained sexual behaviour. Summarises corresponding present social problems. It records what is, and is not, moral sexual behaviour and the unavoidable consequences of depravity. Clearly stated is that the consequences cannot be avoided.

Describes the Pentateuch's social laws and social system for achieving a good life of high quality.

6.4 Nephilim, Dominance and Liberty

The Pentateuch's social laws and social system for achieving and keeping liberty and a good life of high quality are described.

Genesis chapter 6 adds and considers the gaining and misuse of power over others. Corresponding present social problems are summarized. We are told the consequences of allowing some people to misuse their abilities to manipulate, control and enslave others.

The flood follows and from here onwards Genesis shows a conscious knowledge developing of good and evil, stressing consequent reward and punishment, justice and retribution.

And the Pentateuch states and describes the social laws of behaviour and the social system which have to be kept as they enable people to gain and keep liberty and good lives of high quality.

6.5 Differentiating Between Good and Evil

Human beings are shown to be becoming numerous and spreading out, behaving much as before the flood. Different communities developed different customs, traditions, ways of behaving.

Shows that with the life and travels of the Patriarchs, some learned to know the difference between good and evil, learned to behave humanely.

6.6 Meaning and Significance of the Names of God in Genesis

Manfred Davidmann includes his published findings which proved the meaning and significance of the different names of God which had been lost. He describes and proves the meaning and significance of the names of God which are used in Genesis and which are of greatest importance for understanding the meaning of the text of the Bible.

6.7   Meaning and Intent of Genesis: Essential Notes on Hebrew Grammar

Here he includes his already published findings, stating the fundamental rules which were ignored at time of translation because required background knowledge was not available at that time, with consequent mistranslations. He lists and illustrates the grammatical rules which help to differentiate between references to individuals and references to groups or life forms. Essential information for understanding the meaning of Genesis.

6.8   Bible Translations, Versions, Codes and Hidden Information in Bible and Talmud

Here Manfred Davidmann includes the report he published some time ago which proved how changes made in the past obscured the original intended meaning. He also describes the ways in which hidden information has been encoded and labeled so that its original meaning could not be misunderstood or misinterpreted.

Chapter 2

The Real World in which We Live

2.1   The Social Costs of Unemployment

The social costs of unemployment to people as individuals, to their families, and to the community as a whole, are:

INDIVIDUALS
   Poverty, lack of spending money
   Frustration, despair
   Young people without full-time work experience
   Social disillusionment
   Ill health
   Reduced life span
   Mental illness
   Increasing suicide rate
   Drug abuse, crime

FAMILIES
   Increased family breakup
   Homelessness
   Domestic violence

COMMUNITY
   Higher and rising crime rates
   Brutalisation of lifestyle
   Lost Income:
      (1) Loss of income tax from those now unemployed.
      (2) Loss of National Insurance contributions which would have been received from both employees and employers.

(3) Loss of Value Added Tax as the unemployed reduce their spending.
Increased Expenditure
(4) Increased cost of Unemployment Benefit.
(5) Increased cost of Social Security support payments.
(6) Increased costs for Health Service, Police and Prisons.

Note that persistent lack of care and consideration towards its members leads to a view of society as being hostile and unrewarding. We now see this taking place and see its effects.

The social cost of unemployment to the community is the total cost to the community, is the sum of all the items listed here.

Prices used to be based on 'cost plus reasonable mark-up', and unhindered competition was meant to ensure that the mark-up was reasonable. Prices are now based on what people can be persuaded to pay for what they can be persuaded to buy. The mark-up between producing in a low-wage country, and then selling in a high-wage country, can be enormous.

Manfred Davidmann pointed this out in 1996, also saying that imports were now being priced at what the market will bear, or just under. The enormous profit margins then cause production to move from high-wage to low-wage countries. The consequence is a lowering of standard of living in high-wage countries to that in low-wage countries, instead of a raising of standard of living in low-wage countries to that in high wage countries.

The large additional profits which result from transferring operations abroad then do not result from doing a better job, or from providing better, or more needed, or more effectively produced, goods or services. These additional profits result from importing unemployment into the UK, are the result of dismissing British employees. {1}

It is an accepted principle of economics, that the social costs of an enterprise's operations have to be paid by the enterprise, expressed by the maxim 'The polluter pays'. In other words, the social costs of unemployment have to be paid by the enterprise which caused the unemployment. {2}

To the extent to which an enterprise fails to allow for, and pay, the social costs of its operations, to that extent are its profits derived from passing its operating costs to the community, is it making profits at the expense of the community, is it exploiting the community and its members.

26

The social costs of unemployment, however, are in the end paid by the unemployed (who are part of the community) and to some extent by the community as a whole. So the enterprise has passed on to the community this part of its operating costs, is making a profit at the expense of the community.

Owners and directors in this way profit from the unemployment and the lower standard of living their operations cause in the home-country. They will continue to profit from increasing unemployment and its consequences as long as they do not have to pay these social costs of their operations. In other words, as long as they are allowed to pass this part of their operating costs to the community.

Sources and References

{1} Exporting and Importing of Employment and Unemployment
Manfred Davidmann, 1996, 2002
solhaam.org/

{2} Community Economics: Principles
Manfred Davidmann, 1992, 1996
solhaam.org/

2.2   Bureaucracy and the Meaning of Democracy

Manfred Davidmann outlined the battlefield, the real struggle, in his report 'Multinational Summits and Agreements, Top-level Decision-taking and Democracy' {2}, in these terms:

Participative (democratic) organisation rests on the population electing representatives, on the basis of each person having one vote. Representatives are responsible to, and accountable to, the population for putting into effect policies decided by the population.

What underlies participative organisation (democracy) is decision-taking by the people at the level of the people.

What needs to be stressed is that in a participative (democratic) organisation policies are decided by a well-informed population at the level of the population and that policies then become binding on management or government.

And representatives, governments or government officials do not have the authority or right to reduce or sign away the participative (democratic) rights of the electors, of the population.

In an authoritarian organisation, the policy decisions are taken at the top or near the top by the hierarchy (establishment) and are binding on the organisation's members. Decision-taking at the top is sometimes referred to as 'deciding centrally'. Authoritarian organisation is the opposite of democracy and underlies dictatorship.

So what we see is conflict between authoritarian minds wishing to dominate, control and exploit on the one hand and, on the other hand, citizens wishing to maintain and improve the standard of living and quality of life for the population as a whole.

And the real struggle is not between political left and right, but is a struggle for participation, that is for the right of the population to be well-informed and to take the decisions which then become binding on management or government. {1, 2}

Sources and References

{1} Democracy, Socialism and Communism: The Worldwide
    Struggle for a Better Life
    Manfred Davidmann
    solhaam.org/

{2} Multinational Summits and Agreements, Top-level Decision-taking and Democracy
Manfred Davidmann
solhaam.org/

2.3 Multinational (Global) Operations, and Government Of, By, and For the People

How individuals in responsible positions or authority, in local and national government, are managing our affairs on our behalf and for us, is of crucial importance to every citizen.

Government has to make ends meet, has to bring about a rising standard of secure living, social security and an increasing quality of life for its citizens. There can be ups and downs but, says Manfred Davidmann, "failure to make ends meet is just as directly and surely the result of bad leadership and management as it is in any commercial enterprise."

This is a severe criticism also of the kind of experts and consultants used, and of the way they are used. "The quality of one's experts and whether and how their expertise is used, and applied, are of decisive importance."

Multinational Operations

It was Manfred Davidmann who twenty years ago demolished the then-current economic myths about 'Price Inflation' and 'Wage Inflation', and about inflation and unemployment. He coined the phrase 'Exporting Employment and Importing Unemployment', and pointed to, and warned about, the social and economic consequences of what is now often euphemistically called 'outsourcing' or 'globalisation'.

In 1996, for example, Manfred Davidmann pointed out that imports were now being priced at what the market will bear, or just under. The enormous profit margins then cause production to move from high-wage to low-wage countries. The consequence is a lowering of standard of living in high-wage countries to that in low-wage countries, instead of a raising of standard of living in low-wage countries to that in high wage countries. {1}

In 1991, Manfred Davidmann showed that multinational companies were minimising their liability for corporation tax by transfer pricing, that is by making book entries which transfer profits to the country with the lowest corporation tax.

> Say a multinational has increased its profits in such ways. As the government's expenses have not changed it must make up this shortfall elsewhere. From its other tax payers, say from its citizens. So its citizens pay more tax, the government can now

30

spend the same amount as before, the multinational's profits have increased.

This tax avoidance is legal and governments have not legislated to prevent this practice.

The multinational, and this means the owners and directors of the multinational, are thus in effect taxing the country's citizens, its population, in this way increasing the multinational's profits and thus their own incomes and wealth. {3}

> Studies published in the USA, for example, tell us much about the extent to which multinationals can avoid paying tax on their profits. These present a disturbing picture.

It is an accepted principle of economics, that the social costs of an enterprise's operations have to be paid by the enterprise, expressed by the maxim 'The polluter pays'. In other words, the social costs of unemployment have to be paid by the enterprise which caused the unemployment. {2}

However, multinationals tend to regard profit as the sole consideration, regardless of the consequences to the community, regardless of the cost to people. Instead of producing more effectively and competitively at home, owners and directors find it easier and more profitable to import from low-wage countries. Unemployment increases at home, and increasing unemployment and social need is used to force down wages and living standards. {4}

Owners and directors in this way profit from the unemployment and the lower standard of living their operations cause in the home-country. They will continue to profit from increasing unemployment and its consequences as long as they do not have to pay the social costs of their operations. In other words, as long as they are allowed to pass this part of their operating costs to the community.

Employers should pay wages which will provide a good life for employees and their families. But the lower the wage paid, the higher the profit. And there will be employers who are more interested in their own profits than in the welfare of their employees.

Some employers may then pay wages which are so low that employees are forced to work long hours merely to survive. A government may then make up such wages with income-support benefits to a poverty-existence level. Which is apparently what happened in the UK while minimum-wage requirements ceased to be applied. And which is also being done in Germany.

In such ways taxpayers' moneys are used to subsidise the profits of companies (corporations), of their owners. {5}

MAI stands for 'Multilateral Agreement on Investment'. But its name does not reflect those aspects which are of deep concern. What is disturbing are not only the provisions of this proposed treaty but also that the provisions were debated in almost complete secrecy. {6, 7}

It appears that representatives of multinationals and governments representing the 29 richest industrialised countries, all OECD members, had been developing the MAI's provisions at the OECD (Organisation for Economic Co-operation and Development) since 1995. This seems to have been done in complete secrecy till a leaked copy became available on the Internet in 1997.

It seems that the agreement was to have been finalised in February 1998. Apparently it was adverse publicity relating to its restrictive provisions which delayed completion as concerned groups of citizens publicised their concerns. And some governments then withdrew their support.

So let us look at the kind of provisions this almost-agreed agreement on 'Multilateral Agreement on Investment' contained:

Democratically elected governments

- Would have had to allow multinationals access to the country.
- Would have been prevented from discriminating against foreign firms, would not be able to refuse any form of investment in any sector apart from defence.
- Would have been prevented from reducing or controlling a multinationals profits, say by minimum-wage or anti-pollution legislation, or by legislation to ensure local employment.

Multinationals would have had the right to

- Sue national governments for any profits lost through laws which discriminated against the multinational, and which harmed a multinational's interests.
- Sue national governments in an international court which would have been closed to public scrutiny.

We saw that multinationals can legally avoid paying corporation tax by transfer pricing. Unitary taxation can overcome this tax avoidance by assessing the actual profits being generated by a multinational in a particular country. Multinationals could, under MAI, have refused to be taxed by a system of unitary taxation. {5}

So it appears that under MAI the national governments would have handed over control, that is authority to act, over much of the economic and social welfare of their citizens to multinational corporations (that is to those who own and direct these corporations), if they had agreed to this treaty.

In other words, multinationals would have been given overriding authority over democratically elected governments.

Governments recently promised to provide vast money handouts to what appear to have been speculative financial institutions when commercial banks considered these institutions too great a risk and refused to continue lending money to them.

Following which multinational motor manufacturers were claiming that they would have to seriously curtail or close down their operations in major industrialised countries, thus increasing unemployment, apparently hoping or clamouring for similarly enormous money handouts.

With governments seriously considering the motor manufacturers' requests and apparently agreeing, at least in principle, to the handing over of vast sums to them.

Socially responsible and caring governmental legislation has to take precedence over the profit-motivated activities of corporations (including financial institutions)

No elected representative, government or government employee has the authority

1. to hand over to corporations (that is to those who own and control them), or to anyone else, an overriding control over the present and future, economic and social, welfare of its people, or
2. to sign away the democratic rights of their people for the self-determination of key fundamental aspects of their lives.

Sources and References

{1} Exporting and Importing of Employment and Unemployment
   Manfred Davidmann
   solhaam.org/

{2} Community Economics: Principles
   Manfred Davidmann
   solhaam.org/

{3} Multinational Operations: Transfer Pricing and Taxation
Manfred Davidmann
solhaam.org/

{4} Creating Unemployment for the Sake of Private Profit;
Multinational (Global) Operations and the Exporting of
Employment
Manfred Davidmann, 2009
solhaam.org/

{5} Taxing the Population for Private Profit
Manfred Davidmann
solhaam.org/

{6} Democracy Under Attack: Top-level Leadership and Decision-
taking
Manfred Davidmann
solhaam.org/

{7} Multinational Summits and Agreements (Top-level Decision-
taking and Democracy)
Manfred Davidmann
solhaam.org/

2.4 Men and Women, Family and Children; Dominance, Oppression and Exploitation {1 - 4}

We are here dealing with the root causes of our major social problems, showing how to resolve the problems by dealing with their basic causes.

Family and Children

200 million years of evolution are behind us, from reptilian beast through mammalian animal to human being. Human beings are mammals and we are unique in that our children need protecting and bringing up in a humane, emotionally and mentally stimulating environment for between 18 and 25 years, to enable them to mature into socially responsible adults. Men and women co-operate with each other and look after each other and their children, within the family, to achieve this.

The family looks after the interests of all its members, as individuals as well as collectively. Members of a family stand by, support and help each other in times of need.

This gives great strength to each member of the family in the struggle for daily bread, security and happiness. Hence human beings work primarily for their family and the family is the basic unit of society.

Men and Women

Co-operation between men and women, within the family and as equals, would seem to be essential when bringing up their children under modern conditions of rapid change at an accelerating rate of change.

It is women who generally look after the young and other family members as people. This is the key role within the family and it occupies women full-time for some years if it is to be done well, and for more years on an at least part-time basis.

But we live much longer and the time spent full-time at home looking after the family places women at a disadvantage when returning to work outside the family after the children have been brought up. So women need to be supported when returning to work.

The family compensates women for the life-long effects of their contribution towards the upbringing of the children. It is the role of the spouse, of the husband, to continue to provide for the family. A life-long contribution from him which means she does not lose out for the rest of her life because she stayed at home to look after the children, the husband's input into the family balancing her input of bringing up the children and looking after the family's members.

Women, after children have grown up and with the family's backing, can choose work outside the family to fulfil themselves as pay is less important for a second income.

It is largely women who, caring for the welfare of the community, are generally the prime movers in self-help, support, protest and pressure groups, pushing forward also with other social and welfare issues.

Such work and public demonstrations and protests on such issues, are now an essential survival mechanism under beginning-of-twentyfirst-century conditions.

A key characteristic which distinguishes human beings from animals is that we can control the sex urge. Sex is habit-forming and addictive but can be controlled when the will is there, when the individual is motivated to control it.

In the USA steps are being taken to halt and reverse the increasing corruption of their communities by teaching the young the gains to be achieved by abstaining from sexual activity outside marriage.

There are ways of teaching social responsibility, of teaching the young how to take responsibility for others, how to care for, work with and look after other people. Social responsibility, the caring, giving and sharing with others, the taking on of responsibility for others including conflict management, can be and is being taught.

Dominance, Oppression and Exploitation

When one member of a family dominates others, then competition, conflict and struggle replace co-operation and teamwork. Dominance weakens all the family's members, robbing them of emotional and economic support, and so makes it easier to exploit them through their needs. All the family's members suffer as a result.

In the working environment we see a world-wide struggle to achieve a humane way of life, each family, person or community struggling to advance at their own level of development, struggling against those who wish to dominate, exploit, oppress. A struggle whose successful outcome depends on trustful co-operation, companionship and teamwork.

We know that dominating does not work in normal circumstances. Authoritarian organisations are much less effective than participative ones. In authoritarian organisations morale is low, people cease to care and tend to work against each other instead of co-operating with each other for the benefit of the organisation. Which applies equally well to a family.

Strength to resist oppression and exploitation comes from men and women co-operating with each other and so men and women struggle together to achieve a better life, a humane way of living and of government, and social security.

Human rights are based on controlling primitive dominating behaviour, on concern, care and affection for our young and our families, for people and for our communities. Human rights express themselves in co-operation and teamwork between men and women to achieve a good life of high quality.

It is in democracies that a high standard of living has been achieved. In democracies people can struggle openly for a better life but we see that what has been gained has to be defended and extended.

Sources and References

{1} See chapter 5: 'Family, Community, Sex and the Individual'.
Manfred Davidmann, 1998, 2011

{2} Democracy, Socialism and Communism:
The Worldwide Struggle for a Better Life
Manfred Davidmann, 2008
solhaam.org/

{3} Style of Management and Leadership
Manfred Davidmann, 1981, 2006
solhaam.org/

{4} How the Human Brain Developed and How the Human Mind
Works
Manfred Davidmann, 1998, 2006
solhaam.org/

2.5 Family's Role and Life in the Real World; Protecting, and Caring for, the Next Generation; Causes of Social Break-up {1}

The Family

For human beings, primitive (reptilian) instinctive urges and behaviour are overlaid by mammalian care and affection for one's young and human care and affection for one's family and community. {2}

Compared with most, if not all, animals we also have much longer lifespans and it takes a long time before a human baby becomes an adult. Born after nine months in the mother's womb, followed by 4 to 5 years as infant, then 8 to 10 years as child being educated, and say 6 to 9 years as adolescent, about 18 to 25 years old when becoming an adult and independent member of the community.

So the role of the family is

To struggle as a family to survive.

To protect and support mother and children until children become mature and independent adults capable of providing for themselves.

To provide a good standard of living and a life of high quality. Which includes struggling against oppression and exploitation. And sometimes one has to fight to preserve a good way of life.

To serve the interests of, and to support, each member of the family. In turn, each member of the family supports the family.

Hence human beings work primarily for their family and members of a family stand by, support and help each other in times of need. The family is the basic unit of society and it looks after the interests of all its members, as individuals as well as collectively. This gives great strength to each member of the family in the struggle for daily bread, security and happiness.

Protecting and Caring for the Next Generation

It is women who generally look after people, after the welfare and well-being of the members of the family. Care, concern, affection and love, feelings and emotions, are important and matter, and women developed, and have, much skill and expertise in such matters. It is generally men who struggle outside the family to secure survival and good living for the family. A struggle for survival in a seemingly hostile environment engineered by other humans. {3 - 4}

Primarily the family exists to protect and support its young, and this means supporting and looking after the female bearing the child within her body, through birth and while she is protecting and teaching the young how to behave. It is usually the woman whose role it is to ensure the family provides the young with the humane, emotionally and mentally stimulating environment they need to enable them to mature into socially responsible adults. She is assisted in this by her spouse, depending on her needs and depending on his own work. But it is usually the woman who copes with the personal and emotional problems of the family's members and this is challenging, demanding and difficult work demanding social ability and skills as well as care, affection, understanding and concern for people.

When women are persuaded to regard work outside of the family as more important than caring for the young or the family's members, they are in effect handing over the family's key role to outsiders such as day-care businesses and television programme makers, with disastrous results on the way in which the young perceive home life and adult behaviour.

Such outsiders tend to condition the young into behaving like fictional and unreal role models, for example concerning sexual behaviour. Instead of gaining an adult understanding of the reality of living, of family values and relationships, instead of understanding and experiencing socially-responsible behaviour caring for and living with other people, instead of seeing adults (parents) behave in socially responsible way struggling together in a hostile environment to do the best they can for the young and for each other.

Behaviour and Community

Society corrupts itself when human care, affection and concern for one's own family, and for other people, is weakened, is bypassed by self-interest at expense of others.

There is increasing wanton antisocial behaviour such as vandalism and mugging. There is a loss of internal security, by loss of property and by attack against the person. The quality of life is lowered even further by those who pursue personal gain regardless of its cost to other people.

Destructive aggression, viciousness and brutality of people towards each other, disregard of the value of the individual and of life itself, are not normal behaviour. People who behave in such ways become isolated and divided against each other.

Partnerships and marriages break up when difficulties arise. People leave without regard or concern for the interests of the other members, of partner, spouse or children. They leave when they would be better off alone, when there is illness, when their present partner becomes unemployed, when a younger or wealthier 'partner' becomes available.

Basic is that people behave in a way which enables them to trust and assist each other, that men and women co-operate with each other in a way which will protect and strengthen both, behaving in a way which ensures that all benefit from gains made.

So within a family, between husband and wife, it is the other person who comes first. When each spouse tries to make the other spouse happy, when each will go without something so as to make the other happy, then both can be happy.

Family's Role and Life in the Real World

Human beings work primarily for their family and members of a family stand by, support and help each other in times of need.

Smash the family and you undermine the strength of the people. I understand the resulting disruption was so marked in Russia that they had to back-pedal. One of the first things the Khmer Rouge did in Cambodia was to smash the family to make the people dependent on the state.

It is tough when you have to go to work to earn the money, do the shopping, look after the kids and do everything yourself. The one thing you cannot afford to be is to be ill. And you have no time for the kids either. And in a one-parent family, what the children miss is the parent's caring co-operative behaviour, is the example of responsible people looking after each other. The boy being brought up by the mother knows that both of them were left to look after themselves by the father and that is not a good example to model himself on. If you are struggling on your own so as to survive you don't have time or energy to think of freedom or to work for the community or for the betterment of humankind.

In the kibbutzim, that is in Israel's co-operative settlements, children were brought up communally in age groups, away from their parents. One age group would progress together from creche to nursery and then to school, living together during the week and seeing their parents, or living with their parents, only at weekends.

This may have freed both parents for work and defence in the initial struggle for survival. But the practice was continued when successful, possibly to free women for work and so increase production. But it was done at the expense of the family.

Of any group in the country, the kibbutz children consequently showed the highest incidence of mental problems. The kibbutzim have had to backtrack and now give their children a more normal and strengthening family-life experience with their parents. {5}

Each member of the family gets strength from the others. Two heads are better than one, and work divided between two people in such a way that each can become expert in his or her own area is done much better than one person trying to do it all. The family gives people enormous emotional and economic strength to overcome life's problems. Husband and wife battle on together back-to-back and they do so successfully regardless of how tough the struggle may be. You cannot win all the battles but what cements the relationship is not just battles won but battles fought together. The depth of such a relationship between husband and wife and the wealth of strength it gives regardless of the opposition, this you know as well as I do. The children follow the example of their parents, gain the same strength and pass it on. It all depends on deep and secure emotional involvement between two people, between husband and wife.

Sources and References

{1} See chapter 5: 'Family, Community, Sex and the Individual'.
Manfred Davidmann, 1998, 2006, 2011

{2} How the Human Brain Developed and How the Human Mind Works
Manfred Davidmann, 1998, 2006
solhaam.org/

{3} Style of Management and Leadership
Manfred Davidmann
solhaam.org/, 1981, 1982, 1988, 1995, 2006

{4} Motivation Summary
Manfred Davidmann, 1982, 1995, 1998
solhaam.org/

{5} Kibbutzim
Manfred Davidmann, 1996
solhaam.org/

Chapter 3

The God-given Human Rights, Social Laws and Social System

Introduction

This chapter is a comprehensive statement of the God-given human rights which underlie all human freedom, liberty and independence, and which underlie and determine a good life of high quality. People at all stages of development are struggling to achieve these rights and benefits, all over the planet.

Directly relevant to today's social and economic problems, these rights and obligations determine the quality of life in areas such as social and economic security, social responsibility and accountability, ownership and decision-making, government and management, humane behaviour, teamwork and trustful cooperation.

These human rights, these social rules and this social system, are the very foundation of the three main religions of Judaism, Christianity and Islam.

When the Pentateuch <1> was written, people had but little knowledge about science or evolution compared with what is known today. So concepts for which we now have precise terms were described rather than stated. Instead of the term 'scientific law' being used, for example, we see described that 'what is written applies to all people, present or absent, past or future, will happen regardless of how one feels about it, that the results of certain actions are reversed if the actions are reversed'. <2>

And concepts and descriptions were expressed in religious terms so that they could be understood and followed by the population.

What these religions have in common is that in each case a ruling elite succeeded in bypassing or overturning the religion's essential God-given benevolent social provisions and human rights {1, 2, 14-15, 6-9}, in this way exposing their communities and whole populations to oppression and exploitation.

Now that our technological progress so vastly exceeds our social organisation and behaviour, the survival of our species is in doubt. Hence the urgency of the need to apply these rules of behaviour in our daily lives. Here the aim is to show what needs to be done and how it can be achieved.

What Manfred Davidmann has done with his works on the Pentateuch and the Bible, on religion and church-state relations, is to expose and correct the misinterpretations and mistranslations of the past. His works are major breakthroughs, constituting essential information for understanding the meaning and significance of the Pentateuch and the Bible.

In his "Meaning and Significance of the Names of God in Genesis", Manfred Davidmann proved the meaning and significance of the different names of God which had been lost. In "Meaning and Intent of Genesis: Essential Notes on Hebrew Grammar," he stated the fundamental rules which were ignored at time of translation because required background knowledge was not available, with consequent mistranslations. And in "Bible Translations, Versions, Codes and Hidden

Information in Bible and Talmud", he showed how changes made in the past obscured the intended meaning.

Further, the Pentateuch records and details the Social Cause-and-Effect Relationship, a fundamental scientific law which is stated as such and which was discovered there by Manfred Davidmann. This states that the consequences of keeping or not keeping the social laws are inescapable, that what happens to one is in the end the inevitable result of one's own behavior. It is stated to enable people to benefit from knowing the effects of their behavior.

Ignorance of these rules of behavior is no excuse and the relationship applies to all. History and social science confirm it, the prophets knew and understood it and predicted accordingly. Jesus confirmed it; the Koran records Prophet Mohammed repeatedly confirming the Pentateuch, referring to it both as a guide and as a warning.

Whole communities prosper or suffer as a consequence of their collective behavior. Manfred Davidmann says, "The consequences of our behavior cannot be avoided but we can change the course of events by changing our behavior."

Good and Evil and the Difference between Them {3}

The first volume of the Pentateuch (Genesis) describes how plants and animals were formed, evolved and populated the planet. It describes how the behaviour of successive life forms changed as they evolved into human beings. {3}

Evolution had turned into a bitter struggle for the survival of the fittest, where the most fittest was the most vicious and violent. The most 'advanced' species was the species which was the most vicious. Life was brutal and dominated by evil. This is how reptiles came to dominate the earth.

Then mammals evolve from reptiles, and develop feelings of care and affection towards others. Genesis describes {3} that from them evolved a mammalian human-like life form (homo erectus) whose behaviour was more beast-like than human, without knowledge of good and evil and unable to distinguish between them.

Genesis states {3} that if there is to be further development towards good then there has to be knowledge of and understanding of good and evil and of the difference between them so that people can choose between them. And that consequently the human brain evolved from the mammalian brain.

44

The increased brain capacity and the evolution of the neocortex {10} enable humans (Homo sapiens) to know the difference between good and evil and human beings with their larger brains spread across the planet and replaced Homo erectus.

In this way the Pentateuch, in religious language, records {3} the evolution (creation) and behaviour of human beings who know of, can distinguish between and can choose between, good and evil.

The human brain underlies free will, enabling us to decide independently whether to do good or evil, that is what to do or not to do.

But this needs to be supplemented with the ability to think clearly, to assess and evaluate on the basis of knowledge of good and evil and of the essential need for behaving humanely, for following (doing) good instead of evil.

It is here that the relevance and importance of the Pentateuch's social laws and teachings <3> become apparent. The Pentateuch adds to mere mechanistic and chance processes the knowledge that human beings need to, and have to, behave humanely if they wish to prosper and succeed. Stating clearly what is, and is not, humane behaviour, clearly defining the difference between good (including human rights and justice) and evil, adding that human beings stand or fall by the way they behave. {12}

And it is the God-given social laws and social system of the Pentateuch which define and state human rights and behaviour which people need to follow if they wish to prosper and succeed, if they wish to have a high standard of living and a life of high quality.

Unavoidable Consequences of One's Behaviour (Social Cause-and-Effect Relationship <2> {12})

A covenant is an agreement in which each of the parties undertakes duties and obligations towards the other. And the Pentateuch records God's promise that human beings will have a good life of high quality as long as human beings fulfil their obligations under the covenant, as long as human beings follow God's laws, as long as they behave like human beings. <4>

This is also recorded in the Pentateuch as a fundamental scientific law, the Social Cause-and-Effect Relationship {12} <2>, in the language of religion. This states that the consequences of keeping or not keeping the Pentateuch's laws are inescapable, that what happens to one is in the end the inevitable result of one's own behaviour. Also clearly stated is that this is a scientific law which was defined and stated using the language of religion so that people would benefit from knowing the effects (consequences) of their behaviour. The relationship is stated in precise terms. History {2} and social science {21} confirm it.

We are told that the relationship applies to all without exception and at all times, wherever one may be, regardless of type of government, form of religion or social system or country. It applies whether you like it or not, agree or disagree.

The consequences of one's behaviour are detailed both ways, clearly and powerfully illustrating intermediate stages between the two ends of the scale, and we are told that the process is reversible: Increasingly disregarding the laws (rules of behaviour) results in greater suffering and oppression, increasingly behaving according to the laws results in greater freedom, liberty, independence and a better life.

The relationship applies to all. Ignorance is no excuse, not knowing the law does not prevent consequences of one's behaviour, and the relationship is stated in a way which enables people to benefit from knowing the effects of their behaviour, even if they do not understand the underlying relationship.

The relationship is clearly stated in the Pentateuch {12}, confirmed by Jesus {1} and then by Mohammed. The Koran records Mohammed repeatedly confirming the Pentateuch, referring to it both as a guide and as a warning {9}, and Arab and Muslim history illustrates the working of the cause-and-effect relationship.

Freedom and independence of mind and person and the quality of life depend on one's behaviour. The consequences of one's behaviour are inevitable, inescapable. Keeping or disregarding the Pentateuch laws has consequences which cannot be avoided. Whole communities prosper or suffer (are 'persecuted') as a consequence of their individual and thus collective behaviour.

Those who behave according to the law have good and satisfying lives, gain social and military strength. Behaviour which is contrary to the law lowers the quality of life, increases internal stress and conflict to the point of social disruption and military weakness.

If we want freedom, independence, good life of high quality, then we have to follow these laws. If we do not, then we lose freedom, independence, good life and the country in which we live. The consequences of our behaviour cannot be avoided but we can change the course of events by changing our behaviour.

Planet-wide Danger

By the end of the twentieth century a new factor had entered the equation. {21}

Up to now when some people suffered, when a village was wiped out in a war fought for the benefit of another establishment, when a whole country and its people were devastated, it did not mean the end of humanity. The point is that as a result of the impact of technology and increasing speed of transport and communication it is possible for the first time in the history of human beings on this planet for just one or only a very few socially irresponsible persons to do something or to introduce changes which could destroy us all as human beings or else make this planet uninhabitable for human beings.

I showed twenty years ago in 'Social Responsibility, Profits and Social Accountability' {21} that we were experiencing a sequence of accidents and catastrophes which were occurring more and more frequently and were affecting more and more people.

Since then most people have become aware of this. But I also showed what could and should be done about this trend of events.

So now we do not have a choice. If we do not now observe and put into effect the social laws (rules) and social system of the Pentateuch and its code of behaviour then the planet will become uninhabitable for human beings.

Humane Behaviour

Trustful Co-operation (Ten Commandments)

The Ten Commandments <5> are so important and are so well known because it is behaviour in accordance with these rules of behaviour which is the basis for people trusting each other and so for people co-operating and working well with each other. They underlie freedom, independence and strength to oppose and resist oppression. Wherever there is any independence of the mind and material freedom today it exists because people followed these rules of behaviour and it exists to the extent to which they do so. To free ourselves from mental manipulation, conditioning and brainwashing we need to follow them. {12}

In other words, following the provisions of the law results in freedom and ensures it, ensures strength and security. {17}

Take these two commandments (principles of behaviour):
    You must not steal.
    You must not desire anything which belongs to your neighbour.

Much trust and community friendliness is gained when people follow these principles.

But look around you. These principles are at times applied ruthlessly to protect the possessions of the rich from the starving poor who see no other way to survive apart from stealing some scraps of food.

I may be overstating the case so as to make a point. But consider that these laws apply equally to the rich and powerful. It is also the rich and powerful who must not steal from the poor even the little which the poor have. It is the rich and powerful who must not cast longing glances at what little the rest of us possess, it is the rich and powerful who must not aim to gain at our expense.

And now consider this {24}:

> Shareholders would not even consider handing their moneys over to a corporation without in return becoming an owner of a corresponding part of the corporation, without getting a corresponding number of shares in return.
>
> But customers are not given a choice. Corporations (their owners) simply take their customers' moneys
>   (a) for getting back money already spent on the business and
>   (b) for expanding the business
> without in return giving customers (or the community) corresponding ownership rights.
>
> To 'rob' is to take unlawfully. But we are here looking at moneys being taken legally and largely without the owners' (customers') knowledge or agreement.
>
> What is taking place is perhaps best described as 'legalised robbery'.
>
> What we see is a people divided against each other, conflict and struggle.

We are resisting oppression and exploitation and building a better world for ourselves and our children. Our strength depends on co-operation between men and women, on the family, on developing our human potential by controlling the sexual urge, on being able to trust each other and rely on each other. Consider these commandments {12}:
    You must not commit murder.
    You must not bear false witness against your neighbour.
    You must not commit adultery.

People who behave promiscuously (permissively) have sexual relations before marriage, or after marriage with a person other than their spouse. Promiscuity turns men against women, and women against men, and robs both of the support of their family {13, 16}. Hence this prohibition of promiscuous behaviour. <6>

Another commandment <5> is

> Honour your father and your mother and willingly accept the stated principles of behaviour, and the tradition, knowledge and life experience of your parents so that you will progress and advance in understanding and in life and so that you will have long and secure lives of high quality in the land in which you live.

In other words, when your parents believe in the principles stated here, and apply them in their daily lives, then one must learn and respect these teachings. One must not be led astray, no matter how plausible the persuading voices or images in one's social environment seem to be. In one's impressionable years one must not be led astray from the principles of behaviour stated here as these principles underlie freedom and independence and a good and secure life of high quality.

Morality (Men and Women, Family and Family Purity) {16}

Genesis <7> shows human beings becoming aware of the existence of good and evil and of the difference between them, shows human beings learning to choose that which is good and gaining social strength and good lives of high quality as a result. It is about human beings struggling to stop behaving like our beastlike primitive ancestors and instead doing what is good, learning to behave like human beings, to behave humanely.

And underlying humane behaviour is the need, the necessity, to control and overcome the brutalising influences we are struggling against, to control the sex impulse, so as to achieve good lives of high quality.

And what we have in the Pentateuch are rules of behaviour which point to the essence of humane behaviour. We know that ignoring them results in social corruption, oppression and exploitation of the many by the few. And we know that following these rules ensures social strength and a good life for all. {12}

Normal for human beings is an exclusive sexual relationship between husband and wife within a monogamous single life-long relationship (family) which ensures the young are protected for the many years before they reach maturity, and which protects and supports husband

and wife as they grow old. On marriage the male accepts responsibility for the resulting family for life. {3, 13}

> For a comprehensive review of the role of the family and of a family's members, of the impact of casual sexual relations on individuals, family and community, on the effect of increasing lifespans, on dominance, oppression and exploitation within and without the family, on teamwork within the family, on the effects of promiscuous behaviour on social strength of individuals and communities, see {13}.

Those who behave humanely, morally, can trust each other, cooperate with each other, grow, gain strength together, prosper.

All other sexual relations are abnormal and we are told {16} the effects (consequences) of inhuman beastlike (unrestrained, uncontrolled) sexual behaviour.

Those who behave immorally weaken their family and social strength. Those who initiate moral behaviour, who behave morally and humanely, gain strength and standing, and those who support them in this are supported in return. Confirmed by history {12, 2}, we see it taking place all around us.

And sexual relations outside marriage are prohibited before and during marriage.

A clear way of stating
> the importance of chastity,
> that human beings can and do control their sexual urges,
> the importance and necessity for the human male to control the beastlike sexual urge lurking at the border of the conscious.

Sodomy, having sexual relations between persons of the same sex, is unnatural and abnormal, corrupting and destructive of human society and humane behaviour, is punished with utmost severity.

And incest, having sexual relations between members of a close or extended family, is abnormal, corrupting and destructive of family trust, family life and family strength. Incest is primitive beastlike behaviour and perpetrators are punished with utmost severity.

The Pentateuch contains detailed statements about what constitutes abnormal, promiscuous, adulterous sexual relations and prostitution, with associated comments and severe penalties. <8>

Morality and family, individual and social strength, are interrelated. Morality more than any other factor determines the strength and well-being of individuals, families and communities. So morality is of

50

determining importance and these laws of behaviour need to be protected, applied and enforced.

Social and Moral Problems of Our Times

The consequences of immorality cannot be avoided. {12} <2>

The Pentateuch's warnings, punishments and penalties concerning morality are in most cases to the male. It is males who are behind the corrupting of family morality and who are attempting to brutalise women so as to make women more readily available for sex. Even brainwashing and manipulating women into making themselves available. With consequent weakening and breaking up of family, society and quality of life. {13}

Conditioning, persuading, inducing or compelling a person to have sex before marriage, person to person or through the media, is in my opinion an act of rape. The younger the person, the worse is the offence.

Morality has to be protected by punishing immorality, by protecting women and punishing men and women who behave immorally. By punishing those who spread immorality and seduce others into immoral behaviour.

In democracies or when people are struggling for their liberty, authoritarians condone and promote promiscuity so as to weaken the family and weaken the population. People are subjected to conditioning towards immorality to weaken the working population to make them easier to exploit, to weaken the society and democracy. <9>

But when in control, dictatorships of left or right or religious absolutist hierarchies then pedal back to gain strength for their people, so that they will fight for and protect, and slave for, their manipulating rulers. <10>

Hence the importance of morality, of Pentateuch morality and laws of behaviour, of protecting communities and people by restraining immoral behaviour, conditioning and propaganda, by appropriately punishing the perpetrators.

Social Strength

The Pentateuch states what has to be done and what is prohibited, by positive and negative rules of behaviour. {2}

Positive rules state what has to be done so as to create a just and strong society. And point the way ahead towards greater strength, freedom, liberty and a good way of life.

Negative rules (prohibitions) state what must not be done and such rules protect the people from oppression and exploitation, from the antisocial behaviour of others, safeguard the people's strength and freedom.

But support and co-operation have to be two-way flows. The community supports the individual but only if the individual supports the community. Those supported by the community are under obligation to support others in need of support, when able to do so, to share with others who are in need. Where 'need' includes the need for capital to secure their operation, to achieve the general standard of living and quality of life.

Which means that benefits and support from the community are given only to those who believe in its benevolent principles and live accordingly. 'Supporting the community' includes helping to spread knowledge and understanding of its principles. <11>

Throughout, it is only those who themselves keep and apply the benevolent social laws given in this report in their daily lives who are entitled to these rights. Otherwise, to give but one example, funds provided by the community free-of-interest to a non-member (stranger) might be used by the stranger to exploit people by lending funds to others and charging interest so as to enrich himself.

Social and Economic Security

All persons have the right to be free and independent masters of their own fate and no person may oppress or exploit another. Because people can be exploited through their needs there has to be a system of social and economic security which guarantees freedom from needs and so protects people from becoming dependent on others for essential income, protects against loss of material independence and which protects them from losing their spiritual independence.

Every community member is entitled as a matter of right to social security <12>. This means that community members are entitled to be supported by the community not only when they fall on hard times but also to maintain their independence as independent breadwinners for their families. For example, the community has to provide backup funds to those who need them and they have to be provided as and when required.

To prevent people being exploited through their need these funds have to be provided without charging interest. They are called 'loans' because the recipient is under moral obligation to repay them to the community if he can do so. However, such 'loans' are cancelled every seventh calendar year if the borrower has been unable to repay them. <11>

These essential social provisions of the Pentateuch are clear and to the point. This is what is laid down as a matter of law {12}:

The community has to provide ('lend') money to those who need it, free of interest.

1. All such loans, if outstanding, are to be cancelled every seventh year.

Work and Leisure

Weekly Day of Rest

Every seventh day is a day of rest for all, for those who are employed as well as for those who employ. Work stops on the weekly day of rest, the Sabbath, to let those who labour have a regular day of rest. On this day the servant is as free as the master, the worker is as free as the employer. The weekly day of rest has spread and benefits almost all the civilised world. {12} <11>

Sabbatical Year

Community members are entitled to a sabbatical year every seventh year. During this year they are entitled to be freed from work at the expense of the community. <13> {12}

Academics already enjoy regular sabbatical years. During this period they are paid their salaries. {19}

Free to travel, train for more skilled or better work, update knowledge, study, gain greater understanding, qualify. Those on a sabbatical must not work for pay, or produce to sell, during that year but receive the average rate earned by community members during the previous calendar year. <11>

Consider what sabbatical years would mean. For you and for others who would during such a year be free to do as they pleased. We could have much more satisfying lives, we could do much for our own communities, could do much for those in need, for those who are underdeveloped and unable to afford our own expert skills. {19} <14>

Freedom, Liberty and Independence

The words freedom, liberty and independence are usually given subtly different meanings, as follows:

Freedom	The right and power to act, speak, or think freely.
Liberty	The state of being free from oppression or imprisonment.
Independence	Self governing and not depending on another for livelihood or subsistence.

Freedom, liberty and independence go hand-in-hand, support and complement each other. Liberty includes being free from slavery or despotic control by others, means being free from social, economic, political, mental or physical control by others, means being free from antisocial control or manipulation by others. And independence includes not being dependent on, and not being controlled by, another person, group, organisation, or thing.

But it is the social rules and social system of the Pentateuch which in effect state that all are equal, that no person may exploit another or oppress so as to exploit. All have the right to be free and independent masters of their own fate and there has to be a system of social security which guarantees not just freedom from need but also protection against loss of material and spiritual independence.

Government and Management

Here we are looking at the laws of the Pentateuch which control the behaviour and limit the power {12, 2} of government, of top executives and of the establishment, of those in positions of trust, responsibility or authority. The Pentateuch {11} leaves little doubt about what they must not do.

We saw already that

> Positive laws state what has to be done so as to create a just and strong society. And point the way ahead towards greater strength, freedom, liberty and a good way of life.

> Negative laws (prohibitions) state what must not be done and such laws protect the people from oppression and exploitation, from the antisocial behaviour of others, safeguard the people's strength and freedom.

And so the laws quoted here protect people, safeguard their strength and freedom, and need to be applied.

These laws of government relate to 'rulers', apply to all in positions of trust, responsibility or authority, no matter whether secular, religious or military, no matter what the hierarchy or organisation.

Such people may not amass servants and may not oppress the people for their own benefit. They may not amass possessions and wealth, may not grasp power or behave promiscuously.

In other words, they may not put themselves above others by grasping power, may not satisfy personal desires at the expense of others.

And a ruler (person in position of trust, responsibility or authority) has to follow these laws and abide by them every day if he wishes 'to prolong his days in his kingdom, he and his children'. For 'kingdom' read 'position' and include 'influence'.

So the Pentateuch laws quoted here protect people and safeguard their strength and freedom by laying down that those in positions of trust, responsibility or authority may not grasp power, may not oppress the people, may not behave promiscuously, may not enrich themselves. Those in authority must not oppress people so as to increase their own possessions and power, must not form enforcing squads or organisations so as to multiply their own power, must not behave promiscuously, must not gain wives or wealth. {12}

Equality and Ownership

Ownership {24} is the right to possess something and to decide what is to be done with it. If I own something it belongs to me and I decide what is to be done with it. An example would be owning a house.

Possession is having something in one's custody as distinct from owning it. If I possess something it belongs to another but I can decide how to use it. An example would be renting a house.

Another example would be deciding what to do with my money (ownership) or deciding and controlling the use of money belonging to someone else (possession).

And considering the right to ownership, two questions need to be considered. Namely where does the right come from and how is it exercised.

The right to own property varies among societies. Ownership laws which assign ownership 'rights' to owners have been devised by the owners themselves or by those who serve them. {20}

Ownership of land and means of production, of funds and wealth, has always been accumulated at someone else's expense. All belonged to the community, belonged to all alike. And this is what Chapter 5 of Genesis appears to be saying {18}.

A human right is a something one may legally or morally claim, is the state of being entitled to a privilege or immunity or authority to act. Human rights are those held to be claimable by any living person, apply to all living people. Every living person is entitled to them.

So ownership of land and means of production, of funds and wealth, rightfully belongs to the community, belongs to all alike, is a human right. Those who have accumulated them have only possession, which means they can use and apply them but may do so only on behalf of, and for the benefit of, the community and that they are accountable to the community for the way in which they do so. {19}

Hence we have the use of possessions as long as we use them to provide a good living for our family, and beyond that for the benefit of the community. For the benefit of others less able or fortunate, for the benefit of the community around us and then for the benefit of communities abroad.

But we may only support those who themselves genuinely support our benevolent ideals and principles and their application and who themselves live and act accordingly, who behave humanely. {12} <15>

A maximum differential of two, the maximum gross earnings being twice the minimum earnings, within a country and also between countries, would seem a reasonable target to achieve under present more extreme circumstances. {19}

Bearing this in mind, the country's wealth, and this includes productive assets and capital, including land, enterprise and corporation ownership, property, bank deposits and reserves, belongs equally to all community members and needs to be shared out <16>.

To be shared out family by family {12}, where 'family' is a life-long single union {13} between husband and wife. With shares updated at regular intervals of between three and not more than five calendar years <17>. Each receives a share of the community's total net assets <18>, their 'Asset Share'. An Asset Share cannot be sold but the owner has the right to determine its use and to the resulting benefits.

The Worldwide Struggle for God-given Human Rights {17, 13}

Freedom, Liberty and Independence {17}

Humane behaviour is aimed at survival of the young and of the family, and then is for the good of one's family, other people and the community. It is based on feelings of care and affection for others. From this emerges a sense of social responsibility: people matter and are important, need to be treated well and looked after, are entitled to share equally. Backed up by knowledge, understanding and reason. {10}

We know that dominating others is conditioned, that is unnatural, behaviour which is destructive of humane behaviour. A throw-back to the level of the unthinking unfeeling primitive animal. {10}

Genesis says much in chapters 5 and 6. About inhuman behaviour, about possessions, ownership and riches, about domineering, oppression and misusing people by force.

And knowledge of good and evil enables us to choose that which is good (humane) and to overcome that which is inhumane (beast-like, evil).

These themes are continued in Genesis and in the other four volumes (books) of the Pentateuch. We are told about the obligatory social laws and social system which have to be kept if evil is to be overcome, are told about consequent reward and punishment, justice and retribution, so that human beings can have good lives of high quality.

Those who follow and keep the benevolent social laws of the Pentateuch have in the past been opposed by dictatorships of both right and left, by those who wish to establish and support such dictatorships, by those who wish to oppress so as to exploit people. Openly under dictatorship and in more hidden ways under other forms of government. Dictatorships both of the left and of the right, or those who approve or condone such systems, have also attempted to discredit and wipe out from human memory that which God's prophets teach us, namely the social laws and social system of the Pentateuch. {1, 2, 4, 5}

What we see in the working environment is a worldwide struggle to achieve a humane way of life, each person, family or community struggling to advance at their own level of development, struggling against those who wish to dominate, exploit, oppress. A struggle whose successful outcome depends on trustful cooperation, companionship and teamwork. {13, 23, 22}

The struggle is against those who wish to dominate other people. Against those who want primitive power over others, against those who wish to exploit, against those who may brutally and without feeling oppress human beings so as to exploit them. And 'to exploit' includes the whole range of antisocial decisions and activities of those who put profit before people and community. {21}

Human rights are based on controlling primitive dominant behaviour, on concern, care and affection for our young, for our families, people and communities, and express themselves in cooperation and teamwork between men and women to achieve a good life of high quality.

Defence {13}

Sometimes one has to fight to preserve a good way of life, to prevent others from taking what has been achieved. Or one may be expected to fight on behalf of those who dominate and exploit.

Our primitive animal ancestors behaved instinctively. Hunt for food, kill or be killed, fight or flee. Self before others, regardless of needs of others, marking out and defending territory, might being right.

Later mammals tend to have feelings, care and affection for their young. Human beings think as well as feel, and care for and look after their young for many years.

Having to fight, maim and kill amounts to a throwback to primitive animal behaviour, to behaviour which puts self before others. A throwback to beast-like behaviour for those who attack, to beast-like behaviour to counter beast-like behaviour for those who defend.

But one way of countering viciousness is by greater strength. If attacked, we have to defend ourselves.

Authoritarian organisations are much less effective than participative ones. In authoritarian organisations morale is low, people cease to care and tend to work against each other instead of cooperating with each other for the benefit of the organisation. {25-26}

Human beings cooperate well and achieve effective teamwork. Reason and evaluation can temper (add to, or change) emotional and instinct-motivated behaviour and combine with cooperation and teamwork so as to counter, and overcome, threats.

One has to be stronger than the enemy, socially as well as militarily. Essential is greater social as well as military strength. But the authoritarian mind (which includes the military) has to be balanced to prevent it from taking over, has to be motivated towards 'good'.

So we must not allow ourselves to be corrupted by what has to be done when fighting to preserve and secure that which is good, our way of life. Those who fight on our communities' behalf need to know, believe in, and practice, the word of God every day of their lives.

Responsibility and Accountability

Human beings found an effective defence against antisocial manipulations, namely the basic principle that we are responsible and accountable for what we do and how we do it. Obeying an order is no excuse. It does not matter whether the order comes from a secular or religious source or whether it pops up in one's mind. The person taking the decision, the person giving the order, the person carrying out the order, are each responsible for what they do or omit to do, and for the consequences.

Conclusion

So what one aims to achieve is

> to apply in our lives, and in the communities in which we live, the God-given benevolent social laws and social system of the Pentateuch,
>
> so as to achieve a good and secure life of high quality,
>
> by working for the benefit of the community, and
>
> by taking part in the struggle for a better life.

And we need to co-operate with each other as individuals, families and communities, supporting each other in this common struggle for a better life.

It appears that hurt and pain, oppression and exploitation, suffering and hardship, can and should be transformed and countered by an applied sense of social responsibility, by a sense of common purpose and cooperation between people working together in teams. That is by a sense of, and by the satisfaction of, achievement in locating, countering and overcoming the source of the suffering.

Colloquially speaking, there is enough food here for everyone. Pick your ground, pick whichever you think is most important and then use your knowledge, abilities and skills to achieve the good way of life portrayed in this report.

Your life is likely to be a much more rewarding life of higher quality.

Notes <..>

< 1>   Also known as the 'Five Books of Moses' and as 'Torah'.

< 2>   In {12} see section on 'The Social Cause-and-Effect Relationship'.

   The Social Cause-and-Effect Relationship is also listed (in biblical language and in plain English) in Appendix 4 of {12}, with references to the Pentateuch text.

< 3>   The Pentateuch (Five Books of Moses, at times called 'Torah') consists only of the five books of Moses.

   Those wishing to give other writings an appearance of greater authority refer to these other writings as if they were part of 'Torah'. Those doing so appear to be spreading a kind of misleading political propaganda.

< 4>   In {18} see 'Behaviour and Consequences (Genesis Chapter 9)'

< 5>   For a full listing of the Ten Commandments, in biblical and plain English, see Appendix 5 of {12}. For a good discussion of its provisions see {12}.

< 6>   Normal for human beings is an exclusive sexual relationship between a husband and a wife who joined together to form a life-long family so as to ensure that their children are protected for the

many years before they reach maturity. And the family protects and supports husband and wife as they grow old. {3, 13}

People who behave humanely, morally, can trust each other, co-operate with each other, grow, gain strength together, prosper.

All other sexual relations are abnormal, immoral. Those who behave immorally weaken their family and social strength. Those who initiate moral behaviour, who behave morally and humanely, gain strength and standing. {16}

Hence the
      importance of chastity,
      of human beings controlling their sexual urges,
      and for the human male to control the sexual urge lurking at
      the border of the conscious.

And on marriage the male accepts responsibility for the resulting family for life. {13}

< 7>   First volume of the Pentateuch (Five Books of Moses).

< 8>   Largely in Leviticus.

< 9>   See {13}

<10>   See {17}

<11>   For more information about, and other listings of, the Pentateuch's social rules of behaviour and about its social system, see {12, 17, 16, 4}

<12>   Social security also includes provision covering unemployment, ill health and old age, provided cooperatively {19}. <19>

<13>   At present people would take their sabbatical year in turn, one-seventh of the community in any one year, including one-seventh from each of the different occupations.

<14>   It must be up to the individual to select and choose what he wants to do. Sabbaticals are not an opportunity for the government, the state, a political party, a religious hierarchy or the management of an organisation to direct or train

its employees, to condition through some kind of educational scheme, to pressurise one way or another. {19}

<15>   In {18} see 'Social Laws, Social System'

<16>   Companies and corporations present annual accounts to their shareholders including Funds Flow statements. Community accounts should be made available also in form of a 'Funds Flow' statement, as these can show clearly in meaningful terms where the funds have come from and what has been done with them. In terms such as 'Received from Income Tax', 'Received from Corporation Tax', 'Spent on Unemployment Benefit', 'Spent on Payments to Corporations', and so on.

<17>   At the time the Pentateuch was written, the sharing out of assets was to be updated after every 49 years. At present, updating at regular intervals of between three and not more than five calendar years is more appropriate.

<18>   'Net assets' is the amount of money which would be left for distributing among the owners if everything belonging to an enterprise were sold and all its debts paid.

<19>   The level of support (such as what proportion of the community's income is to be spent on health care) needs to be decided by the population, for example by referendum on basis of valid clearly-stated information compiled by concerned community groups.

References {..}

{ 1}   ORIGIN OF CHRISTIANITY and JUDAISM
         Manfred Davidmann, 1994, 2006
         solhaam.org/

{ 2}   History Speaks: Monarchy, Exile and Maccabees
         Manfred Davidmann, 1978, 2007
         solhaam.org/

{ 3}   See chapter 6.1: 'Creation, Evolution and the
       Origin of Evil'
       Manfred Davidmann, 2000

{ 4}   Causes of Antisemitism
       Manfred Davidmann, 1991, 1995
       solhaam.org/

{ 5}   In {27}, see chapter 2.2 'Prophet Mohammed's
       Struggle for a Better Life for All'
       Manfred Davidmann, 2003

{ 6}   In {27}, see chapter 2.4 'The Divine Right to Rule'
       Manfred Davidmann, 2003

{ 7}   In {27}, see chapter 2.5 'Compiling the Koran:
       Hadiths (Traditions) State the Underlying Reality
       Manfred Davidmann, 2003

{ 8}   In {27}, see chapter 2.6 'Uthman's Rearrangement
       of the Chronological (as revealed) Koran's
       Chapters
       Manfred Davidmann, 2003

{ 9}   In {27}, see chapter 2.7 'Prophet Mohammed's
       Word of Allah and the Voice of the Ruling Elite
       Manfred Davidmann, 2003

{10}   How the Human Brain Developed and How the
       Human Mind Works
       Manfred Davidmann, 1998, 2006
       solhaam.org/

{11}   Pentateuch, Deuteronomy 17: 14-20

{12}   See chapter 4 of this book. And see
       Struggle for Freedom: The Social Cause-and-Effect
       Relationship
       Manfred Davidmann, 1978, 2002
       solhaam.org/.

{13}   See chapter 5: 'Family, Community, Sex and the
       Individual'
       Manfred Davidmann, 1998

{14}   At the Time of Jesus, This is What Actually
       Happened in Israel: The Truth about Hillel and his
       Times
       Manfred Davidmann, 1978, 2007
       solhaam.org/

{15}   One Law for All: Freedom Now, Freedom for Ever
       Manfred Davidmann, 1978, 2007
       solhaam.org/

{16}   See chapter 6.3: 'Morality, Sexual Behaviour and
       Depravity'
       Manfred Davidmann, 2001

{17}   See chapter 6.4: 'Nephilim, Dominance and
       Liberty'
       Manfred Davidmann, 2001

{18}   See chapter 6.2 'Pre-flood Evils and the Social
       Problems of Our Time'
       Manfred Davidmann, 2000

{19}   Co-operatives and Co-operation: Causes of Failure,
       Guidelines for Success
       Manfred Davidmann, 1996
       solhaam.org/

{20}   What People are Struggling Against: How Society is
       Organised for Controlling and Exploiting People
       Manfred Davidmann, 1998, 2002
       solhaam.org/

{21}   Social Responsibility, Profits and Social
       Accountability
       Manfred Davidmann, 1979, 1995
       solhaam.org/

{22}   Motivation Summary
       Manfred Davidmann, 1982, 1998
       solhaam.org/

{23}   The Will to Work: What People Struggle to Achieve
       Manfred Davidmann, 1981, 2006
       solhaam.org/

{24}   Understanding How Society is Organised for
       Controlling and Exploiting People
       Manfred Davidmann, 1998, 2002
       solhaam.org/

{25}   Style of Management and Leadership
       Manfred Davidmann, 1981, 2006
       solhaam.org/

{26}   Role of Managers Under Different Styles of
       Management
       Manfred Davidmann, 1982, 1998
       solhaam.org/

{27}   ISLAM: Basis - Past - Present - Future
       Manfred Davidmann, 2003, 2010
       Social Organisation Limited
       ISBN 978-0-85192-053-5

Struggle for Freedom, Liberty and Independence: The Social Cause-and-Effect Relationship

Introduction and Summary

Manfred Davidmann begins by outlining the social and economic environment in which we live, the problems of today, and then discusses uses and misuses of religion in such circumstances. He then outlines the meaning and significance of the Pentateuch's essential but little-known social and economic laws of behaviour, sketched within the environment in which we live and work.

The relevant social laws and the social system of the Pentateuch are described and explained as a self-contained and complete system which prevents people being exploited through need if they fall on hard times and which prevents ownership being concentrated in the hands of a few. The system enables people to live good and satisfying lives in a just and fair society which guarantees freedom and equality. The laws of redemption, for example, are shown to be leasehold laws designed to maintain an equal and fair distribution of income and wealth among the population as a whole. Biblical law underlies all freedom.

This chapter is largely based on, and includes much material from, 'Struggle for Freedom: The Social Cause-and-Effect Relationship' {46}.

Most of the problems now threatening the survival of humankind are caused by the selfish interests of those who are attempting to organise and run society for their own gain. On the other hand are those who resist and struggle on behalf of the interests and benefit of the community at large.

The two sides encourage and spread the kind of behaviour which enables them to gain and keep their own type of society: dictatorship and exploitation on the one hand, freedom and good life on the other.

Hence it is vitally important to know what kind of behaviour serves what kind of ends. If we wish to gain freedom and remain free then we need to know which kind of behaviour gives us strength, enables us to co-operate with each other, helps us to raise the quality of life for all, helps us to lead good and satisfying lives.

It is this which makes the Social Cause-and-Effect Relationship so important. It is stated in the Pentateuch as a fundamental scientific law which applies to all people at all times no matter where they live or what they believe in or what their state of development.

The prophets knew and understood the Social Cause-and-Effect Relationship and how it operates when they predicted what would happen as a result of the way people behave.

Knowledge and understanding of the Social Cause-and-Effect Relationship give us an understanding of how what happens depends on people's behaviour, and a greater understanding of what determines the pattern of events.

Manfred Davidmann details the Social Cause-and-Effect Relationship in biblical language as well as in plain English, detailing the consequences of either following the laws or else of ignoring them.

The legislation shows how people can protect themselves against losing their freedom and how to gain even greater freedom. It opens the door to freedom, to a good life and to government which looks after the interests of its people.

Within Pentateuch law is described the next step ahead towards complete freedom. The strength of individuals and of countries, and even more so the survival of humankind under present conditions, depend on the application of these Pentateuch laws.

The Struggle for Freedom

What people like and what they aim at {44} is to provide for and to satisfy the basic needs for

> shelter, warmth, clothing, food, affection and belonging (within family), friendly and trustful co-operation and companionship, housing, education, good health and good medical services, security against internal and external threats, employment and satisfying work at increasing levels of skill and usefulness and thus of pay, the highest possible standard of living and constructive satisfying leisure activities.

In other words, people wish to live and behave towards each other in a way in which each serves the community which in turn provides for and looks after its members.

They are opposed in this by those who wish to exploit others. Hence the aims of a community have to be achieved by means of struggle, at the level of the human mind and then at the level of events. This is a struggle both for men's minds and for a good life here on earth. It is a struggle which has gone on since one man tried to enslave another.

From Dictatorship to Democracy

Under dictatorship the freedom of the individual is brutally repressed, the individual is at the mercy of state and employer, is told what to do and how to live. The 'state' attempts to destroy that which enables the individual to resist by attempting to weaken and destroy opposing religious beliefs and the strength of the family unit.

Revolutions are successful only when they succeed in replacing an oppressing dictatorship or government by one providing greater personal freedom, such as is obtained by moving away from dictatorship towards democracy. It is in democracies that people have more individual freedom than under dictatorships of the left or of the right, and it is in democracies that people have a far higher standard of living than under dictatorships.

Struggle within Democracy

Successful struggle against dictatorship leads to a democratic form of government and in western democracies there is a large measure of individual freedom, a high standard of living, and the opportunity to struggle and battle freely towards a better life and greater happiness for their citizens. The point of balance has been shifted away from dictatorship towards greater freedom and a better life but the intense struggle taking place within democracies is the same struggle between on the one side those who wish to exploit and oppress, and on the other those who wish to gain, preserve and strengthen freedom.

Correspondingly, there are two ways {43} in which democracies can move, namely on the one side back towards dictatorship and on the other forwards towards a better, more secure and happier life, towards greater freedom from oppression and exploitation, towards a more satisfying life, towards a more egalitarian society.

Those who wish to oppress and exploit use money and the power this provides as a means for doing so. Western democracies are still materialistic societies, money counts and people work for money and material wealth, sometimes regardless of the costs to others or to the community. He who pays the piper calls the tune and the dictates of those who run society, the dictates of those few in whose hands wealth, patronage and power is concentrated, then often seem more important to those whom they employ than the welfare and happiness of the population.

Most of the problems now threatening the survival of humanity are due to this conflict between the selfish interest of those who are attempting to organise and run society for their own personal gain on the one hand, and the interests and benefit of the community at large on the other. There are many examples of which but a few are the man-made Minamata disease {38}, and the cases discussed by Heilbronner {39} and Carson {40}.

The two sides encourage and spread the kind of behaviour which enables them to gain and keep their own type of society: dictatorship and exploitation on the one hand, freedom and good life on the other. Hence it is vitally important to know what kind of behaviour serves what kind of ends.

Impact of Behaviour: Our Troubled Times

It is a well-known fact that the way in which people behave determines their own life and freedom, and the strength and thus freedom of their people as a whole.

68

Behaviour of a particular kind strengthens individuals, strengthens their ability to resist oppression and exploitation. Basic is that people behave in a way which enables them to trust and assist each other, that men and women co-operate with each other in a way which will protect and strengthen both, behaving in a way which ensures that all benefit from gains made.

The younger generation has much to gain from the past experience of their parents, has much to gain from their parents' knowledge of tried and proved beliefs and values. Clearly it is one's parents who have the short and long-term interest of the child and teenager at heart, regardless of other considerations. The family is the basic unit of society and it looks after the interests of all its members, as individuals as well as collectively. This gives great strength to each member of the family in the struggle for daily bread, security and happiness.

It is those who wish to weaken democracy and freedom who condone and thus permit and encourage behaviour which separates people and turns them against each other. They also stress material considerations because religious values emphasize that people are all-important.

An example is immoral behaviour such as having sexual relations before marriage, or after marriage with a person other than one's spouse. Such behaviour turns men against women and robs both of the support of their family.

So you see how important behaviour is and we will now explore this in more detail.

Oppression Through Need

In Egypt there were years of famine but Pharaoh had much grain in his stores. In return for food the people handed over all the money they had, then their horses and farm animals, finally selling themselves to Pharaoh into slavery and selling all their land. The people were then moved from their cities from one end of the land to the other, to drive home to them that they were slaves, that they had to obey regardless of the consequences, that they and the land belonged to their master - Pharaoh. But he had fed his priests so that they had no need to sell either themselves or their land and they glorified Pharaoh in the eyes of the people. From then on the people, Pharaoh's slaves, belonged to him totally and had to pay Pharaoh each year one-fifth of all they produced.

We have not made much progress since then. Much the same situation exists today, much the same techniques are used today to oppress and enslave, in varying degrees in different countries.

For example, the Khmer Rouge in Cambodia took a generous and fine people, drove them away from their towns and homes into the countryside into utter starvation and dependence at great loss of life, thus subjecting and enslaving them. In the USSR the land and all other productive capital belonged to the state, the establishment's communist party controlling the people for its rulers. People had no individual freedom. Job and livelihood depended on following the dictates of the state. The people were effectively enslaved, had to do as they were told, were subjected to vicious inhuman treatment if they protested.

'He who pays the piper calls the tune' applies equally in a democracy as in a dictatorship, applies to political parties no matter whether of right or left. It illustrates what happens when power is concentrated in the hands of a few who run a country. Their influence is extended through wealth and patronage. Those who dispense patronage are those who control jobs, are those who through controlling employment in effect control the means of livelihood and of survival. When these few wish to exploit their people they, and their establishment which depends on them for patronage and income, attempt on the one side to persuade and compel the people to obey and on the other to weaken them so that they become less able to resist oppression. In democracies, freedom and good life are under attack.

Brutality of Man to Man

The consequences of regarding religious values and norms as irrelevant and of thus allowing oneself to be divided against one's fellow, that is the consequences of antisocial behaviour, are very clear. People begin to behave in ways which harm other people, and begin to pursue their own selfish interests. Apathy and neglect towards others result, followed by disregard of community and personal property and by cruelty and viciousness towards others.

There is increasing wanton antisocial behaviour such as vandalism and mugging. There is a loss of internal security, both from loss of property and from attack against the person. The quality of life is lowered even further by those who pursue personal gain regardless of its cost to other people.

Viciousness and brutality of people towards each other, disregard of the value of the individual and of life itself, are not normal behaviour. People who behave in this way become isolated and divided against each other. People who behave in this way do not gain, as in reality they are working for the personal power and wealth of their own brutalised leadership.

Immorality

Those who understand its effects know {41} that sex performs the enormously important function of creating a special single deep emotional relationship between two people which gives them the strength to overcome life's problems, to form a strong family unit which serves and protects all its members. The depth of such a relationship between husband and wife can be appreciated as one sees them both battling on together successfully regardless of how tough the struggle.

In all countries where sex education has been introduced the same corruptive pattern of social change has been observed {42}: sexual experimentation starts and promiscuity increases. Promiscuity leads to increasing sexual dissatisfaction, to the weakening of family life and marriage bonds and to sexual excesses. The substitute satisfactions of smoking, drinking, and drug-taking increase and there is a lowering of the age of those involved. There is an upsurge in wanton destructive aggression in the community and a rise in aggressive juvenile delinquency. There is increasing concern over the harm done on young children by the practices and by the lack of concern and commitment of their parents, and concern has already been expressed over increasing male impotence. These effects are now obvious to any intelligent reader of the informed press.

It is well known that those who engage in sexual relations outside marriage find themselves looking in vain for the affection which is missing to an ever greater extent from their relationships, become less and less able to commit themselves to the other person, mean ever less to each other. Increasing divorce rates, the resultant delinquency of children, the completely casual and inhuman ways some parents treat each other and their children, are almost the direct outcome of pre-marital and adulterous, that is promiscuous, sexual relations.

History shows that free societies which allow themselves to become 'permissive' (promiscuous) weaken themselves to the point where their civilisation destroys itself, or is destroyed by outsiders. Those who wish to weaken democracy condone and/or encourage 'permissiveness'. On the other hand, those who restrict sex to within marriage gain creativity and increase their strength. {41}

The family is the basic unit of society. Its strength depends on the ability of the partners to commit themselves to each other and that means on those who restrict sexual relations to within marriage. Men and women who do so practice a form of self-control which enables them to form a deep and lasting relationship, which in turn lays the basis for happy and contented family life for themselves and their children. The relationship between them is based on mutual trust and respect arising from the sure knowledge that they are in a vital exclusive relationship to each other, that they are working and co-operating with each other for the common good of themselves and their children.

Those Responsible

The media are at present being used to persuade and condition people into thinking that religion is irrelevant, that antisocial behaviour will not have unpleasant consequences. However, the cost to the community of the kind of negative and antisocial behaviour outlined in the sections above, of the lowering of the quality of life, of loss of freedom for the individual, and of loss of satisfaction from the work we do, is enormous. {45}

To answer the question: "Who encourages antisocial behaviour?" we need to ask: "Who benefits from antisocial behaviour?"

It is those who have power through controlling patronage, money and wealth who benefit from antisocial behaviour and who are thus responsible for permitting and encouraging the different forms of antisocial behaviour we have discussed.

Today's Battle for Freedom

Pentateuch (Biblical) Law

The Ten Commandments are so important and are so well known because it is behaviour in accordance with these laws which is the basis for people trusting each other and so for people co-operating and working well with each other. They are here listed both in biblical language and in plain English.

When Moses brought the tables of the law he brought 'freedom upon the tables'. It is the Ten Commandments as a whole which underlie freedom, independence and strength to oppose and resist oppression. Wherever there is any spiritual and material freedom today it exists because people followed these laws (rules) of behaviour and it exists to the extent to which they do so. In other words, following the provisions of the law results in freedom and ensures it, ensures strength and security.

The statement that there is one God and one God alone who delivered us from slavery in Egypt means that only these laws, only this code of behaviour, enables you to gain freedom and stay free.

If you follow advice given by those who want you to behave differently then you are in fact praying to another god, no matter whether this so-called 'god' attempts to influence you through the attitudes and opinions of your external enemies or through opinions and practices being spread internally.

History shows that in the past the people have been betrayed again and again, by non-observant leaderships no matter whether right or left and by so-called orthodox or fundamentalist leaderships who weakened the application of the law so as to be able to oppress the people in order to exploit them. It was those who did not follow the law who in the past grasped power and then weakened and defeated the hope for achieving freedom and a good life for the people and thus in due course for all humanity.

It is equally certain that the same battle is being fought today and it is just as certain that on the one hand is the opportunity to gain freedom while on the other hand our defeat can only result in mankind rapidly destroying itself.

The rules of behaviour of the Ten Commandments are based on a knowledge of what goes on in peoples' minds, of the inner workings of communities and societies, and of democratic and authoritarian organisation. To free ourselves from mental conditioning and brainwashing we have to follow the Ten Commandments and apply the social laws and the social system of the Pentateuch.

Ten Commandments {47}

Religious Language	**Plain English**
	1
I am the Lord your God, who brought you ... out of the house of bondage.	This is the voice of freedom. I proved this by freeing you from enslavement.
And the tables were the work of God, and the writing was the writing of God, freedom upon the tables {47}.	What is being given to you is the pattern of behaviour which underlies all freedom.
You shall have no other gods before Me.	If you want freedom and a good life then there is no other way.
	2
You shall not make for yourself a	You shall not bow down to or serve

73

graven image, even any manner of likeness, of anything that is in heaven above, or that is in the earth beneath, or that is in the waters under the earth.

You shall not bow down to them, nor serve them.

For I the Lord your God am a jealous God, visiting the iniquity of the fathers upon the children, and upon the third and upon the fourth generation of them that hate Me, but showing mercy to the thousandth generation of those who love Me and keep My commandments.

any other kind of god or image or likeness of anything whatsoever.

Those who respect and serve other gods, respect or serve oppressing, exploiting or enslaving beliefs or ideologies, they hate me and they and their children will suffer the consequences even on the fourth generations.

But those who love Me and keep My commandments are shown mercy to the thousandth generation.

3

You shall not take the name of the Lord your God in vain; for the Lord will not hold him guiltless who takes his name in vain.

You shall not use God's name to lend authority to a statement which it would not otherwise have or to a false or misleading statement.

4

Observe the Sabbath day, to keep it holy, as the Lord your God commanded you. Six days shall you labour, and do all your work;

Observe the Sabbath day, the seventh day which is a day of rest from work for all,

but the seventh day is a Sabbath to the Lord your God: in it you shall not do any manner of work - you, nor your son, nor your daughter, nor your man-servant, nor your maid-servant, nor your ox, nor your ass, nor any of your cattle, nor the stranger who is within your gates;

on which all are equal and rest,

that your man-servant and your maid-servant may rest as well as you.

And you shall remember that you were a servant in the land of Egypt, and the Lord your God brought you out from there by a mighty hand and by an outstretched arm; therefore the Lord your God commanded you to keep the Sabbath day.

on which your servants rest just as you do.

You shall remember that it was God who freed you from most brutal service by a mighty hand and by an outstretched arm.

Therefore God commanded you to keep the Sabbath day.

5

Honour your father and your mother, as the Lord your God commanded you; that your days may be long, and that it may go well with you, on the land which the Lord your God gives you.

Honour your father and your mother and willingly accept God's commands and the tradition, knowledge and life experience of your parents so that you will progress and advance in understanding and in life and so that you will have long and secure lives of high quality in the land God will give you.

6

You shall not murder.

7

You shall not commit adultery.

8

You shall not steal.

9

You shall not bear false witness against your neighbour.

10

You shall not covet your neighbour's wife; neither shall you desire your neighbour's house, his field, or his man-servant, or his maid-servant, his ox, or his ass, or any thing that is your neighbour's.

From Oppression to Freedom, From Exploitation to Good Life

Vast power to control our environment is at our beck and call. During the short interval of only about eighty years we have learned to travel by car, to fly, explore space and land on the moon. We communicate with each other within seconds all around the planet by sound and sight, have learned to harness the power of the atom and are attempting to control the power of the sun itself. Computers help us to store and retrieve the ever increasing flood of data, enable us to carry out intricate calculations in the twinkling of an eye which previously would have taken months to do. We have made enormous progress in technology and science. A good and satisfying life for all can be ours here and now.

The same period has also seen the concentration camps of Europe, the damage done by thalidomide and that by mercury in the Bay of Minamata, what has been done to the Cambodians, the misuse of psychiatry in Russia and the misuse of power within some American corporations. Our increasing technological and scientific skills are so far unmatched by similar progress in human relations, in our knowledge about why people behave as they do, about how people should behave towards each other, about what needs to be done and can be done to help people co-operate with each other.

The increasing problems which threaten our environment are eloquent witness to our lack of progress in the field of human relationships. These problems, increasing in frequency as well as in sheer size and in number of people affected by them, are in the end caused by people, caused by the way people treat each other, by the way people co-operate with each other. We see the daily increasing cost.

Daily it is becoming more essential for people to co-operate with each other for the common good. People are becoming more and more aware of this.

Daily more and more people speak up and get together and make their opinions felt, becoming more and more aware of basic causes. They co-operate and struggle successfully towards better life and greater freedom.

The key to this is behaviour, the way in which people behave towards each other. It is only now that we are beginning to understand why people do what they do and why they behave as they do. We now know some qualitative cause-and-effect relationships between what people do and the effects of their actions on themselves and on others.

If we wish to become free and remain free then we need to know which kind of behaviour gives us strength, enables us to co-operate with each other, helps us to raise the quality of life for all, helps us to lead good and satisfying lives.

Indeed this is the reason we are looking at the Social Cause-and-Effect Relationship, illustrating this from 3,000 years of continuous human history.

Predictions of the Prophets

The warnings of the prophets are discussed in 'History Speaks' {48} and their role is discussed in 'One Law for All' {49}. Here we are looking at their predictions in relation to the Social Cause-and-Effect Relationship.

The prophets foretold what would happen as a result of how people were behaving if people continued to behave as they did. They foretold that Israel would be lost if people continued to behave as they did.

A scientist predicts what would happen in the future as a result of some experiment if the experimental conditions are maintained. The prediction, if based on knowledge of proved scientific laws, will be valid.

To someone who has no knowledge or understanding of science and its laws, the scientist's prediction will appear to be a 'prophesy', a foretelling of what will happen as if by divine inspiration.

And so the predictions of the prophets were divinely inspired prophesies to those unaware of the knowledge which the prophets had.

What the prophets said were predictions based on knowledge and understanding of the Cause-and-Effect Relationship in the Pentateuch. This is stated as a fundamental scientific law which applies to all at all times. To understand this relationship means to understand the inevitability of events predicted by them.

The Cause-and-Effect Relationship is just as valid today as then, and it applies to all at all times, no matter where they live or what they believe in or their state of development.

Knowledge and understanding of the Cause-and-Effect Relationship and of how it operates is what the prophets had when they predicted what would happen as a result of the way people behave.

Knowledge and understanding of the Cause-and-Effect Relationship and of how it operates gives us similar understanding to that which the prophets had, of how what happens depends on how people behave, and enables us to understand today's events and what determines the pattern of events.

In History

When talking about results of 'behaviour', what is meant is not just the behaviour of individual persons but also the behaviour of people as a whole. It includes the behaviour of the people, of their leadership, of their religious dignitaries, of their kings and rulers. 'Behaviour' then includes the crime (evil) of allowing their secular and religious leadership to corrupt them, to mislead and oppress them.

The lessons from the past are there for all to see. There is no need to keep repeating the same mistakes. The events speak for themselves.

History clearly and convincingly illustrates the working of the relationship through successive periods of exile and return of the Jewish people to the land of Israel. History shows that behaviour determines events in the way described by the Social Cause-and-Effect Relationship. {48}

The relationship applies to all people and not only to the Jews. However, it is the Jews who retained their belief as a way of life during periods of exile and adversity and who were thus able to survive, return to Israel and regain freedom.

In the Pentateuch

It seems to me that it was not possible to describe the cause-and-effect relationship between social behaviour of individuals and of people, and the resulting freedom or oppression and conflict, three thousand years ago in a way which could have been understood by those then reading the Pentateuch. Hence it was stated to the people in a way which could be understood so as to enable them to follow the law and thus benefit from knowledge of the effect of their behaviour, even if they did not understand at the time the basis of and the reason for the legislation.

There is no mistaking the clear knowledge of the relationship and the deep concern for people which the text indicates: it clearly states the consequences arising from opposite kinds of behaviour and lays down behaviour as a norm which strengthens and protects the individual and the community.

Relatively few scientific papers are able to report their findings in such comprehensive manner, are able to describe and illustrate a complete relationship from beginning to end, clearly stating the extent to which it applies.

The relevant passages from the Pentateuch are listed below in plain English as well as in the Pentateuch's religious language. It is seen that they clearly describe the relationship and the range over which it applies. The relationship itself is clearly illustrated by examples covering the range of effects from one end of the scale to the other.

History and recent social statistics clearly show that behaviour which is contrary to the law lowers the quality of life, increases internal stress and conflict to the point of social disruption and military weakness. Those who behave according to the law have good and satisfying lives, gain social and military strength. {48}

Social Cause-and-Effect Relationship

The Relationship Underlies All Freedom

Plain English	Religious Language
This is the voice of freedom. I proved this by freeing you.	I am the Lord your God, who brought you ... out of the house of bondage. {1}
What is being given to you in the Torah is the pattern of behaviour which underlies all freedom.	And the tables were the work of God, and the writing was the writing of God, freedom upon the tables. {2}
If you want freedom and a good life then there is no other way.	You shall have no other Gods before Me. {3}

Introduction to Relationship

Plain English	Religious Language
You are unable (at your present stage of knowledge and development) to understand the Cause-and-Effect Relationship. However, the information given here enables you to see what will happen	The secret things belong to the Lord our God; but the things that are revealed belong to us and to our children for ever, that we may do all the words of this law. {4}

as a result of your behaviour.

Even if you do not see how that which happens results from your behaviour, the consequences of your behaviour are certain to occur and will be as stated.	I call heaven and earth to witness against you this day ... {5, 6}

Outline of Relationship

Plain English	Religious Language
The quality of your life can range from freedom and a good secure life at one end of the scale to oppression and enslavement at the other end.	See, I have set before you this day life and good, and death and evil, ... {7} ... I have set before you life and death, the blessing and the curse; ... {8}
Where you will be on this scale depends on the way you behave towards each other, that is on the extent to which you follow the law.	
Allow yourself to be persuaded into contrary behaviour and you will be oppressed and enslaved. Follow the law and you will be free and have a good life.	But if your heart turn away, and you will not hear, ... you shall surely perish; ... choose life, that you may live, ... {9}

Extent to Which It Applies

The relationship applies:

Plain English	Religious Language
(1) to all without exception	... your heads, your tribes, your elders, and your officers, even all the men of Israel, your little ones, your wives, and your stranger that is in the midst of your camp, from the hewer of your wood to the drawer of your water; {10}

(2) at all times, to the present as well as to the future

... with him that stands here with us this day ... and also with him that is not here with us this day {11}

(3) here and now, wherever you may happen to be

... it is not too hard for you, neither is it far off. ... It is not in heaven ... neither is it beyond the sea ... {12}

(4) to your mind (thoughts) and to your emotions (feelings)

(It) is very close to you, in your mouth and in your heart, that you may do it. {12}

THE RELATIONSHIP

Plain English	Religious Language	
	Results of Observing the Law	Results of Disregarding the Law
The actual results of behaviour both ways are listed and described, clearly and powerfully illustrating intermediate stages between the two ends of the scale.	Blessed shall you be in the city, and blessed shall you be in the field. {13}	Cursed shall you be in the city, and cursed shall you be in the field. {14}
	Blessed shall be the fruit of your body, and the fruit of your land, and the fruit of your cattle, the increase of your kine and the young of your flock. {15}	Cursed shall be the fruit of your body, and the fruit of your land, the increase of your kine, and the young of your flock. {16}
	The Lord will cause your enemies that rise up against you to be smitten before you; they shall come	The Lord will cause you to be smitten before your enemies; you shall go out

out against you one way, and shall flee before you seven ways. {17}

one way against them, and shall flee seven ways before them; and you shall be a horror to all the kingdoms of the earth. {18}

And the lord will make you over-abundant for good, in the fruit of your body, and in the fruit of your cattle, and in the fruit of your land, in the land which the Lord swore to your fathers to give you. {19}

The fruit of your land, and all your labours, shall a nation which you do not know eat up; and you shall be only oppressed and crushed away; {20}

The Lord will bring you, and your king whom you will set over you, to a nation you have not known, you nor your fathers; and there shall you serve other gods, wood and stone. {21}

...you shall lend to many nations, but you shall not borrow. {22}

The stranger that is in your midst shall mount up above you higher and higher; and you shall come down lower and lower. {24}

And the Lord will make you the head, and not the tail; and you shall be above only, and you shall not be below; if you shall hearken to the

He shall lend to you, and you

commandments of
the Lord your God,
which I command
you this day, to
observe and to do
them; {23}

shall not lend to
him; he shall be
the head and
you shall be the
tail. {25}

Plain English   **Religious Language**

Results of   **Results of**
Observing the Law   **Disregarding the**
                            Law

The process is
reversible.

Increasingly
disregarding the
law results in
greater
suffering and
oppression.

The Lord will
bring a nation
against you from
far {26}

... and he shall
eat the fruit of
your cattle, and
the fruit of your
ground, until you
be destroyed
{27}

... and he shall
besiege you in
all your gates
throughout all
your land {28}

... and you shall
be plucked from
off the land {29}

And the Lord
shall scatter you
among all
peoples, {30}

And your life
shall hang in
doubt before

you; and you
shall fear night
and day and
shall have no
assurance of
your life {31}

Plain English	Religious Language	
	Results of Observing the Law	Results of Disregarding the Law
Increasingly behaving according to the law results in greater freedom and a better life.	... when ... you bethink yourself among the nations, {32} and ... hearken to all that I command you {33} (then) the Lord your God will bring you into the land which your fathers possessed, and you shall possess it; {34} And the Lord your God will put all these curses upon your enemies, and on them that hate you, that persecuted you {35} And the Lord your God will make you over-abundant in all the work of your hand, in the fruit of your body, and in the fruit of your	

cattle, and in the
fruit of your land,
for good; {36}

if you keep His
commandments and
His statutes which
are written in this
book of the law; if
you turn to the Lord
your God with all
your heart, and with
all your soul. {37}

References

{ 1} Exod **20**, 2
{ 2} Exod **32**, 16
{ 3} Exod **20**, 3
{ 4} Deut **29**, 28
{ 5} Deut **30**, 19
{ 6} 'I call heaven and earth to witness against you this day ...'.
      Witnesses are directly concerned with punishing the culprit.
      Heaven and earth will enforce the relationship both ways which
      is equivalent to saying that we have here a direct cause-and-
      effect relationship, that the consequences of given types of
      behaviour will be as stated.
{ 7} Deut **30**, 15
{ 8} Deut **30**, 19
{ 9} Deut **30**, 17-19
{10} Deut **29**, 9-10
{11} Deut **29**, 14
{12} Deut **30**, 11-14
{13} Deut **28**, 3
{14} Ibid, 16
{15} Ibid, 4
{16} Ibid, 18
{17} Ibid, 7
{18} Ibid, 25
{19} Ibid, 11
{20} Ibid, 33
{21} Ibid, 36
{22} Ibid, 12
{23} Ibid, 13

{24} Ibid, 43

{25} Ibid, 44

{26} Ibid, 49

{27} Ibid, 51

{28} Ibid, 52

{29} Ibid, 63

{30} Deut **28**, 64

{31} Ibid, 66

{32} Deut **30**, 1

{33} Ibid, 2

{34} Ibid, 5

{35} Ibid, 7

{36} Ibid, 9

{37} Ibid, 10

{38} The Horror of Pollution: This Water has Maimed a Generation, Sunday Times Magazine, 1973 November 18.

{39} In the Name of Profit, R. L. Heilbronner, Doubleday, New York.

{40} Silent Spring, Rachel Carson, 1962.

{41} If You Want a Future, Read On ..., David Baram

{42} Louise W. Eickoff, Consultant Psychiatrist, Guardian, 1970 September 12

{43} Style of Management and Leadership.
Manfred Davidmann, 1981, 2006
solhaam.org/

{44} The Will to Work: What People Struggle to Achieve
Manfred Davidmann, 1981, 2006
solhaam.org/

{45} Social Responsibility, Profits and Social Accountability
Manfred Davidmann, 1979, 1995
solhaam.org/

{46} Struggle for Freedom: The Social Cause-and-Effect Relationship
Manfred Davidmann, 1978, 2002
solhaam.org/

{47} Deut **5**, 6-18; Exod **20**, 2-14

{48} History Speaks: Monarchy, Exile and Maccabees
Manfred Davidmann, 1978, 2007
solhaam.org/
(See MONARCHY FOLLOWED BY TWO KINGDOMS - Warnings of the Prophets)

{49} One Law for All: Freedom Now, Freedom for Ever
Manfred Davidmann, 1978, 2007
solhaam.org/
(See TELL THE PEOPLE - Role of the Prophets)

Chapter 5

Family, Community, Sex and the Individual

Introduction

The work, analysis and findings reported here investigate casual sex and its effects on individuals, family and community. Also investigated is dominance and confrontation within the family and in the working environment, how men and women relate to each other, and the role of the family in bringing up children.

This report examines root causes of major social problems and shows how to resolve the problems by dealing with their basic causes. The report pulls together information from earlier reports and adds some important sections. The new material deals with how sex affects the individual, with sexual restraint and control, and with the evolution and current role of the family and of its members.

In this report are statements about effects on people, or how people respond, on how people behave, and so on. In all such cases it is understood that in every case there is a range of effects or behaviour from one end of a spectrum to the other, that what applies to one does not apply to another. So while the statements made in the report apply to a whole group or population, they cannot be said to apply to all individuals or to specific individuals.

But the effects I listed in the earlier publications now appear obvious and in the USA steps are being taken to halt and reverse the increasing corruption of their communities.

Role of the Family

How Human Beings Evolved

As far as we know the human brain evolved in three main stages {12}. Its ancient and primitive part is the innermost reptilian brain. Next evolved the mammalian brain by adding new functions and new ways of controlling the body. Then evolved the third part of the brain, the neocortex, the grey matter, the bulk of the brain in two symmetrical hemispheres, separate but communicating. To a considerable extent it is our neocortex which enables us to behave like human beings. {11}

Human emotional responses depend on neuronal pathways which link the right hemisphere to the mammalian brain which in turn is linked to the even older reptilian brain.

For human beings, primitive (reptilian) instinctive urges and behaviour are overlaid by mammalian care and affection for one's young and human care and affection for one's family and community. {11}

So the human brain includes a wide range of emotions, of feelings, of care and affection, and the capability for objective and logical thinking and evaluation.

Compared with most, if not all, other animals we also have much longer lifespans and it takes a long time before a human baby becomes an adult. Born after nine months in the mother's womb, followed by 4 to 5 years as infant, then 8 to 10 years as child being educated, and say 6 to 9 years as adolescent, about 18 to 25 years old when becoming an adult and independent member of the community.

There is a whole scale of behaviour from human to the beast-like, from behaviour based on affection for the other person to, at the other end, uncontrolled behaviour such as rape, and the seduction of the young which I see as another form of rape.

Mammalian and human parts of our brain control our reptilian ancestor's instinctive copulation urges {11}. It seems as if rapists and paedophiles do not restrain and control their bottom-level beast-like instincts, and it seems to be these which urge them on.

The instinctive sex urge aims to ensure the survival of the species. We have been able to adapt and advance by a process of natural selection and a key characteristic which distinguishes human beings from animals is that we can control the sex urge.

Role of the Family

Something like 200 million years of evolution are behind us, from reptilian beast through mammalian animal to human being. Human beings are mammals and are unique in that our children need protecting and bringing up in a humane, emotionally and mentally stimulating environment for between 18 and 21 years, to enable them to mature into socially responsible adults {11}. Men and women co-operate with each other and look after each other and their children, within the family, to do just that.

So the role of the family is

> To struggle as a family to survive.
>
> To protect and support mother and children until children become mature and independent adults capable of providing for themselves.
>
> To provide a good standard of living and a life of high quality. Which includes struggling against oppression and exploitation. And sometimes one has to fight to preserve a good way of life.
>
> To serve the interests of, and to support, each member of the family. In turn, each member of the family supports the family.

Hence human beings work primarily for their family and members of a family stand by, support and help each other in times of need. The family is the basic unit of society and it looks after the interests of all its members, as individuals as well as collectively. This gives great strength to each member of the family in the struggle for daily bread, security and happiness.

Protecting and Caring for the Next Generation

There is a genetic difference between men and women. It is women who bear the child and who need protecting and looking after while bearing the child and after childbirth. There clearly are close emotional bonds between mother and child.

It is women who generally look after people, after the welfare and well-being of the members of the family. Care, concern, affection and love, feelings and emotions, are important and matter, and women developed, and have, much skill and expertise in such matters. It is generally men who struggle outside the family to secure survival and good living for the family. A struggle for survival in a seemingly hostile environment engineered by other humans.

Primarily the family exists to protect and support its young, and this means supporting and looking after the female bearing the child within her body, through birth and while she is protecting and teaching the young how to behave. It is usually the woman whose role it is to ensure the family provides the young with the humane, emotionally and mentally stimulating environment they need to enable them to mature into socially responsible adults. She is assisted in this by her spouse, depending on her needs and depending on his own work. But it is usually the woman who copes with the personal and emotional problems of the family's members and this is challenging, demanding and difficult work demanding social ability and skills as well as care, affection, understanding and concern for people.

In the kibbutzim, that is in Israel's co-operative settlements, children were brought up communally in age groups, away from their parents. One age group would progress together from creche to nursery and then to school, living together during the week and seeing their parents, or living with their parents, only at weekends.

This may have freed both parents for work and defence in the initial struggle for survival. But the practice was continued when successful, possibly to free women for work and so increase production. But it was done at the expense of the family.

Of any group in the country, the kibbutz children consequently showed the highest incidence of mental problems. The kibbutzim have had to backtrack and now give their children a more normal and strengthening family-life experience with their parents. {13}

When women are persuaded to regard work outside of the family as more important than caring for the young or the family's members, they are in effect handing over the family's key role to outsiders such as day-care businesses and television programme makers. With disastrous results on the way the young perceive home life and adult behaviour, tending to condition the young into behaving like fictional and unreal role models, for example concerning sexual behaviour. Instead of gaining an adult understanding of the reality of living, of family values and relationships, instead of understanding and experiencing socially-responsible behaviour caring for and living with other people, instead of seeing adults (parents) behave in socially responsible way struggling in a hostile environment to do the best they can for the young and for each other.

The number of young people who run away from home and family, often becoming homeless, placing themselves at a big disadvantage right at the beginning of their lives, speaks for itself.

The family needs food and shelter and while the female looks after its young and its people, it is usually the male who struggles outside the immediate family to provide it with an income, with a standard of living, to the best of his ability {4, 5}. He is assisted in this when required by his spouse to an extent which depends on her own work within the family. He struggles outside the family to provide it with a good life against those who wish to profit from the family's needs, against those who wish to exploit, who may even wish to oppress so as to exploit.

Sexual Relations

Sex and the Individual

Sex is habit-forming and addictive but can be controlled when the will is there, when the individual is motivated to control it.

Young people are persuaded to have sex for the first time, are seduced, by those who crave for sex regardless of the cost to the young person being misused by being seduced. The cost to the young can be great. The earlier the age of seduction, the more ingrained is the habit, the greater the difficulties of later controlling it.

Having sex for the first time, first intercourse between adults, is a deeply emotional experience which binds people together in a strong bond of care and affection for each other. That is why 'men wish to sleep around but wish to marry virgins', or a succession of virgins if they are rich enough to afford the divorces.

Should the lovers separate, the emotional cost for the seduced is high indeed. Desperate feelings of isolation, loneliness, betrayal. Shock. Almost unbearable. Reluctance to commit oneself again.

With the next relationship there is still commitment, care and affection but more reserved, there is reluctance to commit oneself completely, to commit one's emotions completely, so as to avoid the pain of separation if this should occur again.

After repeated separations, there is little or no emotional commitment or care for the other person. Sex is casual, the individual sleeps around, attempting to gain the pleasure sex can bring. Looking for sex regardless of thought or feelings or care for the other person, regardless of the cost to the other person.

It appears to be well known that those who engage in sexual relations outside marriage find themselves looking in vain for the affection which is missing to an ever-greater extent from their relationships, become less and less able to commit themselves to the other person, mean ever less to each other.

So people who are aware of the likely consequences tend consciously to refrain from promiscuous relationships. When unaware of the consequences, people tend intuitively to put on the brake when tempted to behave promiscuously.

Effect on Behaviour and Community

Some men are persuaded into sleeping around, in turn attempting to persuade women to make themselves available for casual sex. When women were persuaded to make themselves sexually available they relaxed the control which had kept in check the primitive instinctive urge to copulate. Women had protected society by their chastity, had by their chastity compelled men to support and look after the mother (his wife) and their children while support was needed while the young were developing into adults, had protected and maintained the family and the community in this way.

Casual sex weakens and deadens feelings of care and affection for the other person, for partner or spouse, changing feelings of care and affection into a desire to use others for selfish pleasure regardless of the cost to the other person. So people who sleep around, who are addicted to casual sex, use other people to obtain sex, do so without concern or affection for their partners. They may then begin to behave in ways which harm other people, and may begin to pursue their own selfish interests. Apathy and neglect towards others can result.

Society corrupts itself when human care, affection and concern for one's own family, and for other people, is weakened, is bypassed by self-interest at expense of others.

There is increasing wanton antisocial behaviour such as vandalism and mugging. There is a loss of internal security, by loss of property and by attack against the person. The quality of life is lowered even further by those who pursue personal gain regardless of its cost to other people.

All this was clear in the seventies:

> In all countries where sex education has been introduced the same corruptive pattern of social change has been observed {3}: sexual experimentation starts and promiscuity increases. Promiscuity leads to increasing sexual dissatisfaction, to the weakening of family life and marriage bonds and to sexual excesses. The substitute satisfactions of smoking, drinking, and drug-taking increase and there is a lowering of the age of those involved. There is an upsurge in wanton destructive aggression in the community and a rise in aggressive juvenile delinquency. There is increasing concern over the harm done on young children by the practices and by the lack of concern and commitment of their parents, and concern has already been expressed over increasing male impotence. These effects are now obvious to any intelligent reader of the informed press.

> ... Increasing divorce rates, the resultant delinquency of children, the casual and inhuman ways some parents treat each other and their children, are almost the direct outcome of pre-marital and adulterous, that is promiscuous, sexual relations.

Destructive aggression, viciousness and brutality of people towards each other, disregard of the value of the individual and of life itself, are not normal behaviour. People who behave in such ways become isolated and divided against each other.

Women and men may then use sex as a way of getting what they want from their partner, as a way of dominating the partner. While unlikely to be stated in such simple terms between them, their actions convey the message 'do what I want and you can have sex as a reward. Obstruct me or refuse to do what I want and I will not have sex with you' which is a kind of punishment. We see assertiveness and conflict instead of affection and co-operation.

Partnerships and marriages break up when difficulties arise. People leave without regard or concern for the interests of the other members, of partner, spouse or children. They leave when they would be better off alone, when there is illness, when their present partner becomes unemployed, when a younger or wealthier 'partner' becomes available.

People who behave promiscuously (permissively) have sexual relations before marriage, or after marriage with a person other than their spouse. Promiscuity turns men against women, and women against men, and robs both of the support of their family.

Let me put it to you in another way {2}. It is only a few years ago that you went out for the evening without bothering to lock the door. Nowadays you make sure you fasten the windows as well and in some areas keep a light on and the radio going. Just think of what has been happening to crime, delinquency, drug addiction, the younger age of those involved and the increasingly brutal way people treat each other, leaving aside dishonest business dealings. Look at the increasing number of divorces and thus of one-parent families, look at the even larger number of children being brought up in this way. ... it is happening in other democratic countries. And it is nothing new. It has happened again and again. Whenever democracy raised its head, the same knife was used to chop it off.

History shows that free societies which allow themselves to become 'permissive' (promiscuous) weaken themselves to the point where their civilisation destroys itself, or is destroyed by outsiders. Those who wish to weaken democracy condone or encourage 'permissiveness'. On the other hand, those who restrict sex to within marriage gain creativity and increase their strength.

Sexual Restraint and Control

It is control of the sexual urge which distinguishes human beings from animals. Promiscuous unrestrained sexual behaviour indicates cold inhuman, often harsh, behaviour towards others, is characteristic of the cold unemotional behaviour of those who exploit others. Sexual self-control and restraint indicates human caring behaviour.

As permissiveness has increased so we have seen increasing the number of people using others for their own gratification and pleasure without care or concern for them, and also the number of parents behaving brutally towards each other and their children. A process driven by those who want sexual gratification, knowingly or unknowingly without regard to the costs their 'partners' have to pay.

Basic is that people behave in a way which enables them to trust and assist each other, that men and women co-operate with each other in a way which will protect and strengthen both, behaving in a way which ensures that all benefit from gains made.

So within a family, between husband and wife, it is the other person who comes first. When each spouse tries to make the other spouse happy, when each will go without something so as to make the other happy, then both can be happy.

Consider Jewish family law and traditions. When the wife has her period she is considered to be emotionally fragile. So the husband refrains from having sex from a few days before her period starts until a few days after it stops. He refrains out of care, consideration and affection for her, for his wife. She is different, has different needs, his self-denial for her sake continually renews the bonds of affection between them. As does their mutual practice of supporting each other, of putting the other person first when it comes to satisfying each other's needs. Whether or not you agree with the reasoning, sexual control is practised regularly for the sake of the other person and this strengthens the individual and cements the marriage.

Sexual restraint is an exercise in self-control, in controlling and so modifying what in the reptilian-animal part of our brain is a primitive and powerful urge aimed at the survival of the species. Sexual restraint changes it from an animal's instinctive behaviour into human behaviour based on concern and affection for the welfare of others. Not easy to do but it can be done as bereaved spouses or discarded partners can testify. Addiction to casual sex, to sleeping around, to promiscuity, is difficult to control but it can be done and the gains to the person doing so are enormous.

The United States government in 1997 set aside USD 250 million to teach children sexual abstinence, "teaching the social, psychological, and health gains to be realised by abstaining from sexual activity", teaching "abstinence from sexual activity outside marriage as the expected standard for all school-age children". {10}

Restraining and controlling sexual urges by restricting sex to within marriage gives strength to the family, to the individual and to the community, and underlies success in the struggle for a higher standard of living and higher quality of life for each and all.

Dominance

Dominance Within the Family

Within the family we should see co-operation and teamwork between equals who divide up the work which has to be done between them in a functional way so that each becomes expert and effective in his or her part of what has to be done.

But on the whole a family's income is usually earned by the male and income and money pass through his hands to the family. He then may, if he so wishes, use this controlling position to dominate the female. This applies equally well to the female who is a breadwinner, who may then use her controlling position to dominate. And applies also when the income of one is much larger than that of the other.

And both are in the position to use sex as a means of dominating the other, if they so wish. Rewarding compliance with sex, punishing disagreement by withholding sex.

Women have at times been persuaded by traditions or beliefs into accepting domination and sometimes exploitation as the norm. And women have in the past been denied education and full equality with men within the family and in the community in which they live.

The words 'assertiveness' and 'asserting' are used at times to indicate that one person is attempting to dominate the other. Dominating and 'asserting' put one person's personal gain, likes, dislikes against the other person's interests, introduces conflict and competition into what should be co-operation and teamwork.

Considering only women and children, the family protects women and children while children grow to maturity, till children become independent adults. It also protects women from disadvantages resulting from caring for and looking after the family during this period.

What keeps the family in place and gives it strength is restricting sex to within marriage. Men are then motivated to marry, to provide and care for wife and children, and themselves gain much strength from doing so.

When women are persuaded to make themselves available for sex outside marriage they help to dismantle not only their own protection and security but also that of their children.

In such circumstances the selfish instinctive behaviour of the non-feeling primitive animal is asserting itself, is attempting to dominate, overcome and control human feeling of care, affection, concern for members of one's own family and for other people in human societies.

Living in a Hostile Environment

We have seen that when one member of a family dominates others, that competition, conflict and struggle replace co-operation and teamwork. All the family's members suffer as a result.

We know that dominating does not work in normal circumstances. Authoritarian organisations are much less effective than participative ones. In authoritarian organisations morale is low, people cease to care and tend to work against each other instead of co-operating with each other for the benefit of the organisation. Which applies equally well to a family. {7, 8}

In the working environment women are just as oppressed and exploited as men are. When women receive lower wages for work of equal value then this is bad for men and women alike. When some people in a group are being underpaid, the pay of the others is being pushed down.

Outside the family a struggle is taking place. The breadwinner is competing for work and income on behalf of the family. He is also struggling against those who wish to exploit him (and thus his family) and who oppress so as to exploit.

So outside the family we see a widespread struggle against those who wish to dominate other people. Against those who want primitive power over others, against those who wish to exploit, against those who may brutally and without feeling oppress human beings so as to exploit them. And 'to exploit' includes the whole range of antisocial decisions and activities of those who put profit before people and community. {6}

We also saw that on the whole it is men who earn the family's income which then often passes through their hands to the family. And that as a result of the work men do outside the family, it is largely men who gain controlling positions in the working environment.

So on the surface it may seem as if it is men who try to dominate women within the family, that it is men who oppress and exploit women in the working environment.

Anyone who sees men and women co-operating with each other within a family, struggling side by side, back to back, and sees them co-operating with each other and helping each other in the outside working environment, for a more secure and better life for their families, knows how strong and effective they are together.

Blaming men as such, within the family and outside it, when women are oppressed and exploited, amounts to putting women against men, to separating them from each other. A 'divide so as to conquer' process which weakens both in their joint struggle for a better life. It robs men of the support of their families when they are struggling outside the family against being exploited, it robs women of the support of their families while bringing up children to adulthood, when improving their skills or knowledge when returning to work or to improve the quality of their lives.

Dominance and oppression take place within and outside the family, against men and women alike. Both men and women are exploited and oppressed in the working environment to a very considerable degree.

What we see in the working environment is a world-wide struggle to achieve a humane way of life, each person, family or community struggling to advance at their own level of development, struggling against those who wish to dominate, exploit, oppress. A struggle whose successful outcome depends on trustful co-operation, companionship and teamwork. {4, 5}

Sometimes one has to fight to preserve a good way of life, to prevent others from taking what has been achieved, or one is expected to fight on behalf of those who dominate and exploit.

The fighting is usually done by men who are conditioned to fight, maim and kill. Their training weakens and bypasses humane emotions of care, concern and affection for other people, in effect tends to brutalise them.

And we now see in some countries women joining the armed forces, police and security organisations and being trained in somewhat similar ways.

Our primitive animal ancestors behaved instinctively. Hunt for food, kill or be killed, fight or flee, copulate, care for own young for a very short and limited period. Self before others, regardless of needs of others, marking out and defending territory. Later mammals tend to have feelings, care and affection for their young. Human beings think as well as feel, and care for and look after their young for many years.

So conditioning to fight, maim and kill amounts to a throwback to primitive animal behaviour, to behaviour which puts self before others. A throwback to beast-like behaviour for those who attack, to beast-like behaviour to counter beast-like behaviour for those who defend.

But only some people behave in such corrupted ways. There are those many who put people first, who know the difference between human and inhuman behaviour, who believe in participative behaviour and in democratic government.

We saw that casual sex dehumanises, that it blocks affection and increases cold and selfish behaviour against others, that society corrupts itself when promiscuity (casual sex) spreads.

Promiscuity attacks human beings in their struggle for a better life as it:

1. Conditions people into primitive selfish uncaring behaviour which uses other people for personal gain (pleasure), creating a

non-caring society, putting people against each other, at times brutalising them.

2.   Weakens the family and all its members and so adversely affects the young and the way people treat each other. It weakens all the family's members by robbing them of emotional and economic support, and so makes it easier to exploit them through their needs.

Those who behave promiscuously pay a heavy price, namely lose the ability to form a satisfying emotionally deeply binding lasting and shared relationship with one other person. They also lose the emotional strength and economic backup such a shared relationship brings.

The media seem to be concentrating on portraying superstition, violence and casual-sex behaviour as acceptable, so strengthening primitive uncaring and antisocial behaviour towards others. And images penetrate deeply into the human mind.

Sexually explicit and pornographic material would seem to be taking this process even further.

So media are at present persuading and conditioning people into thinking that antisocial behaviour will not have unpleasant consequences. However, the cost to the community of the kind of negative and antisocial behaviour outlined in the sections above, of the lowering of the quality of life, is enormous. {6}

What we see is an almost intentional-seeming conditioning towards antisocial behaviour which breaks up families and so weakens individuals, and which divides people against each other and so weakens them even further.

It looks as if men are being conditioned into opting out of their responsibilities for family, wife and children. Women, on the other hand, are apparently being conditioned into giving away the real support and security they and their children could expect from husband and family, for no real gain.

To answer the question: "Who encourages antisocial behaviour?" we need to ask: "Who benefits from antisocial behaviour?" {6}

So who profits from promiscuity? At first glance it would seem that manufacturers of contraceptives and contraceptive devices have a vested interest as have organisations or associations whose income is derived from selling contraceptives and contraceptive devices. And possibly those whose income depends on advising on the use and application of contraceptives, depending on the extent to which their income depends on this.

And it is those who wish to weaken democracy and freedom who could be expected to condone and thus permit and encourage promiscuous behaviour as promiscuous behaviour separates people and turns them against each other, as it turns men against women and women against men. Indeed, they will condone and encourage any movement which turns men and women against each other so as to rob both of the strength to resist oppression and exploitation, to rob both of the strength which comes from men and women co-operating with each other.

Human rights are based on controlling primitive dominant behaviour, on concern, care and affection for our young, our families, for people, for our communities, and express themselves in co-operation and teamwork between men and women to achieve a good life of high quality.

Men and women are struggling together to achieve a better life, a humane way of living and government, and social security.

And there are ways of teaching social responsibility, of teaching the young how to take responsibility for others, how to care for, work with and look after other people. Social responsibility, the caring, giving and sharing with others, the taking on of responsibility for others including conflict management, can be and is being taught. {14}

It is in democracies that high standards of living have been achieved. In democracies people can struggle openly for a better life but we see that what has been gained has to be defended and extended.

Family's Role and Life in the Real World

The Family

The family is the basic unit of society. Its strength depends on the ability of the partners to commit themselves to each other, that is its strength depends on those who restrict sexual relations to within marriage. Men and women who do so practice a form of self-control which enables them to form a deep and lasting relationship, which in turn lays the basis for happy and contented family life for themselves and their children. The relationship between them is based on mutual trust and respect arising from the sure knowledge that they are in a vital exclusive relationship to each other, that they are working and co-operating with each other for the common good of themselves and their children.

Human beings work primarily for their family and members of a family stand by, support and help each other in times of need.

Smash the family and you undermine the strength of the people. I understand the resulting disruption was so marked in Russia that they had to back-pedal. One of the first things the Khmer Rouge did in Cambodia was to smash the family to make the people dependent on the state.

It is tough when you have to go to work to earn the money, do the shopping, look after the kids and do everything yourself. The one thing you cannot afford to be is to be ill. And you have no time for the kids either. And in a one-parent family, what the children miss is the parent's caring co-operative behaviour, is the example of responsible people looking after each other. The boy being brought up by the mother knows that both of them were left to look after themselves by the father and that is not a good example to model himself on. If you are struggling on your own so as to survive you don't have time or energy to think of freedom or to work for the community or for the betterment of humankind. {2}

Each member of the family gets strength from the others. Two heads are better than one, and work divided between two people in such a way that each can become expert in his or her own area is done much better than one person trying to do it all. The family gives people enormous emotional and economic strength to overcome life's problems. Husband and wife battle on together back-to-back and they do so successfully regardless of how tough the struggle may be. You cannot win all the battles but what cements the relationship is not just battles won but battles fought together. The depth of such a relationship between husband and wife and the wealth of strength it gives regardless of the opposition, this you know as well as I do. The children follow the example of their parents, gain the same strength and pass it on. It all depends on deep and secure emotional involvement between two people, between husband and wife. {2}

Those who understand its effects know that when sex is restrained and controlled, it performs the enormously important function of creating a special single deep emotional relationship between two people which gives them the strength to overcome life's problems, to form a strong family unit which serves and protects all its members. To be strong the relationship has to be unique and secure. It depends on the ability of the partners to commit themselves to each other. The depth of such a relationship between husband and wife can be appreciated as one sees them both battling on together successfully regardless of how tough the struggle may be.

Increasing Lifespans

Tabulating the figures already mentioned and extending the time period to the end of life, key events <1> look something like this:

Length of Period (Years)	Age (Years of Age)	Period	Event
4 - 5		Infant	
8 - 10		Child	
6 - 9		Adolescent	
	18 - 21		Becoming an adult member of family and community.
	25		Adult and independent member of family and community.
	18 - 24		Single
	20 - 26		Marriage (Children born over period of 6 years)
	41 - 47		Children become adults
	75 - 80		Death

Simplifying this a little, we have:

Age (Years of age)	Event or Period
0 - 21	Childhood and adolescence
21 - 23	Adult and single
23	Marriage
23 - 33	Children's childhood
33 - 44	Children's adolescence
44	Children now adult and largely independent
78	Life ends

Only about 100 years ago in the developed countries a person's lifespan was about 45 years, just long enough to bring up the next generation and help them to find their feet in the community. We now live another 35 years or so which enables us to do much more with our lives after our

102

children have become independent. And our lives now look something like this:

Age   **Event or Period**
(Years of
age)

Working outside the family (largely men)
21 - 65 At work
65 - 78 Receiving pension, freed from
         having to work

Within family (largely women)
21 - 23 At work
    23   Marriage
23 - 33 Bringing up the children during
         their childhood
33 - 44 Looking after children during
         their adolescence
44 - 65 At home or at work, as needed or
         as the individual wishes
65 - 78 Receiving pension, free from
         having to work

We saw earlier that the needs of children to be provided with caring and affectionate family life is of overriding importance <2>.

But outstanding is that those looking after people within the family, now have about 20 years of active life which can be spent as they wish, either working outside the family in paid employment, as independent professionals, or serving the community in other ways.

It is not easy to return to paid work as a professional after years of absence looking after one's family. After such a time lapse much has been forgotten and knowledge, equipment and techniques will have changed. And what is missing on returning to professional work is the years of experience which would have been gained had one stayed at work. It is then more than likely that positions of greater responsibility, and promotion to higher levels, will not be gained by those who return to work after such a long absence.

So on returning to work, women are at a disadvantage because of the time spent bringing up the children, and this disadvantage is likely to lower the level at which they can find work or work for the rest of their active life.

The family compensates women for this life-long contribution towards the upbringing of the children. It is the role of the spouse, of the husband, to continue to provide for the family. A life-long contribution from him which means she does not lose out for the rest of her life because she stayed at home to look after the children, the husband's input into the family balancing her input of bringing up the children and looking after the family's members.

As the children grow older, say 14 years old, women can usually spend increasing amounts of time updating or learning and developing skills and abilities for their future or continuing work after the children have grown up. Which is not easy to do and needs the support of her spouse.

Women, after children have grown up and backed by the family, can choose work outside the family to fulfil themselves as pay is less important for a second income.

Much professional work can now be home based. Home working may be less rewarding but is more convenient. Much can be gained by husband supporting his wife as far as he is able.

Looking at life from point of view of one's career, that is from the point of view of those who believe in profiting by compelling people through need to work for less than a fair share of the added value they produce, amounts to sacrificing the interests of one's family, and thus of oneself. The employer profits at the expense of the social and human welfare of the family's members.

What we see outside the family is a pattern of differentials which rewards service to the owners and their establishment rather than ability or service to the community. The nurse, the fire-fighter, the police officer and the teacher are at present paid comparatively little for the work they do. {1}

The community's basic needs are often not met by an uncaring social environment and the community's well-being depends on people, generally women, who use whatever time they have available, for caring for people both within and outside of family life. An employer's profit-orientated work can be well paid, community service-orientated work is not. And it is largely women who, caring for the welfare of the community, are generally the prime movers in self-help, support, protest and pressure groups, pushing forward also with other social and welfare issues.

Such work and public demonstrations and protests on such issues, are now an essential survival mechanism under beginning-of-twentyfirst-century conditions. {6}

104

Women's work in family and society determines individual emotional strength and well-being, the quality of life and the welfare of people as a community, and needs to be recognised and acknowledged.

Teamwork Within the Family

Teamwork implies sharing work and responsibilities in a way which ensures that all that has to be done is done well.

Success is measured by social and mental well-being as well as by standard of living and quality of life, of the family as a whole and of each member.

Key feature of the whole system is that both spouses work for the benefit of their family, of its individual members, and beyond that for the larger community of which the family is a part.

All are equal as people. What has to be done is shared out between them according to individual skill, ability, knowledge and experience. And in the end all share equally in the family's gains and losses. In other words, all are equal, contribute to the best of their ability, and stand or fall together.

The relationship between the two spouses is a functional relationship {9} and functional relationships are often misunderstood and misrepresented.

The spouses share out between themselves what needs to be done, each specialising, concentrating on, areas of work in accordance with their abilities, knowledge, understanding, likes and dislikes of each.

Equal as people, each takes the decisions falling within their own area of competence and responsibility. The husband may decide which car is to be bought or about getting a new job, the wife about which school the children should go to or where the family should live. But each discusses matters with the other family members before deciding from the point of view of what is best for the family as a whole.

They do not waste their time competing with each other but add their knowledge and experience to the decision-taking process of the other. In general, the person who decides would be the one most competent to take such decisions.

Such a functional division of work and responsibilities, of co-operation and teamwork between experts, enables us to survive and do well in the dangerous environment in which we find ourselves.

Consider shopping for food. The shopping expert takes into account the likes and dislikes of the other members of the family. And the expertise involved in shopping can be appreciated by considering what has to be thought about while shopping. How fresh is the food, how long will it have to be stored at home, how much does it cost here compared with elsewhere, has it been genetically modified and what does this mean for us. And what about nitrates in water, heavy metals, herbicides, pesticides, irradiated foods, chemical additives, more expensive organic foods, fat and sugar contents and other health risks.

It would be a waste of time for each to become expert in this field. It would be useless for each of the two people to do so and to argue continually about what is to be done. They would in this way be competing with each other by attempting to show that one is better than the other.

Conclusions

This report deals with the root causes of the major social problems. It shows how to resolve the problems by dealing with their basic causes.

Family and Children

200 million years of evolution are behind us, from reptilian beast through mammalian animal to human being. Human beings are mammals and we are unique in that our children need protecting and bringing up in a humane, emotionally and mentally stimulating environment for between 18 and 25 years, to enable them to mature into socially responsible adults. Men and women co-operate with each other and look after each other and their children, within the family, to achieve this.

Hence human beings work primarily for their family and members of a family stand by, support and help each other in times of need. The family is the basic unit of society and it looks after the interests of all its members, as individuals as well as collectively. This gives great strength to each member of the family in the struggle for daily bread, security and happiness.

Men and Women

Co-operation between men and women, within the family and as equals, would seem to be essential when bringing up their children under modern conditions of rapid change at an accelerating rate of change.

It is women who generally look after the young and other family members as people. This is the key role within the family and it occupies women full-time for some years if it is to be done well, and for more years on an at least part-time basis.

But we live much longer and the time spent full-time at home looking after the family places women at a disadvantage when returning to work outside the family after the children have been brought up. So women need to be supported when returning to work.

The family compensates women for this life-long contribution towards the upbringing of the children. It is the role of the spouse, of the husband, to continue to provide for the family. A life-long contribution from him which means she does not lose out for the rest of her life because she stayed at home to look after the children, the husband's input into the family balancing her input of bringing up the children and looking after the family's members.

Women, after children have grown up and with the family's backing, can choose work outside the family to fulfil themselves as pay is less important for a second income.

It is largely women who, caring for the welfare of the community, are generally the prime movers in self-help, support, protest and pressure groups, pushing forward also with other social and welfare issues.

Such work and public demonstrations and protests on such issues, are now an essential survival mechanism under beginning-of-twentyfirst-century conditions.

The work women do in family and society determines individual emotional strength and well-being, the quality of life and the welfare of people as a community and needs to be recognised and acknowledged.

The report discusses in some detail what is required if husband and wife are to work together as an effective team within the family.

Casual Sex

Casual sex is addictive, weakens and deadens feelings of care and affection for the other person, for partner or spouse, changing feelings of care and affection into a desire to use others for selfish pleasure regardless of the cost to the other person.

So people who sleep around, who are addicted to casual sex, use other people to obtain sex, do so without concern or affection for their partners. Apathy and neglect towards others can result.

Society corrupts itself when human care, affection and concern for one's own family, and for other people, is weakened, is bypassed by self-interest at the expense of others.

Those who sleep around pay a heavy price, namely lose the ability to form a satisfying emotionally deeply binding lasting and shared relationship with one other person. They also lose the emotional strength and economic backup such a shared relationship brings. Promiscuity turns men against women, and women against men, and robs both of the support of their family.

In such ways promiscuity breaks up families, weakens the strength of individuals and thus of the community to resist exploitation and oppression. So it would seem to be those who wish to weaken democracy and freedom who condone and thus permit and encourage promiscuous behaviour.

What keeps the family in place and gives it strength is restricting sex to within marriage. Men are then motivated to marry, to provide and care for wife and children, and themselves gain much strength from doing so. When women are persuaded to make themselves available for sex outside marriage they help to dismantle not only their own protection and security but also that of their children.

A key characteristic which distinguishes human beings from animals is that we can control the sex urge. Sex is habit-forming and addictive but can be controlled when the will is there, when the individual is motivated to control it.

In the USA steps are being taken to halt and reverse the increasing corruption of their communities by teaching the young the gains to be achieved by abstaining from sexual activity outside marriage.

There are ways of teaching social responsibility, of teaching the young how to take responsibility for others, how to care for, work with and look after other people. Social responsibility, the caring, giving and sharing with others, the taking on of responsibility for others including conflict management, can be and is being taught.

Dominance, Oppression and Exploitation

When one member of a family dominates others, then competition, conflict and struggle replace co-operation and teamwork. Dominance weakens all the family's members, robbing them of emotional and economic support, and so makes it easier to exploit them through their needs. All the family's members suffer as a result.

In the working environment we see a world-wide struggle to achieve a humane way of life, each family, person or community struggling to advance at their own level of development, struggling against those who wish to dominate, exploit, oppress. A struggle whose successful outcome depends on trustful co-operation, companionship and teamwork.

We know that dominating does not work in normal circumstances. Authoritarian organisations are much less effective than participative ones. In authoritarian organisations morale is low, people cease to care and tend to work against each other instead of co-operating with each other for the benefit of the organisation. Which applies equally well to a family.

Promiscuous behaviour and casual sexual relationships separate people and turn them against each other, turn men against women and women against men. Promiscuous behaviour and casual sexual relationships break up families, isolate people and rob people of the strength to resist exploitation and oppression.

So it appears that it is those who wish to weaken democracy and freedom who could be expected to condone and thus permit and encourage promiscuous behaviour and casual relationships.

Strength to resist oppression and exploitation comes from men and women co-operating with each other and so men and women struggle together to achieve a better life, a humane way of living and of government, and social security.

Human rights are based on controlling primitive dominating behaviour, on concern, care and affection for our young and our families, for people and for our communities. Human rights express themselves in co-operation and teamwork between men and women to achieve a good life of high quality.

It is in democracies that a high standard of living has been achieved. In democracies people can struggle openly for a better life but we see that what has been gained has to be defended and extended.

Notes and References

Notes

<1> See section on 'How Human Beings Evolved'.

For more background, see section on 'Development of Brain Functions in Humans' in reference {11}.

<2> See section 'Protecting and Caring for the Next Generation'.

The kibbutzim in Israel brought up children communally, away from their parents, and had to backtrack when they became aware of the consequences {13}.

References

{ 1} Work and Pay
Manfred Davidmann, 1981, 2007
solhaam.org/

{ 2} If You Want a Future, Read On ...
David Baram
Social Organisation Limited

{ 3} Sex:
Louise W. Eickoff
Consultant Psychiatrist
Guardian, 1970 Sep 12

{ 4} The Will to Work: What People Struggle to Achieve
Manfred Davidmann, 1981, 2006
solhaam.org/

{ 5} Motivation Summary
Manfred Davidmann, 1982, 1998
solhaam.org/

{ 6} Social Responsibility, Profits and Social Accountability
Manfred Davidmann, 1979, 1995
solhaam.org/

{ 7} Role of Managers Under Different Styles of Management

Manfred Davidmann, 1982, 1998
solhaam.org/

{ 8} Style of Management and Leadership
Manfred Davidmann, 1981, 2006
solhaam.org/

{ 9} Organising
Manfred Davidmann, 1981, 2006
solhaam.org/

{10} Abstinence conundrum
Tamar Lewin
Guardian, 13/05/97

{11} How the Human Brain Developed and How the
Human Mind Works
Manfred Davidmann, 1998, 2006
solhaam.org/

{12} A Triune Concept of the Brain and Behaviour
P D MacLean
University of Toronto Press

{13} Kibbutzim
Manfred Davidmann, 1996
solhaam.org/

{14} To Give or Not To Give
'Everyman' TV documentary
Editor: Jane Drabble; Producer: Angela Kaye
Broadcast on 5/1/92 by BBC 1
Based on book 'The Altruistic Person' by Professor
Sam Oliner

Chapter 6

The Meaning of Genesis

Chapter 6.1

Creation, Evolution and the Origin of Evil

Introduction

The Days of Creation (Genesis Chapter 1)

Evolution and Evil (Genesis Chapter 2)
  Evolution towards Evil (Gen 2: 1-9)
  Eden's Rivers (Gen 2: 10-14)
  Evolution towards Good (Gen 2: 15-25)

Meaning of the Names of God

Garden of Eden (Genesis Chapter 3)
  Further Evolution towards Good (Gen 3: 1-7)
  Consequences (Gen 3: 8-24)

Evolution of Human Beings (Genesis Chapters 2 and 3)

Cain and Abel (Genesis Chapter 4)

The Descendants of Seth (Genesis Chapter 5)

Concluding

Notes and References

Notes   <..>
References   {..}

Names of God (Appendix 1)

Creation of Planet and Life; Evolution of Human Beings
(Appendix 2)

'Adam' and Hebrew Grammar (Appendix 3)

Introduction

When the Pentateuch was written, people had but little knowledge about science or evolution compared with what is known today. So concepts for which we now have precise terms were described rather than stated.

Instead of the term 'scientific law' being used, for example, we see described that 'what is written applies to all people, present or absent, past or future, will happen regardless of how one feels about it, that the results of certain actions are reversed if the actions are reversed'. <1>

And concepts and descriptions are expressed in religious terms so that they could be appreciated and followed by the population.

The abovementioned example of the 'scientific law' illustrates the immense knowledge and understanding which underlies the Pentateuch (of which Genesis is a part) and which could not have been understood or comprehended by those then living. And what is there has been overlaid with the dust of millennia, with accumulated interpretations and comments limited by the then current knowledge, understanding and misconceptions. What is stated in Genesis is thus much more meaningful than is generally appreciated.

So we can expect the text of Genesis to be describing and disclosing what are currently known to be scientific truths in a way which could be understood by those living at the time, using religious language and the words then available.

Hence we can take it that in Genesis the then-beyond-comprehension beginning of life on earth and its evolutionary progress towards humankind is being described to people to whom terms such as 'natural selection' were completely unknown. Every evolutionary change, every new life form, is an act of creation.

And Genesis records 'God' to be that which caused and generated the beginning and development of life on this planet and of its development from the first bacteria to humankind. What we have at the beginning of

113

Genesis is a description of how life developed on this planet, in religious terms.

Understanding this we will see that there is no conflict, no contradiction, no divergence, only astonishing awe-inspiring agreement, between what is stated in Genesis and what we now know. <18>

Discussions between 'Creationism' and 'Evolution' barely scratch the surface of what Genesis is about. Genesis is about matters of enormous significance and importance to humankind at the present time, as you will see.

However, there were some who seemed to think that they knew all there is to be known, that they could decide what is and what is not, that what they were not aware of does not exist, that what they did not understand cannot be meaningful.

And some 150 years ago there were those who wondered why God was being referred to by different names in Genesis. At that time a likely explanation appeared to be that Genesis had been written by a number of people pretending it had all been written by one person but that each author naively referred to God by a different designation. This multiauthor hypothesis has undertones of propaganda aimed at discrediting the Pentateuch (Torah, Five Books of Moses) and its benevolent social teachings, by discrediting its single-author-based religious authority. The multi-author hypothesis was disproved some time ago {2, 13}. And what you will see here is that the different designations for God are not only meaningful but extremely important. <7>

Hebrew grammar distinguishes between proper names of persons and general nouns such as 'life form'. This distinction <17> has been ignored by Bible translators. This report shows that the distinction is meaningful and needs to be made if the text is to be understood as it was intended to be understood, and that Bible translations need to be revised accordingly. <2>

On the whole and when relevant I have tried to present the information by indenting as follows:

As stated in Genesis
      Explanations and comments
            Current knowledge, science
                  Additional notes, comments and quotations

For a quick overview, read the first two, namely 'As stated in Genesis' and 'Explanations and comments'.

The Days of Creation (Genesis Chapter 1)

At the end of every stage of creation is a statement like 'There was evening and there was morning, one day.'

But the Hebrew word 'ereb' equally well means either 'evening' or else means 'to mingle', or 'not to distinguish between them'.

And the Hebrew word 'boker' equally well means either 'morning' or else means 'to search', 'to examine', possibly also 'to check carefully'.

It follows that the Hebrew statement which is being translated as
> There was evening and there was morning

could equally well mean that
> there was a mingling and a uniformity, and a searching for
> differences and an examination of differences. [2]

This second meaning is the more likely when considering the text of Genesis.

Which describes what is now known to be the basis of evolution by natural selection. Hence it appears that 'one day' refers to a stage of evolutionary advance as well as to a stage of creation.

Indeed Genesis, written about 3,400 years ago, describes in religious language the creation (evolution) of humankind, and much more, as follows.

What stands out is that the record of creation in Genesis corresponds in the major steps to the order in which planet and life are known to have been formed and developed.

Stage 1 (one day) (Gen 1: 1-5)

Creation of light. God saw the light, that it was good. God divided the light from the darkness, and called the light Day and the darkness Night. A first stage of creation and evolution had been completed and another began.

> Planet earth came into existence about 4.5 billion
> years ago. [18]

Stage 2 (a second day) (Gen 1: 6-8)

Creation of water and sky. A second stage of creation and evolution had been completed and another began.

About 4 billion years ago there was liquid water on the planet. <18>

Stage 3 (a third day) (Gen 1: 9-13)

Creation of dry land. It happened and 'God saw that it was good.'

And then of vegetation, seed-bearing plants and seeded-fruit trees. After it happened 'God saw that it was good.'

A third stage of creation and evolution had been completed and another began.

> Land began to form about 3.5 billion years ago. Largely covered with shallow water and there was almost no free oxygen. As far as we know, it was the early plant life which fixed carbon dioxide from the atmosphere and gave off oxygen and so made the planet habitable for our kind of life forms. <18>

Stage 4 (a fourth day) (Gen 1: 14-19)

Sun, moon and stars created to mark days and years, to mark the passage of time, and to light the earth. And God saw that it was good. A fourth stage of creation and evolution had been completed and another began.

Stage 5 (a fifth day) (Gen 1: 20-23)

Living creatures in the water and in the air are created. After it happened, 'God saw that it was good.' They are to increase and multiply in diversity and number. A fifth stage of creation and evolution had been completed and another began.

> About 600 to 700 million years ago there were softbodied multicellular animals living in the sea followed by an enormous increase in the number of life forms which appear to have included all the major categories. The land, however, was lifeless.

Stage 6 (the sixth day) (Gen 1: 24-31)

Living creatures on land (such as cattle, creeping things and beasts) are created. After it happened, 'God saw that it was good.'

> About 450 million years ago plants evolved which left the water. Soil accumulated on the land. About 350 million years ago the descendants of fishes, the land vertebrates, had emerged from the sea. About 300 million years ago amphibians and reptiles populated the land.
>
> About 200 million years ago there had emerged small mice-like mammals but reptiles dominated the planet.
>
> By about 65 million years ago, dinosaurs had dominated the planet for something like 170 million years.

"Let us make man in our image, after our likeness. They shall have dominion over" all ... . And man (male and female) is created in God's image.

> A distinction is drawn between image (to look like, referring to appearance) and likeness (with discernment and understanding) <4>. 'Man' is then created but only 'in our image', alike only in appearance.
>
> To me this indicates that we are being told that man is to be alike in appearance to the most advanced life form when Genesis was written, namely humans, but alike only in appearance.
>
> So Man (male and female) is to be a more advanced life form compared with other then existing life forms.
>
> The Hebrew form of Adam used in this sentence is 'eth ha-adam' <14> indicating that what was created were 'human-like life forms' and not just one specific human being.
>
> The Hebrew word 'Elohim' has the form of the plural. That the plural is intentional and meaningful is emphasised by the statement (Gen 1: 26) 'Let us make man in our image, ...'
>
> And the Hebrew word 'Elohim' contains the root 'eleh' (these) which is a plural demonstrative pronoun indicating a 'multiplicity' which has some common characteristics and is thus combined into a unit. <6>

117

Evolution consists of a plurality of individual changes (acts of creation) which are then tried out and evaluated. It is this plurality of change which is described by referring to God in the plural. And we are told that different versions of 'man (male and female)', that is of human-like beings, were created.

They are to be fertile and increase, to fill the earth and subdue it, to be the most advanced of all living things.

Their food consists of all seed-bearing plants and all fruit-bearing fruit. All animals on land and all birds feed off the green plants.

And it was so. And God saw everything that He had made and saw it was very good.

The sixth stage of creation and evolution had been completed and another began.

Stage 7 (the seventh day) (Gen 2: 1-3)

Creation completed, God ceases from all further work like that done before and rests. No further creation. Day of rest.

Animals evolve, are peacefully co-existing and those most suited to available food and prevailing climatic conditions survive and multiply. And all is 'good'.

Up to here all is well, all is 'good', as God intended. All animals and 'man' are plant-eating and live happily side by side.

These three sentences, the first in chapter 2 of Genesis, are the only ones in the whole of chapter 2 which refer to God as the creator of all that is good.

Possibly to alert us to the fact that what follows in chapter 2 of Genesis is a parallel development and not a continuation of chapter 1.

Evolution and Evil (Genesis Chapter 2)

Evolution towards Evil (Gen 2: 4-9)

> The progress and type of evolution (creation) at one point underwent a progressive change towards beastliness (bad, evil) and it is this second form of evolution which is described in this part of Chapter 2 of Genesis.
>
> And the text pointedly refrains from calling the evolutionary developments recorded in Chapter 2 of Genesis as being 'good'.
>
> Genesis has so far referred to God (as creator) by the name Elohim, but now that it describes evolutionary changes it refers to God by the name 'Yhwh Elohim'.
>
> 'Yhwh' means 'He causes to be, He brings into existence' so that Yhwh Elohim refers to God who brings into existence (in the plural), to God (as originator), referring in this way to evolutionary changes. <7>

4 These are the generations of the heaven and of the earth when they were created, in the day that the Lord God (God as originator) made earth and heaven.

> These are the generations, that is the successive development, of life itself beginning with the creation of the first life form (of the coming into existence of the first living cell) from the dust of the earth, right up to human beings.

5 No shrub of the field was yet on the earth, and no herb of the field had yet sprang up; for the Lord God (God as originator) had not caused it to rain upon the earth, and there was not a man to till the ground;

> The land was barren because there was no rain and because no-one was there to work the land.

6 but there went up a mist from the earth, and watered the whole face of the ground.

> About 4 billion years ago there was liquid water on the planet. <18>
>
> Land began to form about 3.5 billion years ago. Largely covered with shallow water and there was almost no free oxygen. <18>

7 Then the Lord God (originator) formed man (Hebrew 'eth ha-adam') from the dust of the ground (Hebrew 'adamah'), and breathed into his

nostrils the breath of life; and man (Hebrew 'ha-adam') became a living soul.

The Hebrew for what has been translated as 'man' shows that it is life forms (or a life form) which are being referred to . There is no mention of 'man' being in God's image or likeness and it is animals which are stated to have a 'living soul' (Gen 1: 30). So this mention of 'man' refers to the first appearance of life on earth, possibly to life in its most primitive form, to primitive life forms.

This corresponds to what we were told in Genesis (Chapter 1) about the creation of life forms. But here there is no mention of these life forms being 'good'.

About 600 to 700 million years ago there were softbodied multicellular animals living in the sea followed by an enormous increase in the number of life forms which appear to have included all the major categories. The land, however, was lifeless.

About 520 million years ago some of the animals living in the sea lived by eating others.

8 And the 'Lord God' (originator) planted a garden eastward, in Eden; and there He put the man whom He had formed.

Hebrew 'mi-kedem' rendered as 'eastward'. It normally means 'from the east' but could also mean 'in the past'.

Gan Eden is either the proper name of a place or a place of pleasure.

So the planting had already been done in a place which was a place of pleasure at the time of planting (which had been 'good' before life forms, or some life forms, were introduced).

About 450 million years ago plants evolved which left the water. Soil accumulated on the land. Soon afterwards the animals followed.

9 And out of the ground made the 'Lord God' (originator) to grow every tree that is pleasant to the sight, and good for food; the tree of life also in the midst of the garden, and the tree of the knowledge of good and evil.

Evolution (creation) is proceeding.

When all animals feed off plants and fruit, then this is 'very good' (Gen 1: 29-31).

Some life forms (animals) live by eating other animals. Genesis pointedly does not mention this, presumably because flesh eating is permitted later (Gen 9: 2-).

At the same time, the evolutionary developments recorded here are pointedly not being called 'good'.

Some life forms (animals) live by eating other animals, are evolving towards greater viciousness and brutality. It is this which is evil. Evil is evolving towards greater evil.

There is good and evil, good and beastliness, but these life forms (animals) do not know this and cannot distinguish between them.

About 520 million years ago some animals lived by eating others and so a brutal vicious element was introduced. In due course peaceful competition for available resources became survival of the fittest where 'fittest' meant 'most brutal, most vicious, most violent, most beastly'. There are predators and prey and animals feed off their prey.

Predators have appeared and evolution turned into a bitter struggle for the survival of the fittest, where the most fittest is the most vicious and violent. The most 'advanced' species is now the species which is the most vicious. Life is brutal and dominated by evil. Reptiles come to dominate the earth.

This kind of evolution consists of changes towards greater beastliness. The evolutionary development towards greater beastliness, oppression and exploitation is thus described and defined as a parallel development, as contrary to good, as evil. 'Bad' and 'evil' are defined in this section of Genesis.

'Eden's Rivers' (Gen 2: 10-14)

10 And a river went out of Eden to water the garden; and from thence it was parted, and became four heads.

11 The name of the first is Pishon; that is it which compasseth the whole land of Havilah, where there is gold;

12 and the gold of that land is good; there is bdellium and the onyx stone.

13 And the name of the second river is Gihon; the same is it that compasseth the whole land of Cush.

14 And the name of the third river is Tigris (Hebrew 'Hiddekel'); that is it which goeth toward the east of Asshur. And the fourth river is the Euphrates.

In these five sentences we are told about a river leaving Eden and splitting into four streams flowing to three different lands.

We are told that in the land of Havilah exist gold, bdellium and lapis lazuli, that is metal, trees and minerals. Life forms are not mentioned, neither animals nor people, and this points to their absence at that time.

The land of Cush and the place Asshur did not then exist, had not been named.

One can conclude that there were no life forms in these lands, that they were uncharted and unpopulated.

Some life forms (animals) at that time lived by eating other animals. Genesis Chapter 2 does not refer to predators as bad or evil, presumably because flesh eating is permitted later (Gen 9: 2-), but also does not refer to them as 'good' <22>.

Predators are pointedly not mentioned in Chapter 2 and so we are told about streams spreading out from Eden. What flowed out of Eden, what spread out from Eden, appear to have been primitive life forms including flesh eating predators.

Following this description of how primitive animals spread out from Eden, Chapter 2 of Genesis continues by describing the evolution of mammalian feelings and life, of hominoids and Homo erectus <23>.

And the next time the names Havilah, Cush and Asshur are mentioned, individually and together, is in Chapter 10 which details the spreading out of human beings (Homo sapiens, modern humans) after the flood. {16}

Which confirms that what spread out from Eden were primitive life forms including flesh eating predators.

About 200 million years ago there had emerged small mice-like mammals but reptiles dominated the planet.

By about 65 million years ago, dinosaurs had dominated the planet for something like 170 million years. A global change of climate apparently lasting hundreds of thousands years (apparently caused by a meteor impact and enormous volcanic outpourings) wiped out about 70 percent of all species, including the dinosaurs.

Mammals then developed and evolved.

And Chapter 2 of Genesis continues by describing the evolution of mammalian feelings and life.

Evolution towards Good (Gen 2: 15-25)

Instincts are a form of behaviour which the animal performs from birth, without being trained to do so. {7}

At the level of evolution of the reptile, behaviour relating to survival of the species, such as sexual behaviour, is instinctive and responses are automatic. Territory is acquired by force and defended. Might is right. {7}

But from about 65 million years ago, mammals developed and evolved.

15 And the 'Lord God' (originator) took the man, and put him into the garden of Eden to dress it and to keep it.

'man': Hebrew 'eth ha-adam' meaning life form or life forms.

16 And the Lord God (originator) commanded the man, saying: 'Of every tree of the garden you may freely eat;

17 but of the tree of the knowledge of good and evil, you shall not eat of it; for in the day that you eat thereof you shall surely die.'

At this point, 'man' (life forms such as vicious reptiles) have no knowledge of good and evil and cannot distinguish between them.

'... you shall surely die.': If you evolve in direction of feeling and thinking, into knowing difference between good (peaceful coexistence and equality) and evil (bitter struggle for survival, beast eating beast) you will die as a species (life form) because you will have evolved into a more advanced life-form which will replace the earlier one.

18 And the Lord God (originator) said: 'It is not good that the man should be alone; I will make him a help meet for him

19 And out of the ground the Lord God (originator) formed every beast of the field, and every fowl of the air; and brought them to the man to see what he would call them; and whatsoever the man would call every living creature, that was to be the name thereof.

20 And the man gave names to all cattle, and to the fowl of the air, and to every beast of the field; but for Adam there was not found a help meet for him.

'Man' learns to communicate which enables co-operation and teamwork with another (others). And lays basis for closer associations between two or more of his own kind.

21 And the Lord God (originator) caused a deep sleep to fall over the man, and he slept; and He took one of his ribs, and closed up the place with flesh instead thereof.

22 And the rib, which the Lord God (originator) had taken from the man, made He a woman, and brought her to the man.

23 And the man said, 'This is now bone of my bones, and flesh of my flesh; she shall be called Woman (Hebrew: ishshah), because she was taken out of Man.' (Hebrew: ish)

Beginning of co-operation between male and female of the same species in bearing, protecting and bringing up the young.

24 Therefore shall a man leave his father and his mother, and shall cleave to his wife, and they shall be one flesh.

Mammalian care and affection for the young and co-operation between parents (together like one person doing all) in looking after the young till they become independent adults.

25 And they were both naked, the man and his wife, and were not ashamed.

'Naked' is here used for referring to sexual behaviour between primitive male and female animals engaging instinctively in sex.

124

Engaging instinctively in sex and forming family connections, just like eating and drinking.

> As mammals evolved from reptiles, there evolved the ability for storing new experiences as they happen and so creating a store of experience-based memories. And so the experience-based recognition of danger and responding to this according to past experience. {7}

> ... and behaviour is less rigidly controlled by instincts. It seems that feelings such as attachment, anger and fear have emerged with associated behavioural response patterns of care, fight or flight. {7}

These verses (Gen 2: 15-25) show that the mammalian brain is evolving, with some feelings of affection and attachment from parents towards their young. So these verses say much, portraying a change from domination by the most vicious towards the emergence of feelings of affection and attachment towards others.

'Man' learns to communicate and so to co-operate with others and there is then co-operation between male and female of the species aimed at bringing up the next generation. The young are helped to maturity and then leave parents to form own family, driven to do so by instinctive sex urge.

> About 3.5 million years ago hominoids, animals resembling humans, had appeared, apparently in East Africa.

>> Hominoids: Erect bipeds with our body shape, intermediate between apes and humans.

> And about 2 million years ago appeared Homo erectus (Erect man), having a much smaller skull size than humans. {3}

Meaning of the Names of God

We have seen that the name used for referring to God clearly points to the meaning of the text. 'Elohim' referred to God as creator of what is good, 'Yhwh Elohim' referred to God as the originator of evolution.

Understanding the meaning and significance of the names by which God is referred to in the Bible is of the greatest importance for understanding the meaning of the Bible text.

And so the meaning and significance of the names of God <7> is as follows:

Hebrew Name	**ELOHIM**	**YHWH ELOHIM**	**YHWH**
Usually translated as	God	Lord God	the Lord
Meaning of Name	**GOD** or **GOD (AS CREATOR)**. God as creator, as creator of all that is good.	**GOD (AS ORIGINATOR)**	**GOD (AS CAUSE)**, as cause of what happened. In other words, this is happening, is what happened.

Example: (Gen 7: 16); And they ... went in(to the ark) ... as God (Elohim) commanded him; and the Lord (Yhwh) shut him in.

Garden of Eden (Genesis Chapter 3)

We know that Homo erectus was followed and replaced by Homo sapiens (Wise man, ourselves, with considerably larger brain size), commonly referred to as humans, human beings, humanity.

And we know that the human brain evolved in three main stages {8}. Its ancient and primitive part is the innermost core reptilian brain. Next evolved the mammalian brain by adding new functions and new ways of controlling the body. Then evolved the third part of the brain, the neocortex, the grey matter, the bulk of the brain in two symmetrical hemispheres, separate but communicating. To a considerable extent it is our neocortex which enables us to behave like human beings {7} and it is the evolution of the neocortex, that is the appearance of Homo sapiens, which is recorded in Chapter 3 of Genesis.

Further Evolution towards Good (Gen 3: 1-7)

It is significant and important that in this chapter of Genesis it is only in the first seven verses that God is referred to as the creator of all that is good, is referred to as God (creator).

In this way we are told that the change (creation) recorded in this chapter of Genesis is a most important move away from the evil of 'survival of the most vicious' and towards that which is 'Good'.

1 Now the serpent was more subtle than any beast of the field which the Lord God (originator) had made. And he said to the woman: 'Has God (creator) said: You shall not eat of any tree of the garden?'

The serpent, itself a predator struggling to survive against other predators, is saying to the female mammal which has some feelings and appreciation of care and affection for her own offspring, whether God (creator of what is good) has told her not to eat from any tree.

'the woman': Hebrew 'ha-ishah', possibly meaning women in general, womankind.

2 And the woman said to the serpent; 'Of the fruit of the trees of the garden we may eat;

3 but of the fruit of the tree which is in the midst of the garden, God (creator) has said: You shall not eat of it, neither shall you touch it, lest you die.'

It was the Lord God (originator) who had said so (Gen 2: 17) but here they are talking about a development towards 'Good' and reference is made to God (creator).

As before, at this point 'man' (life forms such as mammals) have developed feelings of care and affection towards others and some more advanced brain functions, but beyond this have no knowledge of good and evil and cannot distinguish between them.

'Neither shall you touch it': Added by her to God's command. Meaning that we are not to be concerned about, or to think about, the difference between good and evil. In other words, we are unable at this mammalian stage of development to

127

think about right or wrong, good or evil. And a clear statement that this chapter of Genesis is about the evolution of the human brain from the mammalian brain, it being the human brain which includes the thinking part, the neocortex).

4 And the serpent said to the woman: 'You shall not surely die;

5 for God (creator) does know that in the day you eat of it, then your eyes shall be opened, and you shall be as God (creator), knowing good and evil.'

> As said before (Gen 2:17), to 'die' in this context means that 'if you evolve in direction of feeling and thinking, into knowing difference between good (peaceful co-existence and equality) and evil (bitter struggle for survival, beast eating beast) you will die as a species (life form) because you will have evolved into a more advanced life-form which will replace the old one.

> This is what the serpent is saying.

> And the increased brain capacity and the evolution of the neocortex would enable mammals in this respect to become like God the creator of what is good, that is to know the difference between good and evil.

> If there is to be further development towards good then there has to be knowledge of and understanding of good and evil and of the difference between them so that people can choose between them. (From 'You shall be as God (creator), knowing good and evil' so as to choose 'good' instead of evil.)

6 And when the woman saw that the tree was good for food, and that it was a delight to the eyes, and that the tree was to be desired to make one wise, she took of the fruit thereof, and did eat; and she gave also to her husband with her, and he did eat.

> And the mammalian brain became the human brain by adding the massive grey matter (neocortex) which envelopes most of the earlier brain and amounts to about 85 per cent of the human brain mass. {7}

> This massive addition consists mostly of two hemispheres which have, on the whole, different functions and consequently behaviour is not only determined by feelings but also by knowledge, understanding and reason. {7}

>> For comprehensive information on how the human mind evolved and works, see {7}.

The human brain underlies free will, enabling us to decide independently what is good or evil, that is what to do or not to do.

7 And the eyes of them both were opened, and they knew that they were naked; and they sewed fig-leaves together, and made themselves girdles (loin-cloths).

> They learned not to behave instinctively, they learned that to be human one had to control one's instinctive sexual behaviour impulses, they learned to control the sex urge.

> > 'Naked' again refers to sexual behaviour, here to sexual behaviour of human beings.

> > For comprehensive information about the family and how it functions and the pressures which it faces from without and from within, see {10}.

> It takes a long time to give birth (pregnancy) and to provide for upbringing of children to maturity. So sex has to be restrained to within the family (marriage). Human beings behaving humanely control the sex urge.

> > Clothing and modesty are preventatives of sexual stimulation. {9}

Consequences (Gen 3: 8-24)

8 And they heard the voice of the Lord God (originator) walking in the garden toward the cool of the day; and the man and his wife hid themselves from the presence of the Lord God (originator) amongst the trees of the garden.

9 And the Lord God (originator) called to the man, and said to him: 'Where are you?'

10 And he said: 'I heard Your voice in the garden, and I was afraid, because I was naked; and I hid myself.'

> Adam and Eve are shown reacting like early mammals. While reptiles dominated the earth, the early mammals had learned to hide from reptiles in the daytime and ventured out after dark.

11 And He said: 'Who told you that you were naked? Have you eaten of the tree, whereof I commanded you that you should not eat?'

12 And the man said: 'The woman whom You gave to be with me, she gave me of the tree, and I did eat.'

13 And the Lord God (originator) said to the woman: 'What is this you have done?' And the woman said: 'The serpent beguiled me, and I did eat.'

> The changes for good which are taking place are becoming apparent. The pattern of evolution is beginning to change away from vicious beastliness towards feelings of care and affection towards others backed by intellect.
>
> And we are now told what the real-life consequences of this major advance (creation, evolution) are.

14 And the Lord God (originator) said to the serpent: 'Because you have done this, cursed are you from among all cattle, and from among all beasts of the field; upon your belly shall you go, and dust shall you eat all the days of your life.

> Human beings are advancing to a different kind of existence. Reptiles are being left behind, by comparison evolving in a different and downward direction.
>
> > 'Also implying that previously serpents travelled by an alternative mode of locomotion. This is, of course, precisely true: snakes have evolved from four-legged reptilian ancestors ... . Many snakes still retain anatomical vestiges of the limbs of their ancestors.' {9}

15 And I will put enmity between you and the woman, and between your seed and her seed; they shall bruise your head, and you shall bruise their heel.'

> Women's strength is their care and affection for their young and care and concern for people. So they understand 'good' and are the enemy of beastliness, beasts, evil.
>
> Eternal enmity between reptiles and mammals (human beings). Eternal enmity between beastly viciousness, exploitation and oppression on the one hand and humane care and affection for people on the other, eternal enmity between good and evil. And the need to struggle against beastly viciousness, exploitation and oppression.

16 To the woman He said: 'I will greatly multiply your pain and your travail; in pain you shall bring forth children; and your desire shall be to your husband, and he shall rule over you.'

'... greatly multiply your pain and your travail':

This connects the evolution of the human brain with childbirth. Childbirth became much more painful because of greater skull size.

Pregnancy, childbirth, caring for and bringing up the young takes many years until they become self-sufficient and experienced adults.

'... and your desire shall be to your husband.':

It has been suggested <4> that this refers to cohabitation. But this is mutual between male and female and so would not be mentioned only for the female.

The desire is based on need for support and protection while having children and looking after them as they grow older. And so that his cool knowledge, understanding, reasoning can strengthen, add to, and bring about gains in their mutual struggle for achieving that which is good, a humane good life for the family.

> For more comprehensive information about the family and how it functions in tough social environments, and about the pressures it faces from without and from within, see {10}.

'..., and he shall rule over you.':

The husband's strength lies in struggling against external threats, in protecting, and in providing for, the family in a hostile environment.

> For more information about the way in which the neocortex functions and about role of the two halves of the brain, see {7}.

One way of countering viciousness is by greater viciousness or strength. If attacked, we have to defend ourselves. Reason and evaluation can temper (add to, or change) purely emotional, instinctive behaviour (fight or flight) so as to counter and overcome external threats by, for example, co-operation and teamwork among those who are threatened.

The need to survive and overcome external threats means that husband-based decisions based on reason, evaluation and experience, may have to override more humane considerations while an emergency exists.

But the direction of husband-based decisions, like those of the wife, should be motivated by 'Good', and be in direction of 'Good'.

17 And to Adam He said: 'Because you have hearkened to the voice of your wife, and have eaten of the tree, of which I commanded you, saying: You shall not eat of it; cursed is the ground for your sake; in toil shall you eat of it all the days of your life.

18 Thorns also and thistles shall it bring forth to you; and you shall eat the herb of the field.

> What is clear is the functional division of work between men and women which corresponds to women looking after the young for years while men toil to provide for the family's living. A life-long struggle to provide for the family. <9>

> Also clear is the correspondence between their different types of work and the two halves of the brain. One half more suited for dealing with the struggle for food and safety, the other more suited for looking after and caring for the young and thus for people. <10>

19 In the sweat of your face shall you eat bread, till you return to the ground; for out of it were you taken; for dust you are, and to dust shall you return.'

> Birth and death, successive generations, are underlying basic requirement for evolutionary change by natural selection. It is because of this that the way to the 'tree of life' is barred. <20>

20 And the man called his wife's name Eve (Heb. Havvah, that is, Life); because she was the mother of all living.

> '...she was the mother of all living' makes the point that from here on human beings had evolved so that Eve <21> was the mother of all living human beings.

21 And the Lord God (originator) made for Adam and for his wife garments of skins, and clothed them.

22 And the Lord God (originator) said: 'Behold, the man is become as one of us, to know good and evil; and now, lest he put forth his hand, and take also of the tree of life, and eat, and live forever.'

23 Therefore the Lord God (originator) sent him forth from the garden of Eden, to till the ground from whence he was taken.

24 So He drove out the man; and He placed at the east of the garden of Eden the cherubim, and the flaming sword which turned every way, to keep the way to the tree of life.

Evolution of Human Beings (Genesis Chapters 2 and 3)

Peaceful co-existence and equality are good. Bitter struggle for survival, beast eating beast, survival of the most vicious, are evil.

Primitive life forms are told: 'If you evolve in direction of feeling and thinking, into knowing difference between good and evil, you will evolve into a more advanced life-form which will replace the old one.

And mammals evolve from reptiles, and develop feelings of care and affection towards others and develop some more advanced brain functions, but beyond this have no knowledge of good and evil and cannot distinguish between them.

They are told that by evolving further 'You shall be as God (the creator of good), knowing good and evil' so as to choose 'good' instead of evil.

If there is to be further development towards good then there has to be knowledge of and understanding of good and evil and of the difference between them so that people can choose between them.

And the human brain evolves from the mammalian brain. The increased brain capacity and the evolution of the neocortex enable humans to know the difference between good and evil.

Human beings are mortal.

Mortality is essential if evolution towards a better life-form, towards a better way of living, is to proceed by evolution.

Natural selection is improvement by trial and error. Immortality would end the evolution of species and of humankind towards a better life-form, towards a better way of living.

Brutal viciousness, oppression, exploitation, corruption, evil would dominate for ever if it gained the upper hand, and this cannot be allowed to happen under any circumstances.

And this would seem to be, in essence, what Genesis Chapters 2 and 3 say about the evolution of human beings.

Cain and Abel (Genesis Chapter 4)

We saw that

> Evolution had turned into a bitter struggle for the survival of the fittest, where the most fittest was the most vicious and violent. The most 'advanced' species was the species which was the most vicious. Life was brutal and dominated by evil. This is how reptiles came to dominate the earth.
>
> At the level of evolution of the reptile, territory is acquired by force and defended. Might is right. {7}
>
> But mammals had developed some feelings of care and affection towards others but had no knowledge of good and evil and so could not distinguish between them.

And Chapter 4 of Genesis continues the record from this point onwards.

> Genesis is telling a continuous interrelated story and in the whole of this chapter God is referred to by the Hebrew name Yhwh. This means God (as cause), signifying 'this is happening' or 'this is what happened', here meaning 'this is what happened'. <7>
>
>> There is one exception, namely in the second-last sentence (Gen 4: 25) which introduces the subject matter of the subsequent chapter of Genesis.
>
> The use of Yhwh in the whole of this chapter is quite clearly intentional and significant.
>
> It indicates that this chapter of Genesis does not refer to evolutionary change, that this chapter is about what 'man' does, about how a human-like life form is behaving at its level of development.

1 And the man [ha-adam] knew [eth-] Eve his wife; and she conceived and bore [eth-] Cain, and said: 'I have gotten a man with the help of the [eth] Lord.

2 And again she bore his [eth-] brother [eth-] Abel. And Abel was a keeper of sheep, but Cain was a tiller of the ground.

The 'ha' before Adam shows that we are being told about a group of individuals. As 'Adam' consists of many individuals, so 'eth-' before Eve, Cain, brother, Abel indicates that it happened correspondingly many times, as does the 'eth-' before Yhwh.

We are being told what happened to many individuals within a particular life form, by a record apparently relating to an individual.

3 And in process of time it came to pass, that Cain brought of the fruit of the ground an offering to the Lord.

4 And Abel, he also brought of the firstlings of his flock and of the fat thereof. And the Lord had respect unto Abel and to his offering;

5 but unto Cain and to his offering He had no respect. And Cain was very wroth, and his countenance fell.

> Abel choose the finest he had, but that Cain was indifferent, merely discharging his duty {13}. In other words, Abel was 'good', Cain merely appeared to be so.

>> 'was very wroth': "Literally 'it was very hot unto Cain' {13}

>> Cain's name is generally considered to signify 'owner, possession', but the Hebrew word is more likely related to 'jealous'.

>> Abel's name signifies 'of no consequence', possibly 'weakness'.

> So it seems that Cain felt strongly envious of Abel's offering, possibly wanting the offering or Abel's possessions for himself.

6 And the Lord said to Cain: 'Why are you wroth? And why is your countenance fallen?

> Why are you envious?

7 If you do well, shall it not be lifted up? And if you do not well, sin couches at the door; and unto you is its desire, but you may rule over it.'

> What happens is that if you do well, you will feel well.

>> Sin is that which is 'evil' as compared with that which is 'good', and sin has been defined earlier as viciousness, beast against beast, might being right, as oppressing and exploiting fellow beings.

135

Couching: In the background, hiding.

At the door: At the threshold of consciousness.

'And towards you is its desire,': Referring to sin, to the evil inclination, which is continually desiring and craving to make you stumble. <4>

"... it (sin) wishes to master you and to have dominion over you like ..." {13}

So 'sin couches at the door; and unto you is its desire' describes what we know: that the predatory instincts of reptilian ancestors are still within us at the threshold of consciousness and can through our feelings push us towards primitive beastly behaviour, towards doing what is evil, into gaining at expense of fellow beings.

But if you do not do well, then your feelings can push you towards primitive beastly behaviour which is lurking at the threshold of consciousness, but you should be able to control and reject such feelings and thoughts.

8 And Cain spoke to Abel his brother. And it came to pass, when they were in the field, that Cain rose up against Abel his brother, and slew him.

Since Cain 'spoke' to Abel and then killed him, the killing was either thought of in advance or else driven by uncontrolled feelings of envy at the time.

Cain did not control and reject evil feelings and thoughts.

9 And the Lord said to Cain: 'Where is Abel your brother?' And he said:'I know not; am I my brother's keeper?'

Cain does not see or acknowledge that he has done any wrong.

For human beings, primitive (reptilian) instinctive urges and behaviour are overlaid by mammalian care and affection for one's young and human care and affection for one's family, other people and community. {7}

Humane behaviour is based on feelings of care and affection for the young and for the family, and then for other people and the

136

community. From this emerges a sense of social responsibility: people matter and are important, need to be treated well and looked after, are entitled to share equally. And humane behaviour is backed up by knowledge, understanding and reason. {7}

Cain rejects concern, care, affection for others, rejects social responsibility.

Cain does not behave like a human being. His behaviour is that of a primitive animal.

10 And He said: 'What have you done? The voice of your brother's blood cries to Me from the ground.

The Hebrew for 'blood' is in the plural form, indicating more than one 'blood'.

11 And now cursed are you from the ground, which has opened her mouth to receive your brother's blood from your hand.

Here also the Hebrew for 'blood' is in the plural form, again indicating more than one 'blood'.

As said before, we are being told what happened to many people by a story about individuals with individual names. And so verses 10 and 11 refer to blood in the plural, apparently indicating that people were killing each other, that in this way the strong, the most brutal, were dominating others of their own kind.

12 When you till the ground, it shall not henceforth yield to you her strength; a fugitive and a wanderer shall you be in the earth.'

Possibly having to move, or looking for a better place to live.

13 And Cain said to the Lord: 'My punishment is greater than I can bear.

Rashi <4>: 'Is my sin too great to be borne?, that is 'to be forgiven?'

It appears that Cain questions the punishment, does not accept it.

14 Behold, You have driven me out this day from the face of the land; and from Your face shall I be hid; and I shall be a fugitive and a wanderer in the earth; and it will come to pass, that whoever finds me will slay me.'

137

Spreading to other lands. Having to fight for possession, the stronger winning or surviving, might being right.

15 And the Lord said to him: 'Therefore whoever slays Cain, vengeance shall be taken on him sevenfold.' And the Lord set a sign for Cain, lest any finding him should smite him.

> "The verse says, literally, 'any one slaying Cain', not if anyone slays 'you'." {13}
>
> Sevenfold: "Connotes in perfect measure, with the full stringency of the law." {13}

Those who attack them (kill Cain) are to be punished in full measure. In other words, any who attack them are paid back in full measure.

Every one's hand is turned against every one else. Kill or be killed. Dominate or submit.

16 And Cain went out from the presence of the Lord, and dwelt in the land of Nod on the east of Eden.

> 'land of Nod': That is, land of 'wandering' on the east of Eden'.
>
> Here 'kidmath-eden' has been rendered 'east of Eden' but it means 'land that used to be a place of pleasure' <8>. Presumably the reference is to previously unsettled, unoccupied land.

Which appears to mean that Cain dwelt and wandered in the land which used to be a place of pleasure.

This phrase has been used only once before in (Gen 2: 8) and it is not used for the later descendants of Seth. So its use here indicates that the descendants of Cain were the first human-like people to multiply and spread.

17 And Cain knew his wife; and she conceived, and bore Enoch; and he builded a city, and called the name of the city after the name of his son Enoch.

> Wandering and settling down, then more wandering. That is, spreading.

18 And to Enoch was born Irad; and Irad begot Mehujael; and Mehujael (Heb. Mehijael) begot Methushael; and Methushael begot Lamech.

19 And Lamech took to him two wives; the name of one was Adah, and the name of the other was Zillah.

138

Evil here begets greater evil. Lamech has two wives which in normal circumstances would mean that another has to do without a wife.

23-24 And Lamech said to his wives:

"Adah and Zillah, hear my voice; You wives of Lamech, hearken to my speech; For I have slain a man for wounding me, And a young man for bruising me;

If Cain shall be avenged sevenfold, Truly Lamech seventy and sevenfold"

> Seventy-seven fold: in overflowing measure, more than is due, many for one. {13}

> Commits acts of violence and boasts about them. {13}

Lamech is more violent than Cain. He has killed two people for bruising or wounding him and openly boasts about it, saying that those who attack him are being punished not just in full measure (Cain) but in overflowing measure (seventy-seven fold).

Evil, corruption, are spreading and getting worse.

> Power corrupts, competition and opposition is killed, the murderer is protected, and power becomes more absolute, becomes even more corrupt and 'evil' becomes stronger.

25 And Adam knew his wife again; and she bore a son, and called his name Seth: 'for God has appointed me another seed instead of Abel; for Cain slew him.'

> The name Elohim (creator, creator of that which is good) is pointedly used in this verse as the last two sentences of this chapter introduce the subject matter of the immediately following chapter.

At this point, evolution (creation) takes a further step towards that which is good, indicated by God being referred to as God (creator) in this verse.

Another line of descendants from Adam and Eve. Another beginning, another evolutionary development, another life form, a more humane people.

26 And to Seth, to him also there was born a son; and he called his name Enosh; then began men to call upon the name of the Lord.

It is the descendants of Seth who are enumerated in the next chapter. They are aware of the difference between good and evil, are human beings (See Gen 5: 1-3 at the beginning of the immediately following chapter). We are told that each human generation 'begot sons and daughters.' So human beings multiplied and spread.

Hence 'then began men to call upon the name of God (as cause)' tells that from then on the descendants of Cain began to call for help.

What is described in this chapter (Gen 4) about the descendants of Cain is the behaviour of a mammalian human-like life form whose behaviour is more beast-like than human.

This is not human behaviour. It is beast-like behaviour by human-like animals. What is described here appears to relate to the life of Homo erectus who were replaced by humans.

> Homo erectus appeared about 2 million years ago <12>

Thousands
(Thousands
of years
ago)

250   Men with larger brains than Homo erectus began to appear in different parts of the world.

200   Homo erectus largely extinct.

130   Oldest humans (Homo sapiens, Wise man) in Africa.

100   Humans had replaced the other ones (such as Java man in Indonesia, Peking man in China). {3}

> So Homo sapiens (humans) ultimately replaced Homo erectus (Erect man).

The Descendants of Seth (Genesis Chapter 5)

1 This is the book of the generations of Adam. In the day that God created man, in the likeness of God made He him;

2 male and female created He them, and blessed them, and called their name Adam, in the day when they were created.

> Although the story is told about individuals, its content relates to the life form (human beings) as a whole.

3 And Adam lived a hundred and thirty years, and begot a son in his own likeness, after his image; and called his name Seth.

> 'a son in his own likeness': That is, 'in the likeness of God' (See v1 above).

God is here referred to as God (creator), the creator of all that is good, as in Genesis Chapter 1.

> The text in Chapter 1 of Genesis draws a distinction between image and likeness, that is between 'appearance' and 'discernment and understanding'. And man (male and female) are there recorded as having been created only in God's image, alike to God only in appearance. <13>

And 'Adam' (male and female) are here stated to have been created also in the likeness of God. That is, they know good and evil and can distinguish between them (Gen 3: 5, 22).

So this chapter 5 of Genesis is about how human beings multiplied and behaved, is about the descendants of Seth who are human beings.

And every generation has 'sons and daughters'. There were no such statements in the previous chapter about the descendants of Cain. Which tells us that human beings increased in number compared with the descendants of Cain.

> We know that human beings with their larger brains spread across the planet and replaced Homo erectus.

So we are here looking at the development and behaviour of human beings who know of, can distinguish between and can choose between, good and evil.

Thousands
(Thousands
of years
ago)

250	Men with larger brains than Homo erectus began to appear in different parts of the world.
200	Homo erectus largely extinct. {6}
130	Oldest humans (Homo sapiens, modern humans) in Africa.
100	Humans had replaced the other ones (such as Java man in Indonesia, Peking man in China). {3}
50	Humans In Australia
40	Humans In Europe
30	From 30,000 years ago, to the present, all cultures and remains are those of humans.

Concluding

Life as we know it today appears to have developed very, very slowly by a process of trial and error. Each change was evaluated by the extent to which it enabled a life form to survive and multiply in a largely hostile environment in competition with other life forms.

Remarkable is the enormous timescale during which this slow process has enabled ourselves to be created. We are the most complicated and advanced life form and there are many gaps in our knowledge and appreciation of the way in which we exist, function, live and behave.

Alarming is the infinitesimally small period of time in which our technological progress has so vastly exceeded our social organisation and behaviour that now the survival of our species is in doubt.

Evil must not gain the upper hand under any circumstances.

Each person can now have access to vast knowledge undreamt of only a few years ago. <19>

But this needs to be supplemented with the ability to think clearly, to assess and evaluate reliability and applicability, on the basis of knowledge of good and evil and of the essential need for behaving humanely, for following (doing) good instead of evil.

It is here that the relevance and importance of the Pentateuch's social laws and teachings become apparent. The Pentateuch adds to mere mechanistic and chance processes the knowledge that human beings need to behave humanely if they wish to prosper and succeed. Stating clearly what is, and is not, humane behaviour, clearly defining the difference between good (including human rights and justice) and evil, adding that human beings stand or fall by the way they behave. {1}

The meaning and intent of Genesis is explored further in 'Pre-flood Evils and the Social Problems of Our Time' {15}. It begins with the hidden description of pre-flood evils in Chapter 5 of Genesis and discusses the flood and its consequences, showing that a major planet-wide happening corresponds to what is recorded in Genesis about the Flood, occurring at the right time in the history of human beings.

Notes and References

Notes

< 1>   See chapter 4: 'The Social Cause-and-Effect Relationship'.

< 2>   I gratefully acknowledge the assistance I received from Esther Shouby without whose professional knowledge of Hebrew I might not have been able to explain the meaning of the ancient Hebrew texts.

< 3>   TV documentaries presented by Aubrey Manning {3}.

< 4>   See {4}: Commentary by Rashi.

< 5>   This brings together many ancient sayings and bible interpretations. The first six volumes are about Genesis.

< 6>   See {5}: Kasher 1: 72: Commentary on Gen 1: 31

< 7>   In chapter 6.1, see Appendix 1: Names of God

< 8>   See corresponding note to (Gen 2: 8) about 'mi-

kedem' having been rendered as 'eastward'.

<9>   For more comprehensive information about the family and how it functions in tough social environments, and about the pressures it faces from without and from within, see {10}

<10>   For more information about the way in which the neocortex functions and about role of the two halves of the brain, see {7}.

<11>   See {3}: Parts 5 and 6.

<12>   See comments on, and immediately following, (Gen 2: 25). Also, in chapter 6.1, see Appendix 2: 'Creation of Planet and Life; Evolution of Human Beings'.

<13>   See my earlier comments in 'Stage 6 (the sixth day) (Gen 1: 24-31)'

<14>   Commonly supposed to refer to one person but the text says otherwise. In chapter 6.1, see Appendix 3: 'Adam' and Hebrew Grammar.

<15>   The Pentateuch consists only of the five books of Moses and is at times referred to as 'Torah'.

However those wishing to give other writings an appearance of greater authority refer to these other writings as if they were part of the 'Torah'. Those doing so appear to be spreading a kind of misleading political propaganda.

<16>   The Pentateuch text used in this report is generally that of The Soncino Chumash (Bible) {4} which consists of Hebrew text, English translation and selected commentaries. But archaic words such as 'thou' and 'shalt' were changed to 'you' and 'shall'.

<17>   In chapter 6.1, see Appendix 3: 'Adam' and Hebrew Grammar

<18>   Relevant information about the history of the planet and evolution of human beings, from the planet's creation onwards to the present, is summarised in chapter 6.1, Appendix 2: 'Creation of Planet and Life; Evolution of Human Beings'.

<19>   In chapter 6.1, in Appendix 2: 'Creation of Planet and Life; Evolution of Human Beings', see notes on External Memory under time sub-heading 'Years: Now'.

<20>   See below, verse 24.

<21> Eve (Hebrew: Havvah, that is, Life): Derived from 'chayyah' meaning 'living'. <4>

<22> Compare with Genesis Chapter 1

<23> Erect man, much smaller skull size than modern humans.

References

{ 1} See chapter 4: 'The Social Cause-and-Effect Relationship'
And see
Struggle for Freedom: The Social Cause-and-Effect Relationship
Manfred Davidmann, 1978, 2002
solhaam.org/

{ 2} Genesis, Wellhausen and the Computer
Y. T. Radday, H. Shore, M. A. Pollatschek and D. Wickmann
Zeitschrift fuer die Alttestamentliche Wissenschaft
94. Band, Heft 4, 1982
Walter de Gruyter, Berlin, New York

{ 3} Earth Story
Presented by Aubrey Manning
Learning Channel Co-Production, BBC, 1998
Series Producer David Singleton

{ 4} The Soncino Chumash
Edited by Rev. Dr. A. Cohen
Soncino Press, 1947.

{ 5} 'Encyclopedia of Biblical Interpretation'
Menahem M Kasher
American Biblical Encyclopedia Society, 1953. <5>

{ 6} The Origin of Modern Humans: Multiregional and Replacement Theories
http://www.linfield.edu/-mrobert/origins.html
Michael Roberts, Dec 1999

{ 7} How the Human Brain Developed and How the Human Mind Works
Manfred Davidmann, 1998, 2006
solhaam.org/

{ 8} A Triune Concept of the Brain and Behaviour
P D MacLean
University of Toronto Press, 1973

{ 9}   The Dragons of Eden
       Carl Sagan
       Hodder and Stoughton, 1978

{10}   See chapter 5: 'Family, Community, Sex and the
       Individual'
       Manfred Davidmann, 1998

{11}   Homo Erectus: Out of Asia
       TV Documentary
       Horizon, 1997

{12}   Supervolcanoes
       TV Documentary
       Horizon, Feb 2000

{13}   A Commentary on the Book of Genesis.
       Part 1: From Adam to Noah;
       Part 2: From Noah to Abraham.
       By U. Cassuto (1944)
       Translated from the Hebrew by Israel Abrahams
       (1961)
       The Magnes Press, The Hebrew University,
       Jerusalem.

{14}   Encyclopaedia Judaica
       Keter Publishing House Jerusalem Ltd, 1974

{15}   See chapter 6.2: 'Pre-flood Evils and the Social
       Problems of Our Time'
       Manfred Davidmann, 2000

{16}   See chapter 6.5: 'Differentiating Between Good and
       Evil'
       Manfred Davidmann, 2001

Names of God (Appendix 1)

Translations into English from the Hebrew text refer to God using three designations, namely God, Lord God, and Lord.

Hebrew	English
Elohim	God
Yhwh Elohim	Lord God
Yhwh	the Lord

Yhwh

This designation is generally represented by its four consonants.

It was apparently regularly pronounced with its vowels until the destruction of the First Temple. But its pronunciation was avoided from the third century BCE. From then on the Hebrew word consisting of the consonants Yhwh was pronounced 'Adonay' and translated as 'the Lord' although 'Adonay' means 'my Lords'. Hence Yhwh is being translated as 'the Lord'. {14}

The true pronunciation of Yhwh was apparently 'Yahweh', meaning 'He causes to be, He brings into existence'. In the Middle Ages vowel points were added to the consonantal form of the Bible. 'Those used for Yhwh produced the form YeHoVaH and Christian scholars then introduced the name Jehovah.' {14}.

So Yhwh, regardless of how you pronounce it, means 'He causes to be'.

Elohim

The word 'Eloha' means God, and its plural 'Elohim' means 'gods'. Elohim is usually translated as if it meant 'God'.

Yhwh Elohim

Yhwh means 'He causes to be' and also 'He brings into existence'. 'Elohim' means 'gods' but here also is usually translated as if it meant 'God'.

So 'Yhwh Elohim' means God brings into existence.

Meaning and Significance of the Names of God

Hence the meaning and significance of the names of God is as follows:

Hebrew Name	ELOHIM	YHWH ELOHIM	YHWH
Translated as	God	Lord God	the Lord
Derivation of Name	God who creates, Creating God	God who brings into existence, God who originates, Originating God	He causes to be, What took place was, What happened was, What is happening
Meaning of Name	GOD or GOD (AS CREATOR). God as creator, as creator of all that is good.	GOD (AS ORIGINATOR)	GOD (AS CAUSE), as cause of what happened. In other words, this is happening, is what happened.

Example 1: (Gen 7: 16)

And they ... went in (into the ark) ... as God (Elohim) commanded him; and the Lord (Yhwh) shut him in.

Example 2: From {15}

In (Gen 3: 17) the ground is cursed by God (Yhwh Elohim, as originator), meaning that it will be so.

(Gen 5: 29) states that God (Yhwh, as cause) has cursed, meaning that it is happening, that it is so.

Creation of Planet and Life; Evolution of Human Beings
(Appendix 2)

The summary information in the following table has been compiled from a number of sources {3, 6-7, 11-12} as a kind of overview over current knowledge. It is an aid towards understanding that the known sequence of events parallels what is recorded in Genesis.

Some of what follows is uncertain. Being current knowledge {3 <11>, 6} it is likely to change as more knowledge is gained. Where there are disagreements I have tried to indicate this by quoting alternative viewpoints.

Definitions

Primate	An animal of the highest order of mammals, including apes, monkeys, and man
Hominoid	An animal resembling a human
Homo erectus	Erect man, much smaller skull size than that of humans
Homo sapiens	Modern humans, larger brain size than Homo erectus, humans, human beings

Years Ago
(Of the order of; as far as we know)

Billions
(Billions of years ago)

4.5	Planet formed
4	There was liquid water on earth.

| 3.5 | Land beginning to form. Largely covered with shallow water. Virtually no free oxygen. |

Early plant life fixes carbon dioxide and gives off oxygen and so makes planet habitable for our kind of life forms.

Large land areas formed.

Millions
(Millions
of years
ago)

| 600 | Massive ice age. First mass destruction of life on earth. About 70 percent of life on earth was killed. |

Continents broke apart, more circulation of warm water and this finished the ice age.

| 600/700 | When the ice age finished, the water rose, covered part of the land resulting in shallow coastal areas. Right conditions for life to evolve. |

Soft-bodied multicellular animals living in the sea. Followed by explosion of life forms. All the major categories of animals had already evolved then.

| 520 | Some of the animals lived by eating others. Predators and prey. |

Only in the ocean so far. Water teemed with different animals and plants. Land barren and lifeless.

| 450 | Plants made the evolutionary step which allowed them to leave the water. Soil built up. Soon afterwards the animals followed. |

As far as we know, it was the early plant life which fixed carbon dioxide from the atmosphere and gave off oxygen and so made the planet habitable for our kind of life forms.

350   First fossilised footprint on land. At the same time, descendants of fishes, the land vertebrates, had also emerged from the sea.

300   The land was alive with amphibians and reptiles. For example, reptiles which could chew and breathe at the same time and which were the first reptiles to dominate the world.

250   Massive volcanic eruptions and outpourings in the region of Siberia seem to have lasted for several million years. About 90 percent of land and marine life was destroyed.

       Some of the reptiles survived.

200   By this time a new group of much smaller animals had evolved. True mammals. Small mice-like.

       Reptiles were more suited to the conditions of the time.

65   Dinosaurs had dominated the earth for something like 170 million years.

       Another mass extinction. Land, air and sea life disappeared. About 70 percent of all plant and animal species were wiped out, including the dinosaurs. Mammals had previously been held down by the reptiles but now the primates emerged and eventually ourselves.

       Apparently caused by meteor strike [Yucatan] and by massive volcanic outpourings (series of eruptions, India). Global climate apparently altered for hundreds of thousands years.

3.5	Hominoids, animals resembling humans, appeared about this time. Erect bipeds with our body shape. Intermediate between humans and apes. Appear in East Africa.
2	It seems that Homo erectus (Erect man, much smaller skull size than that of humans) appeared about two million years ago. {3}

Thousands
(Thousands
of years
ago)

600/700	Rapid fluctuations between wet and dry periods. Uncertainty of environment.
250	Men with larger brains than Homo erectus began to appear in different parts of the world.
230	Only Neanderthals in Europe.
200	Homo erectus largely extinct. {6}
130	Oldest humans (Homo sapiens, Wise man) in Africa.
120	Some humans stayed in Africa. Rest migrated out of Africa and had reached Asia and Europe by 40,000 years ago.
100	Humans had replaced the other ones (such as Java man in Indonesia, Peking man in China). {3}
75	About 75 thousand years ago there was a massive volcanic eruption in Sumatra which severely affected the climate causing a planet-wide (average) drop in temperature of something like 5 degrees C. It seems that at roughly the same time there was apparently an enormous reduction of world population. It has recently been estimated from a reduction in genetic diversity which occurred at about this time that only a few

thousand (say 5 to 10 thousand) humans
could have survived. The two events appear
to be connected.

70   Humans in Africa.

50   Humans In Australia

40   Humans In Europe

35   The Neanderthals were gone.

30   From 30,000 years ago, to the present, all
              cultures and remains are those of humans.

Homo erectus may have evolved separately
in different parts of the planet {3} or may
have evolved in Africa and moved out of
Africa into Asia {6}.

And similarly we do not know whether
humans (Homo sapiens) evolved from Homo
erectus
(1) by local evolutionary steps in several
places, or
(2) by an initial evolutionary step in one
place followed by migration to others.

But we do know that from mammals evolved
hominoids (animals resembling a human)
which were later replaced by Homo erectus
(Erect man), themselves later replaced by
Homo sapiens (larger brain size than Homo
erectus, humans, human beings).

Now (A few years)

And now we have created External Memory, the vast mass of
externally prepared and stored information which is
accumulating. It has accumulated ever since people told stories to
their young who in turn retold them to later generations and ever
since writing was invented and the printed word accumulated,
followed by pictures, photographs, films and videos, television
and computerised manipulation of text and images. All of which
spread and proliferated together with corresponding search
(recall, retrieval, associating and selecting) procedures. {7}

External memory expanded enormously and became immediately accessible a few years ago, includes the Worldwide-web or Internet, is rapidly expanding planet-wide.

'Adam' and Hebrew Grammar (Appendix 3)

Eth   'Eth' is put before the object of the sentence if the object is either a definite noun (has article 'ha') or a proper noun (proper name).

Example:
Jim ate the bread.
'Jim' is the subject, the doer of the action.
Bread is the object of the action.

Eth adam   'Adam' is the proper name of one person, refers to the person whose name is 'Adam'.

Ha-adam   Life form(s). Example: Human beings.

If Adam stands for 'life form', then one can put 'ha' in front.

If 'Adam' is a proper name, one cannot say 'ha-adam'.
In other words, 'ha-adam' does not refer to a person named 'Adam'.

Eth ha-adam   The life form is the object of the sentence. The life forms are the object of the sentence.

Chapter 6.2

Pre-flood Evils and the Social Problems of Our Time

Introduction

Descendants of Seth (Behaviour of Human Beings; Genesis Chapter 5)

The Flood (Genesis Chapters 6-8)

Behaviour and Consequences (Genesis Chapter 9)

Humane Behaviour

Social Background
> Domineering, Oppression, Exploitation, Misuse of Others
> Armed Forces, Military Strength. Dictatorship and Authoritarianism
> Possessions, Ownership and Riches

Social System and Social Laws of the Bible
> Government; Positions of Trust, Responsibility and Authority; hierarchies
> Ten Commandments
> Social Cause-and-Effect Relationship
> Social Laws, Social System

Explanations, Comments, Notes and Analysis
> Appendix 1 Descendants of Seth (Genesis Chapter 5)
> Appendix 2 The Flood (Genesis: Chapter 6-8)
> Appendix 3 Behaviour and Consequences (Genesis Chapter 9)

Notes and References
> Notes   <..>
> References   {..}

Introduction

Chapters 1-4 of Genesis <8> describe in religious language the creation of planet earth and of life, the evolution of animals to human beings, the origin of evil and the behaviour of early human-like beings. What distinguishes human beings from earlier life forms is that we have the ability to know good and evil, to distinguish good from evil and to choose good instead of evil. {1}

Genesis states {1} that there is eternal enmity between beasts and human beings. Eternal enmity between beastly viciousness and

157

oppression on the one hand and humane care and affection for people on the other, eternal enmity between good and evil.

And Genesis showed that human beings learned that to be human one had to control instinctive behaviour and urges, and to struggle against viciousness and oppression.

Here, in this report, we start with Chapter 5. In Chapter 5, and in later chapters, Genesis looks at how human beings spread across the planet, describes how people behaved and behave, how humane behaviour contrasts with beast-like behaviour. We are told that human beings are human beings only to the extent to which they behave humanely, that inhuman (beastly) behaviour is evil.

Inhuman behaviour is defined, at times in secretive ways, and Genesis and the other books of the Pentateuch (Torah, Five Books of Moses) <2> add the elements of human rights, of justice and morality, of retribution for doing evil.

One's understanding of Genesis depends to a considerable extent on how the ancient text has been translated in the past. For a deeper understanding of Genesis, see chapter 2.6 'Meaning and Significance of the Names of God in Genesis' and chapter 2.7 'Meaning and Intent of Genesis: Essential Notes on Hebrew Grammar'. {2, 3}

Where relevant I have presented information by indenting as follows:

As stated in Genesis
      Explanations and comments
           Current knowledge, science
                 Additional notes, comments and quotations

Descendants of Seth (Behaviour of Human Beings) (Genesis Chapter 5)

Chapter 5 of Genesis is about how human beings increased in numbers and about how human beings behaved.

And for the last few thousand years, people have read chapters 5 and 6 of Genesis and wondered in what ways 'the wickedness of man was great in the earth' and 'every imagination of the thoughts of his heart was only evil continually (Gen 6: 5), causing God (as creator of all that is good) {3} to say that 'all flesh had corrupted their way upon the earth' (Gen 6: 12).

On the surface, this chapter appears to be a list of successive generations of human beings, generation by generation, a person by person listing in direct line of descent from Adam to another Lamech, the number of people in each generation increasing.

What had also remained unexplained until now was why it was necessary to list in detail how old they were when their first child was born, how long they lived after that, and how old they were when they died. The answer is that Chapter 5 of Genesis contains an underlying and important message about evil, contains a hidden description of corrupt and evil behaviour.

Where Pentateuch and Talmud contain hidden information, then this is pointed to, stated and confirmed, at the same time and in a number of different independent ways, to ensure the message is understood as it was intended to be understood. <10>

The complete analysis, with explanations, comments and notes, is in Appendix 1 'Descendants of Seth'. Based on the work recorded in Appendix 1, we continue here by looking at the inner meaning and significance of the text.

Chapter 5 of Genesis begins by telling us that from now on we are being told about human beings and about their behaviour.

In one case a lifespan is stated to have been 365 years.

All the ages and life spans mentioned in this chapter of Genesis are either exact multiples of five, or else multiples of five with the addition of seven. In one case, seven is added twice. {13}

> Cassuto pointed out the abovementioned numerical system, but failed to realise its significance.

All numbers can, in general, be constructed by combining (adding or subtracting) multiples of five and seven. The number 36, for example, is $(5 \times 10)-7-7$. But in this chapter there are five occasions when a single number seven is added to the basic number. Occurring five times this is most unlikely due to chance alone.

And Lamech's lifespan is given as 777 years which pointedly continues this series of numbers, the same name 'Lamech' being the second and confirming pointer:

Ch 4, v15	Cain	7 fold
Ch 4, v24	Lamech	77 fold
Ch 5, v31	Lamech	777 years

The numerical system is a means towards an end. An important statement is being made but it is hidden. The text is telling us something much more important than implausible-seeming ages and life spans of individuals. There has to be good reason for the secrecy and Table 1 illustrates the age-related information listed in this chapter.

Table 1: Life Spans (Genesis 5:)

Name	Age at which first child born (Years)	Years alive after first child born (Years)	Lifespan (Years)
	Column 1	2	3
Adam	130	800	930
Seth	105	800+7	905+7
Enosh	90	815	905
Kenan	70	840	910
Mahalalel	65	830	895
Jared	155+7	800	955+7
Enoch	65	300	365
Methuselah	180+7	775+7	955+7+7
Lamech	175+7	595	770+7=777

The sevens are added in seemingly random fashion in the first two columns of the table. Three sevens are added in column 1 and two sevens are added in column 2.

But all the numerical pointers come together, appear, in the last column. Hence it would seem to be the life spans which point to hidden meaning.

And that column contains a lifespan of 365 years which is much smaller than all the others. But 365 is also the number of days in a year. Which means that the number '365' also has another obvious and well-known meaning quite separate from 'lifespan of 365 years'. And this seems to confirm that the other life spans point to hidden meaning.

Further, the first person to have a seven added to his life span is Seth, the last person to have a seven added is Lamech. This would seem to be significant as the generations here being enumerated begin with Seth and finish with Lamech.

The first four (Seth to Mahalalel) have a life span which is roughly constant, almost the same, ranging from 895 to 912 years. The second four (Jared to Lamech) have life spans which fluctuate enormously by comparison, ranging from 365 to 969. In this way a clear distinction is drawn between these groups of people, of generations, of descendants who follow each other.

Which leads one to look at the meaning of their names and these are listed in Table 2 <6>:

Table 2: Meaning of Names (Genesis 5:)

Name	Pointer	Life Span	Meaning of Name
Seth	+7	912	Foundation.
Enosh	----	905	Human being.
Kenan	----	910	Owner, possession, gain. Variant of Cain.
Mahalalel	----	895	Praise of God, God lets his light shine.
Jared	+7	962	Going down, descent.
Enoch	365	365	Teacher. Beginning.
Methuselah	+7+7	969	Man of spear (or sword or weapon).
Lamech	+7=777	777	Strong. He who overcomes.

The names of those unmarked by pointers tell a clear story when looked at in the sequence of the generations. Some start as ordinary human beings, gain possessions, are successful materially. As all belongs to all, their gains are made at the expense of others. Their success is indicated by the meaning of Mahalalel's name. God has favoured them, they are successful.

The names of those marked by pointers tell quite a different story which is clear at least in outline.

Human beings know and are capable of distinguishing between good and evil and we are now told what is happening:

Enoch and Lamech stand out. They are pointed to by their unusual life spans. The second pointer to them is that their life spans are the only ones stated using 'and was' (v23 and v31).

Enoch 'walked with God' (v22), behaved humanely, died when young. What is taking place resembles what happened to Abel but without killing being mentioned. The names of Jared and Enoch together appear to confirm the resemblance to what took place in the previous chapter.

Methuselah's life span tells that he perished in the Flood, which seems to indicate that he did not follow God's ways <15>. In Chapter 4 of Genesis, those attacking Cain are paid back in full measure (7 times) and the later Lamech is more violent and hits out in overflowing measure (77 times). The Lamech (same name being a pointer) in Chapter 5 has a lifespan of 777 years, the hidden meaning being that he is much more violent. Here also the similarity of meaning of the names of Methuselah and Lamech confirms the intended meaning.

The good are disadvantaged, might and physical strength dominate, apparently even more so than before. Human beings are not behaving humanely, using their abilities towards evil instead of towards good. Evil, corruption, are spreading and getting worse.

But this is a continuous story from Seth to Lamech and the next chapter of Genesis records (Gen 6: 5) that 'the wickedness of man was great in the earth, and that every imagination of the thoughts of his heart was only evil continually.'

So what is recorded here is that some people obtained possessions, amassed wealth, at the expense of others. The 'good' were weakened and became disadvantaged as self-interest (greed, ownership, exploitation, so-called materialism) increased and the strong used their strength and viciousness so as to dominate, misuse or exploit others for personal gain.

And corruption here is more severe than among descendants of Cain (777 here compared with 77 before).

Again, overall, the good are disadvantaged, brutal strength dominates. Human beings have the potential for behaving humanely, but are not doing so. Power corrupts. Evil, corruption, are spreading and getting worse.

162

Power corrupts, absolute power corrupts absolutely. What is stated here in Genesis is parallelled by what is known to have happened later under the Monarchy and under the Hasmonean (Maccabean) dynasty, apparently for the same cause and in the same way. {5}

And all this has been encoded, hidden from view. Why this secretive way of telling?

Because of hidden struggle between 'good' and 'evil' at the subconscious level?

At the threshold of consciousness, evil is straining to dominate and use people but human beings can reject, overcome and control evil. {1} <11>

Because of authoritarian brutality of life at time the Pentateuch was written?

Possibly because of authoritarian power of secular ruling, religious or wealthy hierarchies or families.

According to our present knowledge, both explanations (causes) may be correct and the second follows from the first when people behave inhumanely.

Or because the Pentateuch is not a textbook (guide) on how to do evil, but a guide to doing good, to behaving as human beings.

But later generations distorted the word of God {6, 7, 12}, distorted in different ways the Pentateuch's message of what is good and humane, on how human beings need to behave so as to have good lives of high quality, on how 'good' can, must and will overcome 'evil'.

It seems to me that if evil had been defined more clearly, then it would have been much more difficult to distort the Pentateuch's meaning and message.

However, one cannot look at chapter 5 of Genesis in isolation as each chapter is a unique part of, makes specific contributions to, the

Pentateuch's developing story of the beginning (creation and creating) of human life and humane living, of good and evil, of reward and punishment.

The Flood (Genesis Chapters 6-8)

Chapter 5 and 6 of Genesis are about human beings who have the ability to distinguish between good and evil but do not use it, who continue to behave like their animal-like ancestors, who seem to be using their greater mental powers towards greater beastliness.

There was no objective knowledge of what constituted good, humane, behaviour. There were no rules of behaviour to enable people to resist and overcome the temptations of evil.

Genesis from here on stresses justice and retribution. Chapters 6-8 record the events of the Flood, linking what happened to the inhuman ways in which human beings behaved. Their behaviour included the evils described in Chapters 5. And those who choose to do evil suffer inevitable consequences, cannot avoid punishment.

'The wickedness of man was great in the earth' and 'every imagination of the thoughts of his heart was only evil continually (Gen 6: 5), causing God (as creator of all that is good) to say that 'all flesh had corrupted their way upon the earth' (Gen 6: 12), that 'the end of all flesh is come before Me; for the earth is filled with violence through them' (Gen 6: 13), that God would 'bring the flood of waters upon the earth, to destroy all flesh, wherein is the breath of life' (Gen 6: 17).

But there are to be some survivors, those who are 'righteous', who are 'wholehearted', who 'walked with God', are to survive (Gen 6: 9). Those who follow God's ways survive (Gen 7: 1) and repopulate the planet (Gen 9: 1).

From then on Genesis, the first volume (book) of the Pentateuch, defines evil more closely and describes and lays down what humane behaviour is and how it can be achieved. The social rules (laws) of behaviour set out in the Pentateuch enable people to resist, counter, overcome beastly temptations, to compare good with evil so as to choose good, to live good lives as human beings.

> For detailed analysis, with explanations, comments and notes, see Appendix 2 'The Flood' from which the following information in this chapter was extracted.

(Genesis: Chapter 6: 5-8)

Human beings are capable of comparing good with evil and of choosing good, but the thoughts people are imagining are evil continually. Human beings as a whole are using their thinking and evaluating abilities towards evil, towards evil behaviour.

Life forms are evolving towards greater viciousness (evolution by the survival of the strongest, most vicious), human beings are misusing and exploiting each other for personal gain. So they were wiped out, Noah was the exception.

(Genesis: Chapter 6: 9 to Chapter 8: 19)

Human beings were more corrupt and evil than their more beast-like predecessors and the flood occurred as a consequence.

We are told that the flood is a development towards good, a step ahead in the struggle for good against evil, for good against violence and corruption, that evil does not go unpunished, is being punished so as to control and overcome it.

It is God (as creator of all that is good) who shows Noah, who has behaved righteously, how to survive. All life forms are to be wiped out with the exception of Noah and those with him.

The Flood happened just as God (as creator of all that is good) had told Noah.

God (as creator, as creator of that which is good) ends the flood and tells Noah to leave the ark and the life forms are to repopulate the planet.

(Genesis: Chapter 8: 20-22)

What is stated is that since then life as a whole has not been destroyed for a second time because the thoughts of human beings are evil from youth.

Genesis then states (Gen 8: 22) that 'While the earth remains, seedtime and harvest, and cold and heat, and summer and winter, and day and night shall not cease.'

> It may be that the list seedtime and harvest, and cold and heat, and summer and winter, and day and night refers to essential

environmental characteristics on which depends the continuation of human life on the planet.

So these are happening and the earth is remaining.

As far as we know, the history of life on this planet tells of a major planet-wide happening which corresponds to what is recorded in Genesis about the Flood, occurring at the right time in the history of human beings. As follows <12>:

Thousands
(Thousands of years ago)

120	Some human beings stayed in Africa. Rest migrated out of Africa.
75	About 75 thousand years ago there was a massive volcanic eruption in Sumatra which severely affected the climate causing a planet-wide (average) drop in temperature of something like 5 degrees C. It seems that at roughly the same time there was apparently an enormous reduction of world population. It has recently been estimated from a reduction in genetic diversity which occurred at about this time that only a few thousand (say 5 to 10 thousand) human beings could have survived. The two events appear to be connected.
70	Human beings in Africa.
50	Human beings in Australia
40	Human beings in Europe
30	From 30,000 years ago, to the present, all cultures and remains are those of human beings.

Following the description of events of the Flood in religious terms and as a consequence of the evil behaviour of human beings, Genesis begins to describe what constitutes humane, good, behaviour and makes the point that if human beings wish to survive and prosper they need to follow the rules of behaviour laid down by God.

Behaviour and Consequences (Genesis Chapter 9)

This chapter of Genesis begins to describe, to make people aware of, some primitive aspects of human behaviour. And human behaviour is shown to include the punishing of inhuman behaviour.

> The detailed analysis with explanations, comments and notes is given in Appendix 3 'Behaviour and Consequences (Wrongdoing and Retribution).
>
> What follows here is information extracted from Appendix 3.

Human beings are to be the most advanced life form and human beings may eat all that grows and all that moves and lives.

Animals must not be eaten while alive.

And God (as creator) says in effect 'Life is mine and there is an accounting for every human life. Human life must not be taken by animals nor must it be taken by other human beings.

Whatever or whoever takes the life of a human being, their life is to be taken in return by other human beings.

> At this point of the Pentateuch this is a basic principle, part of the basic constitution. Later legal frameworks were developed to establish facts, circumstances, responsibility. Man-made legislation can be fair or unfair, just or corrupt (such as when applying one law for the poor and another to favour the rich).

Verse 9 records God as saying 'As for Me, behold, I establish My covenant with you, and with your seed after you;

> A covenant is an agreement in which each of the parties undertakes duties and obligations towards the other.

It is not a one-sided promise or obligation.

And God is saying: 'As for Me, behold': On my part (as long as you do your part, as long as you behave like human beings), I ...

So far we have been told that animals must not kill human beings and human beings must not kill human beings.

Whatever or whoever takes the life of a human being, their life is to be taken in return by other human beings.

And God (as creator, as creator of all that is good) tells human beings that as long as they behave like human beings the planet will not be rendered uninhabitable.

From here on, Genesis and the other books of the Pentateuch contain much information about what kind of behaviour is good and righteous, about what kind of behaviour is wicked, evil, corrupt, immoral or violent, and about the resulting consequences when behaving one way or the other.

And rules of behaviour to strengthen that which is good, to enable human beings to gain strength and have good lives of high quality in the struggle against beastliness, against evil.

Humane Behaviour

Humane behaviour is aimed at survival of the young and of the family, and then is for the good of family, other people and the community. It is based on feelings of care and affection for others. From this emerges a sense of social responsibility: people matter and are important, need to be treated well and looked after, are entitled to share equally. Backed up by knowledge, understanding and reason. {9}

We know that dominating others is conditioned, that is unnatural, behaviour which is destructive of humane behaviour. A throw-back to the level of the unthinking unfeeling primitive animal. {9}

And knowledge of good and evil enables us to choose that which is good and to overcome that which is inhumane, which is evil.

Chapter 5 of Genesis said much. About inhuman behaviour, about possessions, ownership and riches, about domineering, oppression and misusing people by force. Emphasized by the statement that whatever pre-flood human beings were considering was evil.

These themes are continued in Genesis and in the other four volumes (books) of the Pentateuch. We are told about the obligatory social laws and social system which have to be kept if evil is to be overcome, so that human beings can have good lives of high quality.

What follows reviews present social background corresponding to the evils listed in Chapter 5 of Genesis. This is followed by a short summary of the social laws and social system of the Pentateuch in so far as these relate to the evils described in Chapter 5 of Genesis.

Social Background

Domineering, Oppression, Exploitation, Misuse of Others

What we see in the working environment is a world-wide struggle to achieve a humane way of life, each person, family or community struggling to advance at their own level of development, struggling against those who wish to dominate, exploit, oppress. A struggle whose successful outcome depends on trustful cooperation, companionship and teamwork. {10, 15, 16}

The struggle is against those who wish to dominate other people. Against those who want primitive power over others, against those who wish to exploit, against those who may brutally and without feeling oppress human beings so as to exploit them. And 'to exploit' includes the whole range of antisocial decisions and activities of those who put profit before people and community. {17}

Human rights are based on controlling primitive dominant behaviour, on concern, care and affection for our young, for our families, people and communities, and express themselves in cooperation and teamwork between men and women to achieve a good life of high quality.

Armed Forces, Military Strength. Dictatorship and Authoritarianism {10}

Sometimes one has to fight to preserve a good way of life, to prevent others from taking what has been achieved, or one is expected to fight on behalf of those who dominate and exploit.

Our primitive animal ancestors behaved instinctively. Hunt for food, kill or be killed, fight or flee. Self before others, regardless of needs of others, marking out and defending territory.

Later mammals tend to have feelings, care and affection for their young. Human beings think as well as feel, and care for and look after their young for many years.

Having to fight, maim and kill amounts to a throwback to primitive animal behaviour, to behaviour which puts self before others. A throwback to beast-like behaviour for those who attack, to beast-like behaviour to counter beast-like behaviour for those who defend.

Authoritarian organisations are much less effective than participative ones. In authoritarian organisations morale is low, people cease to care and tend to work against each other instead of cooperating with each other for the benefit of the organisation. {18, 19}

One way of countering viciousness is by greater strength. If attacked, we have to defend ourselves.

Human beings cooperate well and achieve effective teamwork. Reason and evaluation can temper (add to, or change) emotional and instinct-motivated behaviour and combine with cooperation and teamwork so as to counter, and overcome, threats.

One has to be stronger than the enemy, socially as well as militarily. Essential is greater social as well as military strength. But the authoritarian (which includes military) mind has to be balanced to prevent it from taking over, has to be motivated towards 'good'.

Possessions, Ownership and Riches

Ownership {20} is the right to possess something and to decide what is to be done with it. If I own something it belongs to me and I decide what is to be done with it. An example would be owning a house.

Possession is having something in one's custody as distinct from owning it. If I possess something it belongs to another but I can decide how to use it. An example would be renting a house.

Another example would be deciding what to do with my money (ownership) or deciding and controlling the use of money belonging to someone else (possession).

And considering the right to ownership, two questions need to be considered. Namely where does the right come from and how is it exercised.

The right to own property varies among societies. Ownership laws which assign ownership 'rights' to owners have been devised by the owners themselves or by those who serve them. {21}

Ownership of land and means of production, of funds and wealth, has always been accumulated at someone else's expense. All belonged to the community, belonged to all alike. And this is what Chapter 5 of Genesis appears to be saying.

A human right is a something one may legally or morally claim, is the state of being entitled to a privilege or immunity or authority to act. Human rights are those held to be claimable by any living person, apply to all living people. Every living person is entitled to them.

So ownership of land and means of production, of funds and wealth, rightfully belongs to the community, belongs to all alike, is a human right. Those who have accumulated them have only possession, which means they can use and apply them but may do so only on behalf of, and for the benefit of, the community and that they are accountable to the community for the way in which they do so. {22}

Hence we have the use of possessions as long as we use them to provide a good living for our family, and beyond that for the benefit of the community. For the benefit of others less able or fortunate, for the benefit of the community around us and then for the benefit of communities abroad.

But we may only support those who themselves genuinely support our benevolent ideals and principles and their application and who themselves live and act accordingly, who behave humanely. <14>

Social System and Social Laws of the Bible

Government; Positions of Trust, Responsibility and Authority; Hierarchies

Here we are looking at the laws of the Pentateuch which control the behaviour and limit the power {4, 5} of government, of top executives and of the establishment, of those in positions of trust, responsibility or authority. The Pentateuch {11} leaves little doubt about what they must not do.

Positive laws tell what has to be done so as to create a strong and just society, point the way ahead towards greater strength, freedom and a good way of life.

Negative laws (prohibitions) state what must not be done and such laws protect the people from oppression and exploitation, from the anti-social behaviour of others, safeguard the people's strength and freedom. {5}

So the laws quoted here protect people and safeguard their strength and freedom.

These laws of government relate to 'rulers', apply to all in positions of trust, responsibility or authority, no matter whether secular, religious or military, no matter what the hierarchy or organisation.

Such people may not amass servants and may not oppress the people for their own benefit. They may not amass possessions and wealth, may not grasp power or behave promiscuously.

In other words, they may not put themselves above others by grasping power, may not satisfy personal desires at the expense of others.

And a ruler (person in position of trust, responsibility or authority) has to follow these laws and abide by them every day if he wishes 'to prolong his days in his kingdom, he and his children'. For 'kingdom' read 'position'.

So the Pentateuch laws quoted here protect people and safeguard their strength and freedom by laying down that those in positions of trust, responsibility or authority may not grasp power, may not oppress the people, may not behave promiscuously, may not enrich themselves.

Ten Commandments

The Ten Commandments {8} <13> are so important and are so well known because it is behaviour in accordance with these laws which is the basis for people trusting each other and so for people cooperating and working well with each other.

When Moses brought the tables of the law he brought 'freedom upon the tables'. It is the Ten Commandments as a whole which underlie freedom, independence and strength to oppose and resist oppression. Wherever there is any spiritual and material freedom today it exists because people followed these laws (rules) of behaviour and it exists to the extent to which they do so. {4}

In other words, following the provisions of the law results in freedom and ensures it, ensures strength and security.

Social Cause-and-Effect Relationship <1> {4}

In 'Behaviour and Consequences (Genesis Chapter 9)' we saw that a covenant is an agreement in which each of the parties undertakes duties and obligations towards the other. God promises that certain things will be so, as long as human beings fulfil their obligations under the covenant, as long as human beings follow God's laws, as long as they behave like human beings.

In the language of religion the Pentateuch later on states a fundamental scientific law, the Social Cause-and-Effect Relationship {4} <1>, which is that the consequences of keeping or not keeping the Pentateuch laws are inescapable, that what happens to one is in the end the inevitable result of one's own behaviour. Also clearly stated is that this is a scientific law which was defined and stated using the language of religion so that people would benefit from knowing the effects (consequences) of their behaviour. The relationship is stated in precise terms. History {5} and social science {17} confirm it.

We are told that the Social Cause-and-Effect Relationship applies to all without exception and at all times, wherever one may be, regardless of type of government, form of religion or social system or country. It applies whether you like it or not, agree or disagree.

The consequences of one's behaviour are detailed both ways, clearly and powerfully illustrating intermediate stages between the two ends of the scale, and we are told that the process is reversible. Increasingly disregarding the Law results in greater suffering and oppression, increasingly behaving according to the Law results in greater freedom and a better life.

The relationship applies to all. It is stated in a way which enables people to benefit from knowing the effects of their behaviour, even if they do not understand the underlying interrelation.

Freedom and independence of mind and person and the quality of life depend on one's behaviour. The consequences of observing the Law are described and so are those of disregarding the Law. The consequences of one's behaviour are inevitable, inescapable. Keeping or not keeping the Pentateuch laws has consequences which cannot be avoided.

Those who behave according to the law have good and satisfying lives, gain social and military strength. Behaviour which is contrary to the law lowers the quality of life, increases internal stress and conflict to the point of social disruption and military weakness.

Social Laws, Social System

It is the social laws of the Pentateuch which in effect state that all are equal, that no person may exploit another or oppress so as to exploit. All have the right to be free and independent masters of their own fate and there has to be a system of social security which guarantees not just freedom from need but also protection against loss of material and spiritual independence. In effect, oppression can be and has to be resisted, struggled against and opposed.

The essential social provisions of Pentateuch law are clear and to the point. This is what the Pentateuch lays down as a matter of law {4}:

1. Every seventh day is a day of rest for all, for those who are employed as well as for those who employ. Work stops on the weekly day of rest, the Sabbath, to let those who labour have a regular day of rest. On this day the servant is as free as the master, the worker is as free as the employer. The weekly day of rest has spread and benefits almost all the civilised world.

2. The community has to provide ('lend') money to those who need it, free of interest.

3. All such loans, if outstanding, are to be cancelled every seventh year.

4. The country's wealth, and this applies particularly to productive capital such as land, belongs equally to all and needs to be shared out. Inhabitants are also entitled to have a sabbatical year every seventh year. During this sabbatical year they are entitled to be freed from work at the expense of the community.

Every person is entitled as a matter of right to social security. This means that people are entitled to be supported by the community not only when they fall on hard times but also to maintain their independence as independent breadwinners for their families. For example, the community has to provide backup funds to those who need them and they have to be provided as and when required.

To prevent people being exploited through their need these funds have to be provided without charging interest and such 'loans' are cancelled every seventh year if the borrower has been unable to repay them.

The community supports the individual but only if the individual in turn supports the community. Those supported by the community are under obligation to support others in need of support, in due course and when able to do so, to share with others who are in need. Where need includes the need for capital to secure their operation, to achieve the general standard of living and quality of life.

It is those who themselves keep and apply these benevolent social laws, who keep Pentateuch law, who are entitled to these rights.

Explanations, Comments, Notes and Analysis

On the whole and when relevant I have tried to present the information by indenting as follows:

As stated in Genesis
        Explanations and comments
                Current knowledge, science
                        Additional notes, comments and quotations

For a quick overview, read the first two, namely 'As stated in Genesis' and 'Explanations and comments'.

Appendix 1:

Descendants of Seth (Genesis Chapter 5)

1 This is the book of the generations of Adam. In the day that God created man, in the likeness of God made He him;

2 male and female created He them, and blessed them, and called their name Adam, in the day when they were created.

> Although the story is told about individuals, its content relates to the life form (human beings) as a whole. {2}

3 And Adam lived a hundred and thirty years, and begot a son in his own likeness, after his image; and called his name Seth.

> And begot 'a son': This phrase is used only twice in this chapter. See v29 below.

> 'a son in his own likeness': That is, 'in the likeness of God' (See v1 above).

> God is here referred to as God (creator), the creator of all that is good, as in Genesis Chapter 1. {3}

The text in Chapter 1 of Genesis draws a distinction between image and likeness, that is between 'appearance' and 'discernment and understanding'. And man (male and female) are there recorded as having been created only in God's image, alike to God only in appearance. <9>

And 'Adam' (male and female) are here stated to have been created also in the likeness of God. That is, they know good and evil and can distinguish between them (Gen 3: 5, 22).

Hence this Chapter 5 of Genesis is about how human beings multiplied and behaved, is about the descendants of Seth who are human beings.

So we are here looking at the development and behaviour of human beings who know of, can distinguish between and can choose between, good and evil.

Having told us that we are considering human beings from now on, Chapter 5 of Genesis continues:

4 And the days of Adam after he begot Seth were eight hundred years; and he begot sons and daughters.

5 And all the days that Adam lived were nine hundred and thirty years and he died.

6 And Seth lived a hundred and five years, and begot Enosh.

7 And Seth lived after he begot Enosh eight hundred and seven years; and begot sons and daughters.

8 And all the days of Seth were nine hundred and twelve years; and he died.

Then follow statements similar to v6-8 for a number of generations, from Seth to Lamech, with different ages and time spans. However, there are some exceptions and these are given below in the sequence in which they occur.

9 And Enosh lived ... and begot Kenan. ...

12 And Kenan lived ... and begot Mahalalel. ...

15 And Mahalalel lived ... and begot Jared. ...

18 And Jared lived ... and begot Enoch. ...

21 And Enoch lived sixty and five years, and begot Methuselah.

22 And Enoch walked with God (as creator) after he begot Methuselah three hundred years, and begot sons and daughters.

> 'And Enoch walked with God': Compare with Gen 6: 9 'Noah was in his generations a man righteous and wholehearted; Noah walked with god'. (With God (as creator). So the phrase signifies that Enoch walked in God's ethical ways. {13}

23 And all the days of Enoch were three hundred sixty and five years.

> Stated as a rule that all the days of so-and-so WERE (vajiyu). But in two places the text states 'AND WAS' (singular) (vajehi). (This v23 about Enoch, and v31 about Lamech). {13}

24 And Enoch walked with God (as creator), and he was not; for God (as creator) took him.

> So Enoch followed and applied that which was 'good'. Did not harm other beings, did not domineer, exploit, oppress, use his strength against others on his own behalf.

25 And Methuselah lived ... and begot Lamech. ...

27 And all the days of Methuselah were nine hundred sixty and nine years; and he died.

> "... 969 years after his birth the Flood came upon the world. This implies that he perished in the flood. {13}

28 And Lamech lived a hundred eighty and two years, and begot a son.

29 And he called his name Noah, saying: 'This same shall comfort us in our work and in the toil of our hands, which comes from the ground which the Lord has cursed.'

> And begot 'a son': Pointedly used only twice in this chapter of Genesis. In v3 above, Seth represents a forward move, referring to the evolution (creation) of human beings. Here in v28 Noah represents another forward move, referring to human beings after the Flood as beginning to become conscious of what is 'good' and what is 'evil' so as to choose good instead of evil.

'which the Lord has cursed' refers to Gen 3: 17 on expulsion from Eden, refers to life after evolving into human beings. In Gen 3: 17 the ground is cursed by God (as originator).

But here (Gen 5: 29) states that God (as cause) has cursed, meaning that it is happening, that it is so. <5>

It is a tough struggle and hard work to obtain a living from the ground.

There appears to be an intended parallelism with Gen 4: 26 where we see that to Seth is born a son and then began men (another life form) to call on God (as cause) for help. They (early human beings, Homo erectus) were struggling to obtain a living against pressure of another life form (human beings).

The problem here in v29 is not overcoming another life form but the tough struggle to obtain a living against a harsh environment.

'This same (this person Noah) shall comfort us':

The text should have either 'this one WILL GIVE US REST' (yenichenu) or, (nachman) - 'this one WILL BRING US COMFORT' (yenachamenu). {13}

That is, there are two possible meanings of the Hebrew text. (1) 'will give us rest' from work, or reduce the work. (2) 'will bring us comfort', adding something.

'This same shall comfort us': The bringing of comfort may refer to bringing comfort from internal pressures, possibly due to there being less evil and more good in the world after the flood.

30 And Lamech lived after he begot Noah five hundred ninety and five years, and begot sons and daughters.

31 And all the days of Lamech were seven hundred seventy and seven years; and he died.

> Stated as a rule that all the days of so-and-so WERE (vajiyu). But in two places the text states 'AND WAS' (singular) (vajehi). (This v31 about Lamech and v23 about Enoch). {13}

32 And Noah was five hundred years old; and Noah begot Shem, Ham, and Japheth.

> Instead of 'and Noah lived' the wording in verse 32 is 'and Noah was ... old' {13}. So presumably this statement about Noah is to be regarded as referring to an individual.

Appendix 2: The Flood

Genesis: Chapter 6: 5-8

> The English text refers three times to 'man'. In each case the Hebrew word is 'ha-adam' meaning life form, here human beings, humans. {2}

> In each of these four verses God is referred to by the Hebrew designation 'Yhwh', that is as cause, as cause of what happened. In other words, this is what happened. {3}

5 And the Lord saw that the wickedness of man was great in the earth, and that every imagination of the thoughts of his heart was only evil continually.

> Human beings are capable of comparing good with evil and of choosing good, but the thoughts people are imagining are evil continually. Human beings as a whole are using their thinking and evaluating abilities towards evil, towards evil behaviour.

6 And it repented the Lord that He had made man on the earth, and it grieved Him at His heart.

7 And the Lord said: 'I will blot out man (ha-adam meaning life form) whom I have created from the face of the earth; both man, and beast, and creeping thing, and fowl of the air; for it repenteth Me that I have made them.'

8 But Noah found grace in the eyes of the Lord.

Some sources maintain that the flood was brought about because of what is recorded in the first eight verses of this chapter of Genesis.

Life forms are evolving towards greater viciousness (evolution by the survival of the strongest, most vicious), human beings are misusing and exploiting each other for personal gain. So they were wiped out, Noah was the exception.

Genesis 6: 9 to 8: 19

We have just seen that human beings were more corrupt and evil than their more beast-like predecessors and that the flood occurred.

In the remaining verses of this chapter God is referred to as God (as creator, as creator of all that is good) {3}. So we are told that the flood is a development towards good, a step ahead in the struggle for good against evil, for good against violence and corruption, that evil does not go unpunished, is being punished so as to control and overcome it.

The different designations used for God again add meaning to these chapters. {3}

9 These are the generations of Noah. Noah was in his generations a man righteous and whole-hearted; Noah walked with God (eth-ha'Elohim).

'Noah walked with God.': "... walking with God means walking in those ways in which God walks, namely, in the ways of righteousness and justice; ..." {13}

10 And Noah begot three sons, Shem, Ham, and Japheth.

11 And the earth was corrupt before God (ha'Elohim), and the earth was filled with violence.

'Chamas': Translated as 'violence'.

"All the commentators, both ancient and modern, are accustomed to explain the word to mean lawlessness perpetrated by force. ... . In the rabbinic idiom, as in modern Hebrew, the word 'chamas' connotes a deed of outrage and violence. ... (but) the reference is to wickedness generally, to

180

> unrighteousness as a whole" and should be rendered unrighteousness. {13}

12 And God (Elohim) saw the earth, and, behold, it was corrupt; for all flesh had corrupted their way upon the earth.

13 And God (Elohim) said to Noah: 'The end of all flesh is come before Me; for the earth is filled with violence through them; and behold, I will destroy them with the earth.

> Noah is then told how to build the ark.

17 And I, behold, I do bring the flood of waters upon the earth, to destroy all flesh, wherein is the breath of life, from under heaven; every thing that is in the earth shall perish.

18 But I will establish My covenant with you; ...

> It is God (as creator of all that is good) who shows Noah, who has behaved righteously, how to survive.

> Noah is then told who is to be saved.

> All life forms are to be wiped out with the exception of Noah and those with him. This is a step towards greater 'good'.

Genesis Chapter 7:

1 And the Lord (Yhwh) said to Noah: 'Come you and all your house into the ark; for you have I seen righteous before Me in this generation.

9 ... as God (Elohim) commanded Noah.

16 And they that went in, ... , as God (Elohim) commanded him; and the Lord (Yhwh) shut him in.

> And so it happened.

> In other words, the Flood happened just as God (as creator of all that is good) had told Noah.

24 And the waters prevailed upon the earth a hundred and fifty days.

Genesis Chapter 8

> God (as creator, as creator of that which is good) ends the flood and tells Noah to leave the ark and for the life forms to repopulate the planet.

1 And God (Elohim) remembered Noah, and every living thing, and all the cattle that were with him in the ark; and God (Elohim) made a wind to pass over the earth, and the waters assuaged;

16 And God (Elohim) spoke to Noah, saying:

17 'Go forth from the ark, ...

18 And Noah went forth, and ...

19 every beast, every ... , went forth out of the ark.

Genesis 8: 20-22

What is stated is that since then no comparable planet-wide disaster has happened (see v21) as a consequence of the thoughts human beings are imagining being evil from youth. That is, as a consequence of the thoughts arising from their imagination being evil from youth.

20 And Noah builded an altar to the Lord (la'Yhwh); ...

In Hebrew, le ha Yhwh becomes la'Yhwh

21 And the Lord (Yhwh) smelled the sweet savour; and the Lord (Yhwh) said in His heart: 'I will not again curse the ground any more for man's (haadam) sake; for the imagination of man's heart is evil from his youth; neither will I again smite any more every thing living, as I have done.

Lord (Yhwh) 'said in His heart': Relates to thoughts.

Thinking:

'loh osiph': Literally 'I shall not continue'. Here refers to the cursing of the ground. 'any more': more than it is already cursed. <16>

'I shall not continue' to make life more difficult

man's (ha-adam) sake: because of human beings

for the imagination of man's heart (haadam) is evil from his youth:

182

> Because the thoughts of human beings (which arise from their imagination) are evil from youth

> > 'smite' rendered 'destroy' by Cassuto.

> > 'I will never again destroy': I shall not destroy a second time {13}

> > Since then there has not been another ...

> In other words, since then life as a whole has not been destroyed for a second time because the thoughts of human beings are evil from youth.

22 While the earth remaineth, seedtime and harvest, and cold and heat, and summer and winter, and day and night shall not cease.'

> > It may be that the list seedtime and harvest, and cold and heat, and summer and winter, and day and night refers to essential environmental characteristics on which depends the continuation of human life on the planet.

> > So these are happening and the earth is remaining.

Appendix 3:

Behaviour and Consequences (Wrongdoing and Retribution) (Genesis Chapter 9)

1 And God (Elohim) blessed Noah and his sons, and said to them: 'Be fruitful, and multiply, and replenish the earth.

2 And the fear of you and the dread of you shall be upon every beast of the earth, and upon every fowl of the air, and upon all wherewith the ground teemeth, and upon all the fishes of the sea; into your hand are they delivered.

> Human beings are to be the most advanced life form.

3 Every moving thing that lives shall be for food for you; as the green herb have I given you all.

Now including the flesh of all living creatures (compared with Gen 1: 29 which permitted only vegetarian food). {13}

Human beings may eat all that grows and all that moves and lives.

4 Only flesh with the life thereof, which is the blood thereof, shall you not eat.

Animals must not be eaten while alive.

5 And surely your blood of your lives will I require; at the hand of every beast will I require it; and at the hand of man (ha-adam), even at the hand of every man's brother (ish achiv), will I require the life of man (ha-adam).

... of every beast ...: The Hebrew word for beast can also mean 'living creature'.

'even at the hand of every man's brother' quoted by Cassuto as 'and of man, of every man's brother'. {13}

'every man's brother': Hebrew 'ish achiv' meaning 'every human being'.

Meaning of Hebrew words for 'will I require' is 'will I demand'. Meaning 'I hold responsible'.

'blood of your lives': Life

God (as creator) says in effect 'Life is mine and there is an accounting for every human life. Human life must not be taken by animals nor must it be taken by other human beings.

6 Whoso sheds man's (ha-adam) blood, by man (ba'adam) shall his blood be shed; for in the image of God (Elohim) made He man.

In Hebrew, be ha-adam becomes ba'adam

'by man': By the hand of man {13}

Whatever or whoever takes the life of a human being, their life is to be taken in return by other human beings.

Basic principle, part of basic constitution. Later legal frameworks to establish facts, circumstances, responsibility. Man-made legislation can be fair or unfair, just or corrupt (such as one law for the poor and another for the rich).

184

7 And you, be you fruitful, and multiply; swarm in the earth, and multiply therein.'

8 And God (Elohim) spoke to Noah, and to his sons with him, saying:

9 'As for Me, behold, I establish My covenant with you, and with your seed after you;

> A covenant is an agreement in which each of the parties undertakes duties and obligations towards the other.
>
> > It is not a one-sided promise or obligation.
>
> 'As for Me, behold': On my part (as long as you do your part, as long as you behave like human beings), I ...

10 and with every ...

11 And I will establish My covenant with you; neither shall all flesh be cut off any more by the waters of the flood; neither shall there any more be a flood to destroy the earth.'

> 'I will establish My covenant (my rules of behaviour) with you; (so that) neither shall ...'

12 And God (Elohim) said: 'This is the token of the covenant ...

16 '... that I may remember the everlasting covenant between God (Elohim) and every living creature of all flesh that is upon the earth.'

17 And God (Elohim) said to Noah: 'This is the token of the covenant which I have established between Me and all flesh that is upon the earth.'

Notes and References

Notes

< 1> The Social Cause-and-Effect Relationship is listed both in biblical language and in plain English in chapter 4: 'The Social Cause-and-Effect Relationship', with detailed references to the Pentateuch text.

< 2> Pentateuch (Torah, Five Books of Moses <3, 7>

< 3> The Pentateuch text used in this report is generally that of The Soncino Chumash (Bible) {14} which consists of Hebrew text, English translation and selected commentaries. But archaic words such as

'thou' and 'shalt' were changed to 'you' and 'shall'.

< 4> See {14}: Commentary by Rashi

< 5> See {3}.

< 6> See {6} for another detailed example of use of names in ancient Jewish religious writings to convey hidden important information. There see section on 'The Five Pairs (Zugot)' and Table 2 'Names of the Pairs').

< 7> The 'Torah' (Pentateuch, Five Books of Moses) consists only of the five books of Moses.

(Those wishing to give other writings an appearance of greater authority refer to these other writings as if they were part of the Torah. Those doing so are spreading a kind of misleading political propaganda.)

< 8> Genesis: First volume (book) of Pentateuch (Torah, Five Books of Moses) <3>.

< 9> In {1}, see comments to (Gen 1: 24-31) in 'Stage 6 (the sixth day)'

<10> A good example is the hidden way in which the Talmud refers to Christians and early Christian beliefs. In {7} see what is recorded about R. Johanan b. Zakkai's discple Joshua b. Hananiah

<11> In {1}, see discussion and comments on (Gen 4: 7)

<12> In {1}, see Appendix 2: 'Creation of Planet and Life; Evolution of Human Beings'.

<13> The Ten Commandments are listed both in biblical language and in plain English in chapter 4: 'The Social Cause-and-Effect Relationship', with detailed references to the Pentateuch text.

<14> In this chapter, see 'Social Laws, Social System'

<15> In this chapter's 'Appendix 1', see note to v27.

<16> In {13}, see Cassuto II, p119

References

{ 1} See chapter 6.1: Creation, Evolution and the Origin of Evil
Manfred Davidmann, 2000

{ 2} See chapter 6.7: Meaning and Intent of Genesis:

Essential Notes on Hebrew Grammar
Manfred Davidmann, 2000

{ 3} See chapter 6.6: Meaning and Significance of the
      Names of God in Genesis
      Manfred Davidmann, 2000

{ 4} See chapter 4: 'The Social Cause-and-Effect
      Relationship'
      And see
      Struggle for Freedom: The Social Cause-and-Effect
      Relationship
      Manfred Davidmann, 1978, 2002
      solhaam.org/

{ 5} History Speaks: Monarchy, Exile and Maccabees
      Manfred Davidmann, 1978, 2007
      solhaam.org/

{ 6} At the Time of Jesus, The Truth about Hillel and his
      Times
      Manfred Davidmann, 1978, 2007
      solhaam.org/

{ 7} One Law for All: Freedom Now, Freedom for Ever
      Manfred Davidmann, 1978, 2007
      solhaam.org/

{ 8} Deut **5**, 6-18; Exod **20**, 2-14

{ 9} How the Human Brain Developed and How the
      Human Mind Works
      Manfred Davidmann, 1998, 2006
      solhaam.org/

{10} See chapter 5: 'Family, Community, Sex and the
      Individual'
      Manfred Davidmann, 1998

{11} Deut **17**, 14-20

{12} ORIGIN OF CHRISTIANITY and JUDAISM
      Manfred Davidmann, 1994, 2006
      solhaam.org/

{13} A Commentary on the Book of Genesis.
      Part 1: From Adam to Noah;
      Part 2: From Noah to Abraham.
      By U. Cassuto (1944)
      Translated from the Hebrew by Israel Abrahams
      (1961)
      The Magnes Press, The Hebrew University,
      Jerusalem.

{14} The Soncino Chumash

Edited by Rev. Dr. A. Cohen
Soncino Press, 1947.

{15} The Will to Work: What People Struggle to Achieve
Manfred Davidmann, 1981, 2006
solhaam.org/

{16} Motivation Summary
Manfred Davidmann, 1982, 1998
solhaam.org/

{17} Social Responsibility, Profits and Social
Accountability
Manfred Davidmann, 1979, 1995
solhaam.org/

{18} Style of Management and Leadership
Manfred Davidmann, 1981, 2006
solhaam.org/

{19} Role of Managers Under Different Styles of
Management
Manfred Davidmann, 1982, 1998
solhaam.org/

{20} Understanding How Society is Organised for
Controlling and Exploiting People
Manfred Davidmann, 1998, 2002
solhaam.org/

{21} What People are Struggling Against: How Society is
Organised for Controlling and Exploiting People
Manfred Davidmann, 1998, 2002
solhaam.org/

{22} Co-operatives and Co-operation: Causes of Failure,
Guidelines for Success
http://www.solhaam.org/
Manfred Davidmann, 1996

Morality, Sexual Behaviour and Depravity

'Nakedness' and Sexual Behaviour

Primitive mammals engage instinctively in sex, forming family connections, just like eating and drinking. And 'naked' is used in (Gen 2: 25) for referring to sexual behaviour between primitive male and female animals engaging instinctively in sex. <1>

'Naked' is used again, in (Gen 3: 7), for referring to sexual behaviour between male and female human beings when stating that human beings do not behave instinctively, that human beings control instinctive sexual behaviour impulses, that they control the sex urge. <2>

The human brain underlies free will, enabling us to decide independently what is good or evil, that is what to do or not to do.

Human beings learned not to behave instinctively, they learned that to be human one had to control one's instinctive sexual behaviour impulses, that human beings can control the sex urge.

It takes a long time to give birth (pregnancy) and to provide for upbringing of children to maturity. So sex has to be restrained to within the family (marriage). Human beings behaving humanely control the sex urge.

> For comprehensive information on how the human mind evolved and works, see {4}

> For comprehensive information about the family and how it functions and the pressures which it faces from without and from within, see {5}

Sexual Behaviour (Genesis Chapter 6: 1-2, 5)

Genesis Chapter 5 described the behaviour of the 'descendants of Seth', namely Homo sapiens, human beings. Chapter 6 continues the development by describing other aspects of the behaviour of human beings at that time.

Having detailed 'dominating, oppressing and exploiting' in Chapter 5 {10}, Genesis in Chapter 6 adds 'unrestrained sexual behaviour' as a main cause of the flood. Verses 1-2 and 5 of Chapter 6 tell much.

While the information in Genesis Chapter 6 about 'sons of God' and 'daughters of men' appears vague, is among the least understood of the passages of the Pentateuch, it deals with behaviour which underlies evil and is quoted as a direct cause of the subsequent flood.

6: 1 And it came to pass, when men began to multiply on the face of the earth, and daughters were born to them,

> Hebrew ha'adam rendered 'men' but the meaning is 'life form'. {11}

> In Genesis Chapter 5 the descendants 'begot sons and daughters'. But the first sentence of Chapter 6 pointedly refers to 'daughters' in general, to the female of the life form, to women.

6: 2 that the sons of God saw the daughters of men that they were fair; and they took them wives, whomsoever they choose.

'the sons of God' (Hebrew 'bene-ha'elohim':

> The name Elohim used is that of God (creator),
> that is of God as creator of all that is good,
> indicating, as before, potential towards good. {1,
> 2}

> What they have in common is that they are alike
> to God in their ability to understand the
> difference between good and evil.
> > Gen 3: 5 ... you shall be as God, knowing good
> > and evil.
> > Gen 3: 22 ... the man is become as one of us,
> > to know good and evil;

> So 'sons of God' refers to the males of a life form
> which in itself is a development towards good,
> which is alike to God in its ability to understand
> the difference between good and evil, to human
> beings. {1}

> In other words, 'sons of God' refers to 'men'.

'The daughters of men':

> eth-benot ha'adam: The daughters of human
> beings. The reference is to 'daughters' in general,
> to the female of the life form, to women.

'that they were fair':

> 'fair': Hebrew 'tobboth', literally 'good'

'they took them wives, whomsoever they choose.':

> This phrase is generally considered to include:
> Even those married to others <3>
> Even (one) wedded to a man <4>

> Without restraint. Without care or consideration for
> the 'daughters' or other people.

The application of their abilities towards taking whomever
they chose as wives is misuse of others for personal gain
regardless of the feelings and welfare of other peoples, is
corrupt and evil corresponding to unrestrained beastly animal
behaviour from below the level of human consciousness.
Beastly animal behaviour which human beings can, should and
have to control. <5>

191

But human beings are misusing their abilities, misapplying them towards greater evil instead of towards greater good, here towards greater sexual self-gratification without care or concern for others.

It is in these first few sentences of Genesis Chapter 6 that uncontrolled sexual behaviour is added to the list of beastly behaviours carried forward by human beings from their primitive ancestors.

6: 5 And the Lord saw that the wickedness of man was great in the earth, and that every imagination of the thoughts of his heart was only evil continually.

> Human beings on the whole were exploiting and misusing each other for personal gain, as described in Chapters 5 and 6 <6>. So they were almost wiped out by the flood. Noah and his family were saved because he was righteous {10}.

Consequences of Wrongdoing, of Inhuman Behaviour

Genesis has been describing evil as taking place, has been defining it in general terms. But has not been detailing evil behaviour in plain language.

Humans beings, however, are capable of comparing good with evil and of choosing good.

So why is evil not described and its cause stated in plain language? Why the secrecy, the codes, used in Genesis Chapters 5 and 6 to show that people are being exploited, oppressed and misused?

Evil has so far not been detailed because at this point, and on the whole, there is no clear realisation of what kind of behaviour is good, and thus of what is bad, evil, inhuman.

Human beings behaved just like earlier, lower, more beastly, forms of life because there was no objective knowledge of what constituted good, humane, behaviour.

People did not distinguish between humane and beastly behaviour, there were no descriptions of humane compared with beastly behaviour, no rules of behaviour to enable people to resist and overcome primitive instinctive urges.

But from now on Genesis (that is the Pentateuch) defines evil more closely, bringing it from the subconscious to the conscious level, and so enabling people to choose between good and evil. Describing evil behaviour and its serious consequences, describing what humane behaviour is and how it can be achieved.

Immediately following the flood, God is recorded (Gen 9: 9) saying 'As for Me, behold, I establish My covenant with you, and with your seed after you; ... <7>

> A covenant is an agreement in which each of the parties undertakes duties and obligations towards the other. It is not a one-sided promise or obligation. {10}

> And God is saying: 'As for Me, behold': On my part (as long as you do your part, as long as you behave like human beings), I ...

> And God (as creator, as creator of all that is good) tells human beings that as long as they behave like human beings the planet will not be rendered uninhabitable.

And Chapter 9 of Genesis begins to describe, to make people aware of, some primitive aspects of human behaviour <7> which is shown to include the punishing of inhuman, beastlike, behaviour.

From here on, Genesis and the other books of the Pentateuch contain much information about what kind of behaviour is good and righteous, about what kind of behaviour is wicked, evil, corrupt, immoral or violent, and about the resulting consequences when behaving one way or the other. {10}

And contain rules of behaviour to strengthen that which is good, to enable human beings to gain strength and have good lives of high quality in the struggle against beastliness, against evil.

The social rules (laws) of behaviour set out in the Pentateuch enable people to resist, counter and overcome primitive instinctive urges and beastlike behaviour, enable human beings to have good lives of high quality, to know the difference between good and evil and so to choose that which is good.

'Nakedness' Incident (Genesis Chapter 9: 18-27)

Commentators have concentrated their attention on guessing what Ham did to his father Noah and why Noah cursed Ham's son Canaan instead of Ham. And commentators paid much less attention to it being Noah and not God who condemns and praises his sons according to the way they behaved.

As before in Genesis, we see that a generally applicable statement is being made by a story told about individuals. In other words, this is an allegory. We are told that all human beings are the descendants of the three sons of Noah and the story is about the behaviour of human beings, and about what happens as a result.

We are told that these three people (their descendants, people) behaved in very different ways, depending on their sexual and family morality. And Noah states the consequences of their behaviour.

18 And the sons of Noah, that went forth from the ark, were Shem, and Ham, and Japheth; and Ham is the father of Canaan.

> Only Canaan is mentioned of all their descendants.

19 These three were the sons of Noah, and of these was the whole earth overspread.

> We are told that all human beings are the descendants of the three sons of Noah and the story is about their behaviour and what happened as a result. All human beings are descended from them and so what is being said about behaviour, and about resulting consequences, applies to all human beings. A general point is being made by a story which relates to individuals.

20 And Noah the husbandman (forefather) began, and planted a vineyard.

> Hebrew 'Ish ha-adamah', literally 'man of the earth', rendered 'husbandman' in the translations.

> In Gen 2: 7 the first life form 'ha-adam' is formed from the earth 'ha-adamah'. {1}

> Noah similarly is the first man, all human beings who survived the flood are descended from him.

> He is the righteous forefather of all human beings and 'Ish ha-adamah' should be rendered 'the forefather'.

21 And he drank of the wine, and was drunken; and he was uncovered within his tent.

22 And Ham, the father of Canaan, saw the nakedness of his father, and told his two brothers outside.

'the father of Canaan'

> "Ham simply represents here the Canaanites ... and his actions symbolise the practices of the children of Canaan. There is no other possible interpretation of the expression 'the father of Canaan' (abbi: 'father of'). {9}

'Saw the nakedness of'

> 'Naked' has been used previously for referring to sexual behaviour between primitive animals and also to sexual behaviour between male and female human beings. <8>

> 'Saw the nakedness of' is found elsewhere in the Pentateuch in connection with actual sexual relations {9} <9>

> In the Pentateuch, to uncover or see nakedness refers to knowing in sexual union, to sexual relations.

> "The primary sin of Ham (that is of the Canaanites and those who behave like them) was his transgression against sexual morality." {9}

> Sodom and Gomorrah are included in the territory of the Canaanites (Genesis 10: 19). We are informed of their sins <10> which included the same category of offences as that committed here by Ham the father of Canaan. {9}

23 And Shem and Japheth took a garment, and laid it upon both their shoulders, and went backward, and covered the nakedness of their father; and their faces were backward, and they saw not their father's nakedness.

> They restrained their sex urges, behaved like human beings.

> Hebrew 'vajikach', that is 'and he took'

> Rendered 'took'

'The verb is in the singular, because Shem took the initiative in this matter.' <11>

24 And Noah awoke from his wine, and knew what his youngest son had done to him.

25 And he said:
Cursed be Canaan;
A servant of servants shall he be to his brethren.

It is Noah the righteous forefather who is speaking.

'The Canaanites are to suffer bondage not because of the sins of Ham, but because they themselves act like Ham, because of their own transgressions, which resembled those attributed to Ham in this allegory.' {9}

26 And he said:
Blessed be the Lord, the God of Shem;
And let Canaan be their servant.

'... the reference is not specifically to Noah's son Shem but to his descendants.' {9}

'Yhwh Eloheh' rendered 'the Lord, the God': Shem's God (as originator), who originated, caused, the humane moral behaviour of Shem (and of his descendants).

27
God (Elohim) enlarge Japheth,
And He shall dwell in the tents of Shem;
And let Canaan be their servant.

'... the reference is not specifically to Noah's son Japheth but to his descendants.' {9}

God (Elohim) enlarge Japheth: God (creator of that which is good) enlarge Japheth.

Enlarge in the sense of 'make wide', a general wish for success. {9}

'dwell in the tents of': associates and allies of the sons of Shem. {9}

28 And Noah lived after the flood three hundred and fifty years.

> Japheth is the eldest. Ham was the third.
> Shem was consequently the second. {9} <18>

29 And all the days of Noah were nine hundred and fifty years; and he died.

> This allegory is not only about abnormal sexual relations but also about abnormal sexual relations within a family. It is primitive animals who engage instinctively in sex and the allegory is about beastlike lack of control of sexual urges.
>
> Human beings do not behave instinctively, human beings control instinctive sexual behaviour impulses, control the sex urge. Normal for human beings is an exclusive sexual relationship between husband and wife within a single life-long relationship. This ensures the young are protected for the many years it takes before they reach maturity, and protects and supports husband and wife as they grow old. {1, 5}
>
> All other sexual relations are abnormal and we are being told the consequences of inhuman beastlike (unrestrained) sexual behaviour.
>
> Those (Ham, Canaan) who behave immorally weaken their family and social strength, weaken themselves, are to be servants to those (Shem, Japheth) who have higher moral standards. What is to happen is that those (Shem) who initiate moral behaviour, who behave morally and humanely, gain strength and standing, and those (Japheth) who support them in this are supported in return.
>
> Those who behave humanely, morally, can trust each other, cooperate with each other, grow, gain strength together, prosper.
>
> This is what is taking place, this is setting the theme. The next chapter of Genesis (Chapter 10) shows how the planet is repopulated after the flood, shows people spreading out. It is following this that the record shows human beings behaving more like human beings, gaining strength and a good life of high quality accordingly.

Sanctity of Marriage

Human beings were dominating, misusing and oppressing each other for personal gain. {10}

And Gen 6: 2 added 'they took them wives, whomsoever they choose' as another main cause of the flood. They took wives without restraint. Without care or consideration for the women they took or for other people, for self-gratification regardless of feelings and welfare of others. Just like primitive mammalian animals where a wife is protected from the sexual advances of other males by the strength and power of the husband while he is alive.

But then we see three stories from the travels of the patriarchs which form a connected sequence. They are linked by the key phrase <12> that in each case the patriarch is afraid of being killed by local men for the sake of his beautiful wife. That the linking is intentional is confirmed by a second key phrase, namely 'she is my sister'.

As follows:

> Abram in Egypt (Pharaoh). (Genesis Chapter 12)
> > 12: 11 ... you are a fair woman to look upon.
> > 12: 12 ... they will kill me, but you they will keep alive.
> > 12: 19 Why said you: She is my sister? ...
>
> Abraham in Gerar (Abimelech). (Genesis Chapter 20)
> > 20: 2 And Abraham said of Sarah his wife: 'She is my sister.'
> > 20: 11 ... they will slay me for my wife's sake.
>
> Isaac in Gerar (Abimelech). (Genesis Chapter 26)
> > 26: 7 ... he said: 'She is my sister'; for he feared to say: 'My wife'; 'lest the men of the place should kill me for Rebekah, because she is fair to look upon.'

These stories, that is these allegories, and what they record as having been achieved, are:

Abram in Egypt (Pharaoh). (Genesis Chapter 12)

The woman had been taken by Pharaoh simply because he wanted her.

Pharaoh and his house suffer great plagues.

Pharaoh says that if he had known that she was Abram's wife he would not have taken her as his, Pharaoh's, wife.

So that
> The woman is taken to serve as wife by the ruler, simply because he wants her.

And the ruler is
> Forced by God to acknowledge that a married woman is outside his reach, is not to be taken, is protected.

Abraham in Gerar (Abimelech). (Genesis Chapter 20)

The ruler sends for the woman and takes her. Before he has approached her, God speaks to him.

God (Elohim) says that knowingly taking and keeping another man's wife carries the punishment of death for the sinner and all that are his. (Gen 20: 3, 7)

Taking another man's wife is a sin punishable by death.

But if it is done unknowingly and without having touched the other man's wife, the penalty may be avoided by ample compensation which the husband considers adequate.

Abimelech had been made infertile by God (Elohim) and was healed at Abraham's request (prayer) after ample compensation had been received.

Isaac in Gerar (Abimelech). (Chapter 26)

After Isaac has been there a long time, king Abimelech sees Isaac 'sporting' with Rebekah and concludes Rebekah is Isaac's wife.

And tells Isaac that if one of the people had lain with her, they would have become guilty, and lays down to the people (legislates) that who touches this man or his wife shall be put to death.

Summary

So what is recorded in these allegories as having been achieved is:

> The ruler is forced by God to acknowledge that a married woman is outside his reach, is not to be taken, is protected.

> God states that in general, applying to all,
>> The taking of another man's wife is a sin punishable by death, but that if it is done unknowingly and without having touched the other man's wife, the penalty may be avoided by ample compensation which the husband considers adequate.

Laid down, legislated, that he who touches either a husband for the sake of his wife, or his wife, shall be put to death.

Chastity and Rape: The Story of Dinah. (Genesis Chapters 33-35)

> Name 'Dinah' mentioned only once in whole of Bible.

Chapter 33

Jacob came in peace to the city of Shechem, in the land of Canaan, spread his tent, bought the land on which he had settled from the children of the head of the local family.

> From the children of Hamor who is referred to as 'Shechem's father'.

Chapter 34

Dinah, daughter of Jacob and Leah, went out to see the daughters of the land.

She was seen by Shechem the son of Hamor the Hivite, the prince of the land; and he took her and raped her.

> Hivites: Descendants of Canaan, Canaanites. See Gen 10: 17.

Hamor asks for Dinah to be given to his son Shechem as a wife and offers whatever they wish by way of dowry and gift.

Because he had defiled Dinah their sister, the sons of Jacob answered Shechem and Hamor his father with guile, ...

and later two of the sons of Jacob, Simeon and Levi, Dinah's brothers, took each man his sword, and came upon the city unawares, and slew all the males.

> 'City' appears to be a settlement, apparently of one extended family.

They slew Hamor and Shechem his son with the edge of the sword, and took Dinah out of Shechem's house, and went forth.

The sons of Jacob came upon the slain, and spoiled the city, because they had defiled their sister. They took all there was including wealth, wives, children.

And Jacob said to Simeon and Levi: 'I am worried because you have made me be disliked by the local people, the Canaanites and Perizzites. I am few, they will join together against me and I and my house will be destroyed.'

To which they replied: 'Is our sister to be treated like a harlot?

> 'Like a harlot': Like public property (without legal protection). {3}

> She is not a harlot and her wrong (the wrong done to her) must be avenged. <13>

Chapter 35

God tells Jacob to go to Beth-el ... .

Jacob asks his household to put away all strange gods and they gave him all the foreign gods they had, and the rings they had in their ears, and Jacob hid them under the terebinth which was by Shechem.

> To have faith and trust the one and only God.

And the terror of God was upon the cities around them and they were not pursued.

So Jacob and his people came to Luz (Beth-el) in the land of Canaan.

So the allegory tells:

The son of a local Canaanite family raped Dinah.

Rape is so horrendous that it cannot be made good, cannot be undone, by payment of large dowry, gift and subsequent marriage.

The extended family is held responsible for an act of rape committed by one of its members.

Note the severe penalty for rape, including those who condoned what had happened and whose sole concern appears to have been material possessions and not righteousness or morality.

The punishment is death for the male members of the extended family of the rapist, the dissolution and end of their family and households.

Because of the immorality of behaviour taught and practised by the family, community, its members.

A clear way of stating

the importance of chastity,

that human beings can and do control their sexual urges,

the importance and necessity for the human male to control the beastlike sexual urge lurking at the border of the conscious.

Sodomy: The Allegory of Sodom and Gomorrah (Genesis Chapters 18-19)

Lot had moved his tent to, dwelt at, Sodom (Gen 13: 12). Sodom and Gomorrah were in the territory of the Canaanites (Gen 10: 19) and the men of Sodom were wicked and sinned greatly (Gen 13: 13).

So God said to Abraham: Look around you in all directions. All the land you see, the territory of the Canaanites, I will give to you, and to your seed, for ever. (Gen 13: 14-15)

> Hebrew name used here for God is Yhwh meaning 'this is happening, this is so' {2}

In other words, they (the Canaanites) are getting weaker, you (Abraham) are getting stronger.

But always understood, implied: If, and as long as, you follow the word of God, behave like human beings; And as long as you struggle for God and people.

Concerning Sodom, God tells Abraham what He is doing (Gen 18: 17-19), because Abraham's descendants will surely become a mighty nation and a source of blessing to all the people of the earth.

> Hebrew name used here for God is Yhwh meaning 'this is happening, this is so' {2}

That is, Abraham's household and descendants need to be told and taught to keep the way of the Lord (Yhwh), to do righteousness and justice; to the end that the Lord (Yhwh) may bring upon Abraham that which He has spoken of, namely to become a mighty nation and a source of blessing to all people.

In other words, Abraham is being told by God what is going to happen, and why, so that others and future generations can be told and taught how to behave in God's ways, that is how to behave like human beings, so as to gain strength and prosper, so as to avoid being destroyed.

Abraham, addressing God as 'Judge of all the earth' (Gen 18: 25) and as 'Master' (Gen 18: 32), then adds a plea for justice and mercy, for forgiving if there are a sufficient number of righteous people living among the wicked, for not slaying the righteous among the wicked as if they were wicked. (Gen 18: 23-32)

> Abraham here refers to God as 'Master' thus emphasising that it is God who decides. (Gen 18: 32)

> Hebrew word 'ladonaj, meaning 'the master' but translated as 'the Lord'

God agrees that the punishment should be according to the extent of the corruption. But the final determination rests with God, it is God who decides the punishment (Gen 18: 32). <14>

In the next chapter of Genesis (Chapter 19) we are told that Lot has hospitably asked two male travellers to stay in his house for the night.

But all the men of Sodom gather round Lot's house and demand that the two strangers be handed to them 'that we may know them' by sodomy.

> 'that we may know them': That is, vent our lust upon them by sodomy. {3} <15>

Lot tries to dissuade them and offers them his two virgin daughters instead, a most unlikely gesture. The men reject the offer and continue to press for the two strangers to be handed over to them.

> The offer and its rejection is intended to emphasise that the men had been corrupted by the practice of sodomy and were lusting for it, that is were addicted to it. Their sin was the practice of sodomy and they were being punished for the practice of sodomy.

Lot is warned to escape for his life before the place is destroyed. His sons-in-law ignore the warning but Lot escapes with his immediate family to Zoar.

Sodom and Gomorrah and their inhabitants, the plain and the plants which grew, were overthrown. Destroyed, devoid of life.

When God destroyed the cities of the Plain, God remembered Abraham (see abovementioned plea by Abraham on behalf of the righteous), and sent Lot out of the midst of the overthrow, when He overthrew the cities in which Lot dwelt.

The society had been corrupted by sodomy. The level of corruption had been such that God decided to destroy the place and its inhabitants

<16>. The righteous were advised to escape. Those escaped who believed the warning.

Incest: The Allegory of Lot's Two Daughters (Genesis Chapter 19)

Alone with their father and isolated from male human beings, the two daughters separately have sexual intercourse with their father when he is too drunk to be aware of what is happening, so as to ensure the continuation of his family (seed).

Each gave birth to a son.

The older daughter called her son Moab and we are told that his descendants are the Moabites (Gen 19: 37).

The younger called her son Ben-ammi and we are told that his descendants are the 'children of Ammon'. (Gen 19: 38)

Sexual union between close members of the same family, between people too closely related to marry each other, is called incest.

The name Moab indicates the child's origin as being 'from my father', by similarity of words. <17>

The name Ben-ammi veils the child's origin in anonymity as it means 'a son of my people'. <17>

So we are being told that incest is incest regardless of whether it is done openly or secretly.

Also stated are the consequences of incest and they are severe. The descendants of an Ammonite or a Moabite are excluded from the 'assembly of the Lord' for ten generations. (Deut 23: 4)

'assembly of the Lord': Community

For comparison, after the exodus from Egypt and in the same chapter of Deuteronomy, we see 'Do not detest an Egyptian, because you were a stranger in his land'. After so many years of enslavement, the descendants of an Egyptian are also excluded from the 'assembly of the Lord', but only to the third generation. (Deut 23: 8-9)

Morality and Social Strength, Family and Well-being

What we have seen is that Genesis shows human beings becoming aware of the existence of good and evil and of the difference between them, is about human beings learning to choose that which is good and gaining social strength and good lives of high quality as a result.

It is about human beings struggling to stop behaving like our beastlike primitive ancestors and instead doing what is good, learning to behave like human beings, to behave humanely.

And underlying humane behaviour is the need, the necessity, to control the sex impulse. And so this report is about morality and about the struggle to achieve this so as to achieve good lives of high quality.

Which in turn points to those extraordinary inhuman brutalising influences we are struggling against and to the consequent great need to know what is good and what is evil. So that we can choose that which is good because it will give us strength to achieve good lives of high quality and to struggle successfully against that which is evil.

And what we have in the Pentateuch are rules of behaviour which point to the essence of humane behaviour. We know that ignoring them results in social corruption, oppression and exploitation of the many by the few. And we know that following these rules ensures social strength and a good life for all. {7}

Normal for human beings is an exclusive sexual relationship between husband and wife within a single life-long relationship which ensures the young are protected for the many years before they reach maturity, and which protects and supports husband and wife as they grow old. {1, 5}

Those who behave humanely, morally, can trust each other, cooperate with each other, grow, gain strength together, prosper.

All other sexual relations are abnormal and we are told (Chapter 9) the effects (consequences) of inhuman beastlike (unrestrained, uncontrolled) sexual behaviour.

Those who behave immorally weaken their family and social strength, will need to serve and be dependent on those who have higher moral standards. Those who initiate moral behaviour, who behave morally and humanely, gain strength and standing, and those who support them in this are supported in return.

Confirmed by history {7, 8}, we see it taking place all around us.

And we saw that when the planet was repopulated after the flood that people continued to behave much as before. But then there were those who began to distinguish between good and evil, between humane and beastlike unrestrained behaviour. {12}

From the travels of the patriarchs we saw that

> No man may take another man's wife. He who touches either a husband for the sake of his wife, or his wife, is punished with utmost severity.

> Rape is horrendous, cannot be made good, cannot be undone. The rapist's extended family is held responsible for an act of rape committed by one of its members, because of the morality of behaviour taught and practised by family, community, its members. And an act of rape is also punished with utmost severity.

And in this way sexual relations outside marriage were prohibited before and during marriage.

A clear way of stating

> the importance of chastity,

> that human beings can and do control their sexual urges,

> the importance and necessity for the human male to control the beastlike sexual urge lurking at the border of the conscious.

And on marriage the male accepts responsibility for the resulting family for life.

Sodomy, having sexual relations between persons of the same sex, is unnatural and abnormal, corrupting and destructive of human society and humane behaviour, is punished with utmost severity.

And incest, having sexual relations between members of a close or extended family, is abnormal, corrupting and destructive of family trust, family life and family strength. Incest is primitive beastlike behaviour and perpetrators are punished with utmost severity.

The Pentateuch contains detailed statements about what constitutes abnormal, promiscuous, adulterous sexual relations and prostitution, with associated comments and severe penalties, largely in Leviticus.

The Pentateuch and the Problems of Our Times

The Pentateuch legislates in detail, stating what needs to be done and what is prohibited, by positive and negative rules of behaviour. Positive rules point the way ahead towards greater strength and liberty, negative rules (prohibitions) protect people from the antisocial behaviour of others, safeguard the people's strength and liberty. {8}

The Pentateuch's warnings, punishments and penalties concerning morality are in most cases to the male. It is males who are behind the corrupting of family morality and who are attempting to brutalise women so as to make women more readily available for sex. Even brainwashing and manipulating women into making themselves available. With consequent weakening and breaking up of family, society and quality of life. {5}

Conditioning, persuading, inducing or compelling a person to have sex before marriage, person to person or through the media, is an act of rape.

The younger the person, the worse is the offence.

Morality has to be protected by punishing immorality, by protecting women and punishing men who behave immorally. By punishing those who do not restrain their sex urges. By punishing those who spread immorality and seduce others into immoral behaviour.

The consequences of immorality cannot be avoided. {7} <16>

In democracies or when people are struggling for their liberty, authoritarians condone and promote promiscuity so as to weaken the family and weaken the population. People are subjected to conditioning towards immorality to weaken the working population to make them easier to exploit, and to weaken the society to weaken democracy. <19>

When in totalitarian control, dictatorships of left or right or religious hierarchies then pedal back to gain strength for their people, so that they will fight for and protect, and slave for, their manipulating rulers. <20>

Hence the importance of morality, of Pentateuch morality and laws of behaviour, of protecting communities and people by restraining immoral behaviour, conditioning and propaganda, by appropriately punishing the perpetrators.

Notes and References

Notes

< 1> In {1} see 'Evolution towards Good (Gen 2: 15-25)'

< 2> In {1} see 'Further Evolution towards Good' (Gen 3: 1-7)'

< 3> Soncino {6} quoting Nachmanides

< 4> Rashi {3} quoting Bereshith Rabbah (Midrash Rabbah to Genesis)

< 5> In {1} see 'Cain and Abel (Genesis Chapter 4)', Comments to (4: 7).

< 6> See {10} for information on Genesis Chapter 5. See {13} for information on (Gen 6: 3-4).

< 7> In {10} see 'Behaviour and Consequences (Genesis Chapter 9, v 1-17)'

< 8> See 'Nakedness and Sexual Behaviour'

< 9> Cassuto lists 'Lev 20: 10-24, particularly 11, 13 and 20'

<10> Cassuto lists 'Gen 13: 13; 18: 20-; 19: 1-, particularly Gen 19: 5'

<11> Soncino {6} quoting Rashi {3}

<12> For more information about key phrases see {14}

<13> Soncino {6} quoting Sforno

<14> The inevitable consequences of wrongdoing, of inhuman behaviour, are detailed later in the Pentateuch. See {7} on 'Social Cause-and-Effect Relationship.

<15> Soncino {6} quoting Rashi, Ibn Ezra, Rashbam

<16> In {7} see 'Social Cause-and-Effect Relationship'.

<17> Soncino {6} on v37-38 (based on Rashi)

<18> See Gen 10: 21

<19> See {5}

<20> See {13}

References

{ 1} See chapter 6.1: Creation, Evolution and the Origin of Evil

Manfred Davidmann, 2000

{ 2} See chapter 6.6: Meaning and Significance of the
Names of God in Genesis
Manfred Davidmann, 2000

{ 3} Rashi
The Pentateuch and Rashi's Commentary
S. S. & R. Publishing Company, Inc.
New York, 1949

{ 4} How the Human Brain Developed and How the
Human Mind Works
Manfred Davidmann, 1998, 2006
solhaam.org/

{ 5} See chapter 5: 'Family, Community, Sex and the
Individual'
Manfred Davidmann, 1998

{ 6} Soncino The Soncino Chumash
Edited by Rev. Dr. A. Cohen
Soncino Press, 1947.

{ 7} See chapter 4: 'The Social Cause-and-Effect
Relationship'
And see
Struggle for Freedom: The Social Cause-and-Effect
Relationship
Manfred Davidmann, 1978, 2002
solhaam.org/

{ 8} History Speaks: Monarchy, Exile and Maccabees
Manfred Davidmann, 1978, 2007
solhaam.org/

{ 9} Cassuto A Commentary on the Book of Genesis.
Part 1: From Adam to Noah;
Part 2: From Noah to Abraham.
By U. Cassuto (1944)
Translated from the Hebrew by Israel Abrahams
(1961)
The Magnes Press, The Hebrew University,
Jerusalem.

{10} See chapter 6.2: Pre-flood Evils and the Social
Problems of Our Time
Manfred Davidmann, 2000

{11} See chapter 6.7: Meaning and Intent of Genesis:
Essential Notes on Hebrew Grammar
Manfred Davidmann, 2000

{12} See chapter 6.5: Differentiating Between Good and
      Evil
      Manfred Davidmann, 2001

{13} See chapter 6.4: Nephilim, Dominance and Liberty
      Manfred Davidmann, 2001

{14} See chapter 6.8: Bible Translations, Versions, Codes
      and Hidden Information in Bible and Talmud
      Manfred Davidmann, 2001

Nephilim, Dominance and Liberty

Nephilim (Genesis Chapter 6: 3-5)

The information in Chapter 6 about 'nephilim' appears vague, is among the least understood of the passages of the Pentateuch (Torah, Five Books of Moses), and yet deals with behaviour which underlies evil and is quoted as a direct cause of the subsequent flood.

But we are here being told about another key aspect of human behaviour and social organisation which has been carried forward from our primitive ancestors, we are here being given essential core information about the roots of evil.

In Genesis Chapter 6, verses 1 and 2 record that men are misusing their abilities regardless of the cost to others. {4}

Verse 3 states that man's lifespan is to be limited to 120 years.

Verse 4 is about nephilim and about the exceptional abilities of some descendants.

Verse 5 sums up what we have been told in chapters 5 and 6, stating that 'the wickedness of man was great in the earth, and that every imagination of the thoughts of his heart was only evil continually.'

That verses 3 and 4 are connected is indicated by information relating to 'lifespan' and 'descendants'. And we are told about another aspect of human behaviour, namely that there are 'nephilim' and that their behaviour is evil.

To find out who or what the nephilim are, and about their behaviour, we need to look more closely at verses 3 and 4. And what we see is so evident that it raises the question why their meaning has not previously been seen.

3 And the Lord said: 'My spirit shall not abide in man for ever, for that he also is flesh; therefore shall his days be a hundred and twenty years.'

> 'the Lord' (Yhwh): God as cause, as cause of what happened. {2}
>
> 'And the Lord said': In other words, this is happening, is what happened. {2}
>
> 'in man' (Heb. 'ba'adam'): 'ba'adam' stands for 'be ha adam', so that Adam stands for human beings. {6}
>
> 'he also is flesh': Meaning of the Hebrew is 'for flesh is weak'.

> The verse reads 'My spirit' cannot stay in human beings for ever. Flesh is weak and the lifespan of human beings is 120 years.

> Which means that the mind, the soul, stay with the human being as long as the human is alive and the life span of human beings is limited.

4 The nephilim were in the earth in those days, and also after that, when the sons of God came in unto the daughters of men, and they bore children to them; the same were the mighty men that were of old, the men of renown.

'daughters' refers to 'daughters' in general, to the female of the life form, to women. {4}

'sons of God' refers to males among human beings. In other words, 'sons of God' refers to 'men'. {4}

'they bore children to them (who) were ... the men of renown': The abilities of the nephilim are passed on by heredity.

'and also after that': As lifespan is limited (previous verse) this phrase is another pointer towards hereditary passing on of abilities. People die but the abilities of the nephilim are passed on by heredity.

We are being told about human beings.

What verses 3 and 4 have in common is that they deal with extraordinary abilities people have while alive, with mind and soul on the one hand and with the abilities of the nephilim on the other. In this way each of these two verses confirms the intended meaning of the other.

Where Pentateuch and Talmud contain hidden information, then this is pointed to, stated and confirmed, at the same time and in a number of different independent ways, to ensure the message is understood as it was intended to be understood. That verses 3 and 4 confirm each other is intended and meaningful. <1>

And so 'nephilim' are simply human beings without distinguishing physical characteristics who intermarry with others human beings and whose extraordinary abilities and skills are hereditary. Their abilities and skills appear to be somewhat rare.

'Heredity' is the inheritance of mental or physical characteristics from parents or ancestors. So 'hereditary' does not imply 'to all sons' nor does it imply 'in every generation'.

And what else have we been told about the nephilim:

They were so named because they fell (naphal) and caused the world to fall <2>. From the Hebrew 'naphal' (to fall) which can mean a fall, a deterioration, in the moral sense.

213

In the Hebrew language (nephilim) has the meaning of 'giants' {10}. It can refer to mental rather than to physical giants.

'the mighty men':

They were mighty in their rebellion against God. <2>

'ha-gibborim': 'the mighty men'. Also 'the mighty ones'.

'The men of renown'

'anshe ha-shem': People of name (well-known people). <3>

And so 'nephilim' refers to human beings with hereditary abilities which appear extraordinary. These abilities apparently enable them to influence, organise, manipulate, control, dominate other human beings. They are misusing their abilities for their own ends, their behaviour is 'evil'.

Human beings are capable of distinguishing between good and evil and of choosing good while rejecting evil. But they do not do so. And the nephilim among them are corruptly and evilly misusing their extraordinary abilities.

We do not at this point know who the nephilim are. But we know that their abilities are extraordinary and hereditary, that they are with us here and now just as before, within our communities at the present time. That they are referred to as 'fallen' indicates that their capabilities are being used for selfish ends. Their descendants are 'mighty' (powerful) and 'of renown' (well-known, prominent, in the public eye).

In other words, there are among us people with extraordinary abilities which are hereditary and who are using them for their own selfish corrupt ends, and who are likely to be powerful or influential and well-known.

So we need to see what else we are told about them. This matter of the nephilim has remained a mystery to our days, but we are told more. The pattern is becoming clearer and we will see just who and what the nephilim are and become aware of their activities.

5 And the Lord saw that the wickedness of man was great in the earth, and that every imagination of the thoughts of his heart was only evil continually.

The thoughts people were imagining, that is the thoughts arising from their imagination, were evil continually. Human beings as a whole are using their thinking and evaluating abilities towards evil, towards evil behaviour, are misusing and exploiting each other for personal gain. <4>

Genesis is here describing, and defining, evil. Describing it as taking place. But not defining evil openly in plain language. Not stating the cause of evil.

And associating nephilim with evil, possibly as a hidden cause. They are misusing their abilities for personal gain, are corrupting, are dominating.

Wanderings of Nimrod and Asshur (Genesis Chapter 10: 8-12)

Chapter 10 of Genesis records how the planet was repopulated after the flood, tells us about peoples, lands, nations. But exceptional are the few sentences relating the deeds of individuals. So let us see what the Bible tells us about the travels of these individuals.

In the immediately preceding Chapter 9 of Genesis, Ham and his descendants (Canaan) were condemned by Noah because of Ham's (and their) immoral unrestrained behaviour {4}. And about Ham's grandson Nimrod we are told

> 10: 6 And the sons of Ham: Cush, and Mizraim, ... and Canaan.
>
> 10: 8 And Cush begot Nimrod; he began to be a mighty one in the earth.
>
> 10: 9 He was a mighty hunter before the Lord (Yhwh); wherefore it is said: 'Like Nimrod a mighty hunter before the Lord.'

The Bible text specifically refers to Nimrod as an individual. He is called 'mighty' (gibor) three times in two successive verses, and in this way our attention is focussed on the attribute 'mighty'.

Gen 6: 4 made the point that the capabilities of the nephilim are hereditary and that their descendants are the mighty men, the men of renown. That their descendants are 'mighty' (powerful) and 'of renown' (well-known, prominent, in the public eye).

In this way we are told that Nimrod was one of the nephilim.

Which is further confirmed by what we are then told about him. What we are told also tells us that nephilim used their extraordinary abilities

215

for their own benefit, for dominating, organising, manipulating and exploiting other human beings.

10: 10 And the beginning of his kingdom was Babel ... in the land of Shinar.

> Babel: Babylon. The well-known city in South Mesopotamia. {12}

In the immediately following chapter of Genesis we are told that

> 11: 2 And it came to pass, as they journeyed east, that they found a plain in the land of Shinar; and they dwelt there.

> 11: 9 Therefore was the name of it called Babel; because ...

and in this way is Nimrod linked with the events told in the allegory of The Tower of Babel.

Shem, who was praised by Noah in the immediately preceding chapter of Genesis for his moral and considerate behaviour, has a son called Asshur {30}.

And Asshur then leaves Shinar and builds Nineveh and other cities, told as follows:

10: 11 Out of that land went forth Asshur, and built Nineveh, and ...

> 'out of that land went forth Asshur':

> > When Nimrod ruled over that country, Asshur abandoned it, being opposed to his rule. <5>

> > Since Asshur saw his sons listening to Nimrod and rebelling against God by building the tower, he went out from their midst. <6>

> Nineveh: This is the famous city on the river Tigris, which was, after the city of Asshur, the principal city of the kingdom of Assyria. {12}

There was conflict between Babylonia and Assyria, and they struggled with each other, for hundreds of years.

So these verses in Chapter 10 about Nimrod and Asshur show that as people populated the planet, the nephilim were among them and moved with them. And tell us much about their behaviour and who they are.

Summing up, so far:

> Human beings are capable of distinguishing between good and evil and of choosing good while rejecting evil. But the nephilim among them are corruptly and evilly misusing their extraordinary and hereditary abilities to dominate, corrupt, control and manipulate other human beings.

> They are with us here and now just as before, within our communities at the present time. That they are referred to as 'fallen' indicates that their abilities are being used for selfish ends, that their behaviour is 'evil'. Their descendants are 'mighty' (powerful) and 'of renown' (well-known, prominent, in the public eye).

> In other words, there are among us people with extraordinary abilities which are hereditary and who are using them for their own selfish corrupt ends, and who are likely to be powerful or influential and well-known.

The Allegory of 'The Tower of Babel' (Genesis Chapter 11: 1-9)

The allegory <7> of The Tower of Babel describes key and focal events which determined the quality of life itself, and which enabled the development of humane behaviour, life and living, as you will see. Of the greatest importance then, of utter and determining importance at the present time. The fate and future of humankind, of all human beings, is balanced on a razors edge between oppression, exploitation and enslavement on the one side, and liberty, equality and a good life for all on the other side.

It is essential that we understand the deeper underlying meaning and significance of these events and apply the knowledge we will have gained to the way in which we live and organise our lives, to communities, societies and social organisation.

Story

We are told what happened in the land of Shinar in a city called Babel, about the city of Babel and the tower its people attempted to build at a time when all people spoke the same language.

We are then told that, as a consequence of what happened at Babel, different languages developed, that people ceased to understand each

Figure 1   **Relevant Family Trees**   (Genesis Chapter 10)

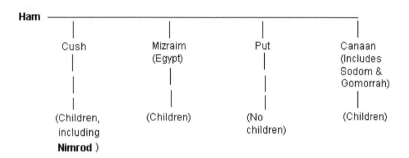

Ham ──

| Cush | Mizraim (Egypt) | Put | Canaan (Includes Sodom & Gomorrah) |

(Children, including **Nimrod**)   (Children)   (No children)   (Children)

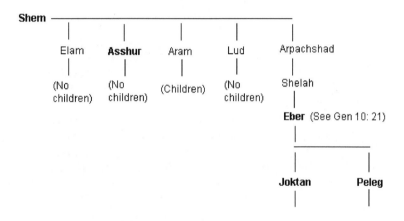

Shem ──────────────────────────────

| Elam | **Asshur** | Aram | Lud | Arpachshad |

(No children)   (No children)   (Children)   (No children)   Shelah

Eber (See Gen 10: 21)

Joktan   **Peleg**

other, that they were scattered from there over all the countries of the world and stopped building the city.

The people were scattered because they were building the tower. Of particular interest is that verse 8 states that they then stopped building the city but pointedly does not mention that they stopped building the tower.

Allegory

There are two intertwined, interwoven and interconnected, stories here. The first is about the scattering of people and their developing different languages, the second is about building the tower.

> Note that in the whole of this allegory (Gen 11: 1-9) God is referred to by the name 'Yhwh' and that God is not mentioned again in this chapter.
>
> Yhwh: God as cause of what happened. In other words, this is happening, is what happened. Here 'this is what happened'. {2}
>
> In Babylonian the name Babel means 'Gate of God'. {12}
>
> Verse 9 (Gen 11: 9) states the city was called Babel because 'the Lord (Yhwh) did there confound the language(s) of ... . So the name 'Babel' in Hebrew is a designation for confusion {12} derived from Hebrew 'balal', to confound {11}.
>
> The Hebrew 'babel' could possibly also stand for 'to create a mixture of'.

What we are told is

11: 1 And the whole earth was of one language and of one speech.

> So that all people could communicate with each other.

> 'All the earth' here means 'all mankind'. It is repeated at the end in a different sense, there signifying 'all the countries of the world'. {12}

219

11: 2 And it came to pass, as they journeyed east, that they found a plain in the land of Shinar; and they dwelt there.

11: 3 And they said one to another: 'Come, let us make brick, and burn them thoroughly.' And they had brick for stone, and slime had they for mortar.

11: 4 And they said: 'Come, let us build us a city, and a tower, with its top in heaven, and let us make us a name; lest we be scattered abroad upon the face of the whole earth.'

> We have already been told that the beginning of Nimrod's kingdom was Babel in the land of Shinar (Gen 10: 10). It was called Babel because of the building of the city and of a tower with its top in heaven and of the resulting scattering of the people (Gen 11: 9).
>
> In this way is Nimrod linked with what happened in Babel, that is with founding the city (Gate of God) and with building the tower 'with its top in heaven'.

11: 5 And the Lord (Yhwh) came down to see the city and the tower, which the children of men builded.

> > 'bnei ha-adam' here rendered 'children of men'. The literal meaning is 'sons of the life form', that is sons of human beings, that is 'men'. {1, 2}
> >
> > Builded: Which they had begun to build (were building). {12}

11: 6 And the Lord (Yhwh) said: 'Behold, they are one people, and they have all one language; and this is what they begin to do; and now nothing will be withholden from them, which they purpose to do.

> > Cassuto records this as:
> > And the Lord said, 'Behold, they are one people, and they have all one language; and this is only the beginning of what they will do; and now nothing will prove too hard for them of all that they purpose to do. {12}

> A settlement or town, even a city, can arise haphazardly, at random, but to build a tower requires resources, planning and organisation of many people.
>
> The driving force behind the building of the tower appears to be Nimrod. The 'fallen' nephilim are selfish, corrupt, dominating, exploiting and oppressing. It is the ability of such

nephilim to manipulate ordinary people into working for the nephil, which is here being pointed out and criticised. Ordinary people are being manipulated into serving nephilim, into working to increase a selfish and corrupt nephil's personal influence and power.

11: 7 Come, let us go down, and there confound their language, that they may not understand one another's speech.'

> Yhwh: God as cause of what happened. In other words, this is happening, is what happened. {2}
>
> And the Hebrew for 'us' refers to the confounder, not to the confounding.
>
> So in 'let us go down' the plural indicates a plurality of change, indicates many such changes, possibly in many places.
>
> 'And there confound their language': 'In this way we shall destroy the prerequisite that assures the success of their work.' {12}

That is, destroy their organisation and their ability to organise on a large, overall dominating, scale by destroying their ability to communicate and cooperate, their teamwork.

11: 8 So the Lord (Yhwh) scattered them abroad from thence upon the face of all the earth; and they left off to build the city.

This verse does not say that they left off building the tower.

> Common explanation for the tower not being mentioned is that it follows that they had to stop building the tower when they were dispersed.
>
> But the tower is the cause of the scattering and so it seems that there is another reason why it is not mentioned.
>
> One likely reason is that they kept on building 'towers' wherever they lived, wherever they built their settlements, on a much smaller, more limited, scale.

Hence they kept on doing what 'building towers' stands for, wherever they lived and built their settlements and communities, but on a much smaller, more limited, scale.

11: 9 Therefore was the name of it called Babel; because the Lord (Yhwh) did there confound the language of all the earth; and from thence did the Lord (Yhwh) scatter them abroad upon the face of all the earth.

> 'All the earth': In the opening sentence it signified 'all mankind', here it signifies 'all the countries of the world'. {12}

Have another look at verse 4:

11: 4 And they said: 'Come, let us build us a city, and a tower, with its top in heaven, and let us make us a name; lest we be scattered abroad upon the face of the whole earth.'

> The story tells that they were scattered by God. So they are opposing God by what they are doing.
>
> And the name they wanted to make for themselves while opposing God was Babel meaning 'Gate of God'.
>
> And the tower was to have its top in heaven.
>
> Aiming to reach heaven and become god-like, to set themselves up in opposition to God. Which means that Nimrod who is referred to as their king is attempting to gain, to assign to himself, god-like authority and power.

> > 'Tower': Organisation, command structure, chain of command of kings, rulers, those with authority, those above.
> >
> > 'Gate of God' and 'top in heaven': In their thinking, they are going to dominate, be divine. Be powerful, supreme, like God.
> >
> > Assuming, taking to themselves, god-like power over people concerning good life or bad life, concerning life or death.

> So they are apparently driven by Nimrod who, being one of the nephilim, is using his extraordinary abilities for setting himself up as all-powerful supremo in opposition to God, that is in opposition to humane behaviour, equality, independence, liberty, shared wealth and good life for all.

And now have another look at verse 8:

11: 8 So the Lord (Yhwh) scattered them abroad from thence upon the face of all the earth; and they left off to build the city.

My comments (verbatim, see above) were

> This verse does not say that they left off building the tower.
>
>> Common explanation for the tower not being mentioned is that it follows that they had to stop building the tower when they were dispersed.
>>
>> But the tower is the cause of the scattering and so it seems that there is another reason why it is not mentioned.
>>
>> One likely reason is that they kept on building 'towers' wherever they lived, wherever they built their settlements, on a much smaller, more limited, scale.
>
> Hence they kept on doing what 'building towers' stands for, wherever they lived and built their settlements and communities, but on a much smaller, more limited, scale.

Now consider this

>> They were stopped from getting together and cooperating (city building) but not from tower building.
>>
>> So it seems they kept on building towers, elsewhere. Elsewhere after having been scattered, divided. Separately, and not all together.
>
> It appears that they stopped building this city and consequently the tower they had been building.
>
> And, having been dispersed, they continued to build cities, smaller cities, elsewhere, each presumably with its own 'tower'.

So the allegory states that if any become too powerful, a threat to that which is humane and good, then they need to be, and are to be, dispersed. In other words, their tower (power, organisation, country, empire, corporation, monopoly, government, rulers, multinational, global corporation) needs to be dispersed.

Power corrupts, absolute power corrupts absolutely. Hence the great need, and the importance of the need, for scattering and dispersal, for multiplicity and variety.

The designation for God's name in the first part of the chapter indicated 'this is happening, this is what happened'.

And in this same chapter of Genesis, what follows is the direct line of descendants to Abram, that is to Abraham the Patriarch.

So the point is being made that 'Good' developed, prospered and gained strength following the scattering of the power-seekers and the development of separate and distinct languages, customs and traditions. {3}

Power corrupts, absolute power corrupts absolutely. Humanity and human behaviour depend on opposition and balance, on democracy. <8>

Enslavement, then Liberty and Good Life for All (Genesis Chapters 41-47)

Joseph, son of Jacob (Israel), is given enormous power by Egypt's Pharaoh. He marries an Egyptian woman, daughter of an Egyptian priest, and has two sons whom he names Manasseh (Making to forget) and Ephraim (To be fruitful).

> In his youth Joseph had previously been sold by his own brothers. There was no appreciation of a human being's right to liberty and to the humane treatment of one person by another.
>
> There is famine and when Jacob's sons come to Egypt to buy food, Joseph's 'father's house' are allowed to settle in Egypt.

Joseph then used their extreme need to compel the people to sell all their land and possessions and themselves to the ruler. He used his extraordinary abilities to create and install an inhuman economic system in which ownership of all land and farm animals, that is property and wealth, belonged to Pharaoh, with the Egyptians enslaved to Pharaoh and sharecropping for him, to the point where he could move them at will from one end of the country to the other (Gen 47: 21).

The priests were serving Pharaoh and retained their lands and freedom. Their role apparently being to use religion to tranquillise the population into accepting their condition (Gen 47: 22).

In due course the Hebrews were also enslaved but were freed by God (Elohim), Creator of all that is good (Exodus 2:), with consequent writing down of rules of behaviour and of a social system which together ensure liberty and a good life for all. {5, 8}

God, People and Behaviour, Help and Protection, Reward or Punishment

God told Moses not to be an enemy of Moab, and not to fight them, because God gave Ar to the children of Lot as a possession. (Deut 2: 9)

And God told Moses not to harass the children of Ammon, and not to struggle with them, because God gave their land to the children of Ammon as a possession. (Deut 2: 19)

But at Shittim, the people began to commit harlotry with the daughters of Moab who called the people to sacrifice and bow down to their gods, to worship Baal-Peor (Numb 25: 1-3). They were causing the children of Israel to break faith with God (Numb 31: 16).

And so we read that because Ammon and Moab did not meet Israel 'with bread and water' when Israel came out of Egypt, because they opposed Israel ('hired Balaam to curse you'; Deut 23: 5), because they opposed Israel instead of supporting it, that

> You shall not seek their peace nor their prosperity all your days for ever (Deut 23: 7).

In other words, one may not aid or support those who oppose (opposed) one on the way to liberty.

And we know that {21}

> God helps, protects and rewards manifold those who act for God and people.

> When people do not act for God and people, then God withdraws his protection from them.

> The consequences cannot be avoided.

Lessons from History

The Monarchy {9}

During the period of the monarchy, that is during the period of Saul, David and Solomon, we see central military authority being more effective in an emergency and see the military leader subsequently taking over the administration, taking over the government. This is followed by increasing centralisation of power and the formation of an establishment (secular and religious) which serves the source of power and is used to oppress the people.

Military personnel are used to give and obey orders but the skills involved are completely different from those expected from an effective manager. In general, while authoritarian organisations are effective in an emergency they are generally ineffective and wasteful at other times {19}. And what took place during the monarchy was increasing centralisation of power, increasing corruption and oppression, increasing enslavement of the people with consequent social stress and subsequent destruction. {9}

Struggle of the Maccabees {9}

The Maccabees were united and struggled against brutal foreign oppression. They struggled for Pentateuch, freedom and the people. Against them were foreign invaders who believed in slavery and who were trying to impose their way of life through imposing their beliefs.

Together they defeated the invaders. But after three generations the situation had changed and we now see very clearly increasing internal confrontation, a struggle between people and Pentateuch on the one hand against their own oppressive rulers and their oppressing establishment on the other.

The oppression of Jew by Jew, of the Jewish people by their own rulers and establishment, and the resulting struggle between them defeated both. It ended Maccabean rule, lost the land which had been gained, resulted in enormous hardship to the people.

What stands out is that the people were unable to restrain their leaders. The result was total destruction of people and country, and the dispersion of the Jewish people. {9}

Humane Behaviour <14>

Humane behaviour is aimed at survival of the young and of the family, and then is for the good of family, other people and the community. It is based on feelings of care and affection for others. From this emerges a sense of social responsibility: people matter and are important, need to be treated well and looked after, are entitled to share equally. Backed up by knowledge, understanding and reason. {22}

We know that dominating others is conditioned, that is unnatural, behaviour which is destructive of humane behaviour. A throw-back to the level of the unthinking unfeeling primitive animal. {22}

And knowledge of good and evil enables us to choose that which is good and to overcome that which is inhumane, which is evil.

Chapter 5 of Genesis said much. About inhuman behaviour, about possessions, ownership and riches, about domineering, oppression and misusing people by force. Emphasized by the statement that whatever pre-flood human beings were considering was evil.

These themes are continued in Genesis and in the other four volumes (books) of the Pentateuch. We are told about the obligatory social laws and social system which have to be kept if evil is to be overcome, so that human beings can have good lives of high quality.

What follows reviews present social background corresponding to the evils of dominating, oppressing and exploiting listed in chapters 5 and 6 of Genesis. This is followed by a short summary of the social laws and social system of the Pentateuch in so far as these relate to these evils.

Social Background

Domineering, Oppression, Exploitation, Misuse of Others

What we see in the working environment is a worldwide struggle to achieve a humane way of life, each person, family or community struggling to advance at their own level of development, struggling against those who wish to dominate, exploit, oppress. A struggle whose successful outcome depends on trustful cooperation, companionship and teamwork. {23, 24, 25}

The struggle is against those who wish to dominate other people. Against those who want primitive power over others, against those who wish to exploit, against those who may brutally and without feeling oppress human beings so as to exploit them. And 'to exploit' includes the whole range of antisocial decisions and activities of those who put profit before people and community. {17}

Human rights are based on controlling primitive dominant behaviour, on concern, care and affection for our young, for our families, people and communities, and express themselves in cooperation and teamwork between men and women to achieve a good life of high quality.

Armed Forces, Military Strength. Dictatorship and Authoritarianism {23}

Sometimes one has to fight to preserve a good way of life, to prevent others from taking what has been achieved. Or one is expected to fight on behalf of those who dominate and exploit.

Our primitive animal ancestors behaved instinctively. Hunt for food, kill or be killed, fight or flee. Self before others, regardless of needs of others, marking out and defending territory.

Later mammals tend to have feelings, care and affection for their young. Human beings think as well as feel, and care for and look after their young for many years.

Having to fight, maim and kill amounts to a throwback to primitive animal behaviour, to behaviour which puts self before others. A throwback to beast-like behaviour for those who attack, to beast-like behaviour to counter beast-like behaviour for those who defend.

Authoritarian organisations are much less effective than participative ones. In authoritarian organisations morale is low, people cease to care and tend to work against each other instead of cooperating with each other for the benefit of the organisation. {19, 26}

One way of countering viciousness is by greater strength. If attacked, we have to defend ourselves.

Human beings cooperate well and achieve effective teamwork. Reason and evaluation can temper (add to, or change) emotional and instinct-motivated behaviour and combine with cooperation and teamwork so as to counter, and overcome, threats.

One has to be stronger than the enemy, socially as well as militarily. Essential is greater social as well as military strength. But the authoritarian (which includes military) mind has to be balanced to prevent it from taking over, has to be motivated towards 'good'.

Possessions, Ownership and Riches

Ownership {27} is the right to possess something and to decide what is to be done with it. If I own something it belongs to me and I decide what is to be done with it. An example would be owning a house.

Possession is having something in one's custody as distinct from owning it. If I possess something it belongs to another but I can decide how to use it. An example would be renting a house.

Another example would be deciding what to do with my money (ownership) or deciding and controlling the use of money belonging to someone else (possession).

And considering the right to ownership, two questions need to be considered. Namely where does the right come from and how is it exercised.

The right to own property varies among societies. Ownership laws which assign ownership 'rights' to owners have been devised by the owners themselves or by those who serve them. {18}

Ownership of land and means of production, of funds and wealth, has always been accumulated at someone else's expense. All belonged to the community, belonged to all alike. And this is what Chapter 5 of Genesis appears to be saying {5}.

A human right is a something one may legally or morally claim, is the state of being entitled to a privilege or immunity or authority to act. Human rights are those held to be claimable by any living person, apply to all living people. Every living person is entitled to them.

So ownership of land and means of production, of funds and wealth, rightfully belongs to the community, belongs to all alike, is a human right. Those who have accumulated them have only possession, which means they can use and apply them but may do so only on behalf of, and for the benefit of, the community and that they are accountable to the community for the way in which they do so. {20}

Hence we have the use of possessions as long as we use them to provide a good living for our family, and beyond that for the benefit of the community. For the benefit of others less able or fortunate, for the benefit of the community around us and then for the benefit of communities abroad.

But we may only support those who themselves genuinely support our benevolent ideals and principles and their application and who themselves live and act accordingly, who behave humanely. <10>

Social Laws and Social System of the Bible

Government; Positions of Trust, Responsibility and Authority; Hierarchies

Here we are looking at the laws of the Pentateuch which control the behaviour and limit the power {8, 9} of government, of top executives and of the establishment, of those in positions of trust, responsibility or authority. The Pentateuch {28} leaves little doubt about what they must not do.

Positive laws tell what has to be done so as to create a strong and just society, point the way ahead towards greater strength, freedom and a good way of life.

Negative laws (prohibitions) state what must not be done and such laws protect the people from oppression and exploitation, from the antisocial behaviour of others, safeguard the people's strength and freedom. {9}

So the laws quoted here protect people and safeguard their strength and freedom.

These laws of government relate to 'rulers', apply to all in positions of trust, responsibility or authority, no matter whether secular, religious or military, no matter what the hierarchy or organisation.

Such people may not amass servants and may not oppress the people for their own benefit. They may not amass possessions and wealth, may not grasp power or behave promiscuously.

In other words, they may not put themselves above others by grasping power, may not satisfy personal desires at the expense of others.

And a ruler (person in position of trust, responsibility or authority) has to follow these laws and abide by them every day if he wishes 'to prolong his days in his kingdom, he and his children'. For 'kingdom' read 'position'.

So the Pentateuch laws quoted here protect people and safeguard their strength and freedom by laying down that those in positions of trust, responsibility or authority may not grasp power, may not oppress the people, may not behave promiscuously, may not enrich themselves.

Ten Commandments

The Ten Commandments {29} <11> are so important and are so well known because it is behaviour in accordance with these laws which is the basis for people trusting each other and so for people cooperating and working well with each other.

When Moses brought the tables of the law he brought 'freedom upon the tables'. It is the Ten Commandments as a whole which underlie freedom, independence and strength to oppose and resist oppression. Wherever there is any spiritual and material freedom today it exists because people followed these laws (rules) of behaviour and it exists to the extent to which they do so. {8}

In other words, following the provisions of the law results in freedom and ensures it, ensures strength and security.

Social Cause-and-Effect Relationship <12> {8}

We saw <13> that a covenant is an agreement in which each of the parties undertakes duties and obligations towards the other. God promises that certain things will be so, as long as human beings fulfil their obligations under the covenant, as long as human beings follow God's laws, as long as they behave like human beings.

In the language of religion the Pentateuch later on states a fundamental scientific law, the Social Cause-and-Effect Relationship {8} <12>, which is that the consequences of keeping or not keeping the Pentateuch laws are inescapable, that what happens to one is in the end the inevitable result of one's own behaviour. Also clearly stated is that this is a scientific law which was defined and stated using the language of religion so that people would benefit from knowing the effects (consequences) of their behaviour. The relationship is stated in precise terms. History {9} and social science {17} confirm it.

We are told that the Social Cause-and-Effect Relationship applies to all without exception and at all times, wherever one may be, regardless of type of government, form of religion or social system or country. It applies whether you like it or not, agree or disagree.

The consequences of one's behaviour are detailed both ways, clearly and powerfully illustrating intermediate stages between the two ends of the scale, and we are told that the process is reversible: Increasingly disregarding the Law results in greater suffering and oppression, increasingly behaving according to the Law results in greater freedom and a better life.

The relationship applies to all. It is stated in a way which enables people to benefit from knowing the effects of their behaviour, even if they do not understand the underlying interrelation.

Freedom and independence of mind and person and the quality of life depend on one's behaviour. The consequences of observing the Law are described and so are those of disregarding the Law. The consequences of one's behaviour are inevitable, inescapable. Keeping or not keeping the Pentateuch laws has consequences which cannot be avoided.

Those who behave according to the law have good and satisfying lives, gain social and military strength. Behaviour which is contrary to the law lowers the quality of life, increases internal stress and conflict to the point of social disruption and military weakness.

Social Laws, Social System

It is the social laws of the Pentateuch which in effect state that all are equal, that no person may exploit another or oppress so as to exploit. All have the right to be free and independent masters of their own fate and there has to be a system of social security which guarantees not just freedom from need but also protection against loss of material and spiritual independence. In effect, oppression can be and has to be resisted, struggled against and opposed.

The essential social provisions of Pentateuch law are clear and to the point. This is what the Pentateuch lays down as a matter of law {8}:

1. Every seventh day is a day of rest for all, for those who are employed as well as for those who employ. Work stops on the weekly day of rest, the Sabbath, to let those who labour have a regular day of rest. On this day the servant is as free as the master, the worker is as free as the employer. The weekly day of rest has spread and benefits almost all the civilised world.

2. The community has to provide ('lend') money to those who need it, free of interest.

3. All such loans, if outstanding, are to be cancelled every seventh year.

4. The country's wealth, and this applies particularly to productive capital such as land, belongs equally to all and needs to be shared out.

5. The country's inhabitants are entitled to have a sabbatical year every seventh year. During this sabbatical year they are entitled to be freed from work at the expense of the community.

Every person is entitled as a matter of right to social security. This means that people are entitled to be supported by the community not only when they fall on hard times but also to maintain their independence as independent breadwinners for their families. For example, the community has to provide backup funds to those who need them and they have to be provided as and when required.

To prevent people being exploited through their need these funds have to be provided without charging interest and such 'loans' are cancelled every seventh year if the borrower has been unable to repay them.

The community supports the individual but only if the individual in turn supports the community. Those supported by the community are under obligation to support others in need of support, in due course and when able to do so, to share with others who are in need. Where need includes the need for capital to secure their operation, to achieve the general standard of living and quality of life.

It is those who themselves keep and apply these benevolent social laws, who keep Pentateuch law, who are entitled to these rights.

Notes and References

Notes

< 1> See {7} for more information and detailed examples illustrating code checks and confirmations.

< 2> Soncino {11} quoting Rashi {10}

< 3> The Hebrew words 'ha-shem' (name) and 'shemamon' (desolation) are similar so that 'anshe ha-shem' could possibly be interpreted to mean 'men of desolation' {10}, later paraphrased to 'men who brought desolation upon the world' <2>. This seems far fetched but may be appropriate.

< 4> In {5} see Appendix 2 'The Flood'

< 5> Soncino {11} quoting Nachmanides and Sforno

< 6> Rashi {10} quoting from Bereshith Rabbah (Midrash Rabbah to Genesis)

< 7> An allegory is a story or description in which the characters and events symbolise some deeper underlying meaning (Oxford Concise Dictionary)

< 8>   See {17, 18, 19, 20}

< 9>   In {15} see Appendix 2 'Holocaust'

<10>   In {5} see 'Social Laws, Social System'

<11>   The Ten Commandments are listed both in
       biblical language and in plain English in chapter
       4: 'The Social Cause-and-Effect Relationship', with
       detailed references to the Pentateuch text.

<12>   The Social Cause-and-Effect Relationship is listed
       both in biblical language and in plain English in
       chapter 4: 'The Social Cause-and-Effect
       Relationship', with detailed references to the
       Pentateuch text.

<13>   In {5} see 'Behaviour and Consequences (Genesis
       Chapter 9)'

<14>   The whole of this section has been reproduced
       here from {5}

References

{ 1}   See chapter 6.1: Creation, Evolution and the Origin
       of Evil
       Manfred Davidmann, 2000

{ 2}   See chapter 6.6: Meaning and Significance of the
       Names of God in Genesis
       Manfred Davidmann, 2000

{ 3}   See chapter 6.5: Differentiating Between Good and
       Evil
       Manfred Davidmann, 2001

{ 4}   See chapter 6.3: Morality, Sexual Behaviour and
       Depravity
       Manfred Davidmann, 2001

{ 5}   See chapter 6.2: Pre-flood Evils and the Social
       Problems of Our Time
       Manfred Davidmann, 2000

{ 6}   See chapter 6.7: Meaning and Intent of Genesis:
       Essential Notes on Hebrew Grammar
       Manfred Davidmann, 2000

{ 7}   See chapter 6.8: Bible Translations, Versions, Codes
       and Hidden Information in Bible and Talmud
       Manfred Davidmann, 2001

{ 8} See chapter 4: 'The Social Cause-and-Effect
      Relationship'
      And see
      Struggle for Freedom: The Social Cause-and-Effect
      Relationship
      Manfred Davidmann, 1978, 2002
      solhaam.org/

{ 9} History Speaks: Monarchy, Exile and Maccabees
      Manfred Davidmann, 1978, 2007
      solhaam.org/

{10} The Pentateuch and Rashi's Commentary
      S. S. & R. Publishing Company, Inc.
      New York, 1949

{11} The Soncino Chumash
      Edited by Rev. Dr. A. Cohen
      Soncino Press, 1947.

{12} A Commentary on the Book of Genesis.
      Part 1: From Adam to Noah;
      Part 2: From Noah to Abraham.
      By U. Cassuto (1944)
      Translated from the Hebrew by Israel Abrahams
      (1961)
      The Magnes Press, The Hebrew University,
      Jerusalem.

{13} Eichmann in Jerusalem - A Report on the Banality of
      Evil
      Dr. Hannah Arendt
      Faber and Faber, 1963

{14} Black Sabbath
      Robert Katz
      Arthur Barker, 1969

{15} Wake Up Israel
      Manfred Davidmann
      Social Organisation Ltd, 1973

{16} Lodz Ghetto
      Alan Adelson and Kathryn Taverna
      TV documentary, Channel 4, 06/05/1991

{17} Social Responsibility, Profits and Social
      Accountability
      Manfred Davidmann, 1979, 1995
      solhaam.org/

{18}   What People are Struggling Against: How Society is
       Organised for Controlling and Exploiting People
       Manfred Davidmann, 1998, 2002
       solhaam.org/

{19}   Style of Management and Leadership
       Manfred Davidmann, 1981, 2006
       solhaam.org/

{20}   Co-operatives and Co-operation: Causes of Failure,
       Guidelines for Success
       Manfred Davidmann, 1996
       solhaam.org/

{21}   Faith
       Manfred Davidmann, 2000

{22}   How the Human Brain Developed and How the
       Human Mind Works
       Manfred Davidmann, 1998, 2006
       solhaam.org/

{23}   See chapter 5: 'Family, Community, Sex and the
       Individual'
       Manfred Davidmann, 1998

{24}   The Will to Work: What People Struggle to Achieve
       Manfred Davidmann, 1981, 2006
       solhaam.org/

{25}   Motivation Summary
       Manfred Davidmann, 1982, 1998
       solhaam.org/

{26}   Role of Managers Under Different Styles of
       Management
       Manfred Davidmann, 1982, 1998
       solhaam.org/

{27}   Understanding How Society is Organised for
       Controlling and Exploiting People
       Manfred Davidmann, 1998, 2002
       solhaam.org/

{28}   Deut 17: 14-20

{29}   Deut 5: 6-18; Exod 20: 2-14

{30}   Gen 10: 22

Differentiating Between Good and Evil

How Evolving Life Forms and Human Beings Populated the Planet

What flowed out of Eden, what spread out from Eden, were primitive life forms including flesh eating predators. Genesis Chapter 2 records they spread out to lands called Havilah, Cush and Asshur. {1} <1>

Chapter 2 continues by describing the evolution of mammalian feelings and family life, of hominoids and Homo erectus (early man) <2>. Genesis then records how human beings evolved {1} and that Homo erectus was replaced by human beings <3>.

The flood left only a few survivors {2} and Chapter 10 describes the spreading out of human beings after the flood. The same names which earlier referred to lands to which primitive animals spread out from Eden, namely Havilah, Cush and Asshur, are all mentioned for the second time in Chapter 10.

The Behaviour of the Sons of Noah (Genesis Chapter 10)

Much effort has been spent in the past in relating the names of the different people listed and mentioned in this chapter to people, tribes, lands or countries. There is no obvious pattern, some of the names are unknown, some names refer to individuals or to communities without clear distinction.

But names of people and places are listed in different lines of descent in different generations to tell us that this chapter is about how human beings populated the planet and that they behaved much alike. That on the whole their behaviour was inhuman like that of their primitive ancestors. Genesis Chapter 10 does not distinguish between different types of behaviour.

The way in which names are listed to show this can be seen by the following two examples.

The three lands mentioned in Chapter 2, namely Havilah, Cush, and Asshur, are here all mentioned for the second time and all together, in the following lines of descent:

Havilah	In Ham's line, also in Shem's line
Cush	In Ham's line
Asshur	In Shem's line

Which seems to confirm that this is a record of the 'spreading out' of human beings regardless of descent, regardless of behaviour.

That no distinction is at this point being made between the descendants of the sons of Noah is confirmed by:

Sheba	In Ham's line, also in Shem's line
Lud	In Shem's line
Ludim	In Ham's line

> The descendants of the sons of Noah are listed for up to two generations. We are given names for their children and grandchildren. There are only two exceptions and 'Sheba' is one of them. 'Sheba' points to the meaning of Genesis Chapter 10 by being listed both in Shem's and in Ham's line of descendants.
>
> Lud and Ludim are another kind of exception in so far as Lud and Ludim (plural of Lud) are not mentioned elsewhere in the Pentateuch.

So Chapter 10 is a record of how the planet was repopulated by people increasing in numbers and spreading out, without distinguishing between good or evil behaviour, without distinguishing between lines of descent from the three sons of Noah as regards behaviour.

But a distinction was drawn by Noah between the behaviour of his sons in Chapter 9 of Genesis, particularly between the behaviour of Ham and Shem. This distinction is taken up again at the end of this chapter 10.

Noah distinguished between moral and immoral behaviour, and the resulting consequences, stating that 'good' gains strength and 'evil' weakens in accordance with the way people behave. And at the end of Chapter 10, and in Chapter 11, we are told that the world became divided, that a distinction was being drawn between good and evil, some behaving one way, some the other.

Differentiating Between Good and Evil (Genesis Chapter 11)

In Chapter 10 are listed the descendants of the sons of Noah for up to two generations. One of only two exceptions has just been discussed, namely 'Sheba'.

The second exception stands out. Shem's grandson Shelah has a son called Eber who has two sons called Joktan and Peleg.

In Chapter 10 are listed the names of thirteen children for Joktan, none for Peleg. But in Chapter 11 are listed the descendants of Peleg for five generations to Abram (the Patriarch), none for Joktan.

In addition, we are told:

Gen 10: 21 And to Shem, the father of all the children of Eber, the elder brother of Japheth, to him also were children born.

Gen 10: 25 And to Eber were born two sons; the name of the one was Peleg <4>; for in his days was the earth divided; and his brother's name was Joktan.

In other words, (Gen 10: 21) states that all the descendants of Eber, that is those of Joktan and of Peleg, are descended from Shem and that (Gen 10: 25) in Peleg's days the earth was divided.

And in Chapter 11, following the story about the tower of Babel, are listed the descendants of Peleg to Abram (the Patriarch Abraham).

So there is a clear division, a separation, between those mentioned in Genesis Chapter 10 and those mentioned in Genesis Chapter 11.

Figure 1   From Inhuman to Humane Behaviour after Being Scattered

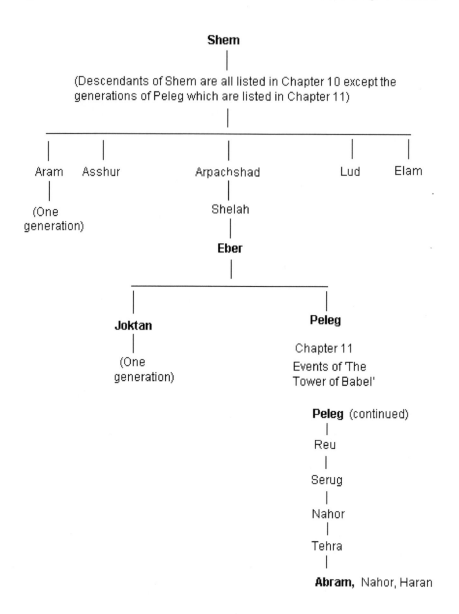

What lies between them are the 'Tower of Babel' events. We are told that as a result people were scattered from there over all lands, that different languages developed and that people ceased to understand each other. So different people would be developing differing customs, traditions, ways of behaving.

And some human beings, namely the descendants of Eber's son Peleg, become more and more aware of the difference between primitive inhuman (beastly) behaviour and of humane behaviour. And in the end learned to behave like human beings, as illustrated by the life and travels of the Patriarchs, learned to distinguish between good and evil, learned to behave humanely. {2, 3, 4}

And so the world was divided between those who continued to behave much as their primitive ancestors had done, and those who, knowing the difference between good and evil, decided to behave according to what was good, decided to behaved like human beings.

Notes and References

Notes

<1>   See {1} on 'Eden's Rivers' (Gen 2: 10-14)

<2>   Homo erectus: Erect man, much smaller skull size than modern humans.

<3>   Homo sapiens: Human beings, modern humans.

<4>   Hebrew 'peleg', that is 'Division'

References

{1}   See chapter 6.1: Creation, Evolution and the Origin of Evil
Manfred Davidmann, 2000

{2}   See chapter 6.2: Pre-flood Evils and the Social Problems of Our Time
Manfred Davidmann, 2000

{3}   See chapter 6.3: Morality, Sexual Behaviour and Depravity
Manfred Davidmann, 2001

{4}   See chapter 6.4: Nephilim, Dominance and Liberty
Manfred Davidmann, 2001

Meaning and Significance of the Names of God in Genesis

Names of God
Meaning of the Names of God
References   {..}

Names of God

Understanding the meaning and significance of the names by which God is referred to in the Bible is of the greatest importance for understanding the meaning of the text of the Bible.

Translations into English from the Hebrew text refer to God using three designations, namely God, Lord God, and Lord.

Hebrew	English
Elohim	God
Yhwh Elohim	Lord God
Yhwh	the Lord

Yhwh

This designation is generally represented by its four consonants.

It was apparently regularly pronounced with its vowels until the destruction of the First Temple. But its pronunciation was avoided from the third century BCE. From then on the Hebrew word consisting of the consonants Yhwh was pronounced 'Adonay' and translated as 'the Lord' although 'Adonay' means 'my Lords'. Hence Yhwh is being translated as 'the Lord'. {1}

The true pronunciation of Yhwh was apparently 'Yahweh', meaning 'He causes to be, He brings into existence'. In the Middle Ages vowel points were added to the consonantal form of the Bible. 'Those used for Yhwh produced the form YeHoVaH and Christian scholars then introduced the name Jehovah.' {1}.

So Yhwh, regardless of how you pronounce it, means 'He causes to be'.

Elohim

The word 'Eloha' means God, and its plural 'Elohim' means 'gods'. Elohim is usually translated as if it meant 'God'.

Yhwh Elohim

Yhwh means 'He causes to be' and also 'He brings into existence'. 'Elohim' means 'gods' but here also is usually translated as if it meant 'God'.
So 'Yhwh Elohim' means God brings into existence.

Hence the meaning and significance of the names of God is as follows:

Meaning of the Names of God

Hebrew Name	**ELOHIM**	**YHWH ELOHIM**	**YHWH**
Translated as	God	Lord God	the Lord
Derivation of Name	God who creates, Creating God	God who brings into existence, God who originates, Originating God	He causes to be, What took place was, What happened was, What is happening
Meaning of Name	**GOD** or **GOD (AS CREATOR).** God as creator, as creator of	**GOD (AS ORIGINATOR)**	**GOD (AS CAUSE)**, as cause of what happened.

all that is
good.

In other
words, this is
happening, is
what
happened.

Example 1: (Gen 7: 16)

And they ... went in (into the ark) ... as God (Elohim) commanded him;
and the Lord (Yhwh) shut him in.

Example 2: From {3}

In (Gen 3: 17) the ground is cursed by God (Yhwh Elohim, as originator),
meaning that it will be so.

(Gen 5: 29) states that God (Yhwh, as cause) has cursed, meaning that it
is happening, that it is so.

For detailed comprehensive discussions, illustrations and comments

on the meaning, significance and use of the different names of God in
the Bible, see reference {2}.

References

{1} Encyclopaedia Judaica
     Keter Publishing House Jerusalem Ltd, 1974
{2} See chapter 6.1: Creation, Evolution and the Origin
     of Evil
     Manfred Davidmann, 2000
{3} See chapter 6.2: Pre-flood Evils and the Social
     Problems of Our Time
     Manfred Davidmann, 2000

Meaning and Intent of Genesis: Essential Notes on Hebrew Grammar

'Adam' and Hebrew Grammar

Eth	'Eth' is put before the object of the sentence if the object is either a definite noun (has article 'ha') or a proper noun (proper name).
	Example: Jim ate the bread. 'Jim' is the subject, the doer of the action. 'Bread' is the object of the action.
Eth adam	'Adam' is the proper name of one person, refers to the person whose name is 'Adam'.
Ha-adam	Life form(s). Example: Human beings.
	As 'Adam' stands for 'life form', one can put 'ha' in front.
	If 'Adam' is a proper name, one cannot say 'ha-adam'. In other words, 'ha-adam' cannot refer to a person named 'Adam'.
Eth ha-adam	The life form is the object of the sentence. The life forms are the object of the sentence.

For detailed comprehensive discussions, illustrations and comments on the meaning and significance of the different forms of 'Adam' used in Genesis, see chapter 6.1 'Creation, Evolution and the Origin of Evil'.

Bible Translations, Versions, Codes and Hidden Information in Bible and Talmud

Introduction

When something does not make sense in a Bible text in the light of current knowledge, that is when we do not understand it, then it is our knowledge and understanding of the text which is inadequate.

When translators do not know or understand the intended meaning of a Bible text or think their then current knowledge or thoughts are way ahead of the Bible's, then their translations can obscure the original meaning of a text, can mislead.

And similarly misleading can be new versions which allow for or include then current popular words or phrases, views or ideologies.

The extent to which this has taken place can be judged by the examples which follow.

Knowledge for Understanding not Available at Time of Translation

Genesis describes the creation and development of the planet and of life, including the evolution of early man and modern human beings, and defines human behaviour stating what is good and what is evil. {1}

This deep knowledge has remained obscured till now because the Hebrew 'ha-adam' meaning 'life form' was ungrammatically taken to refer to an individual called 'Adam' because the term 'life form' could not be understood at that time. {5}

Similarly the meaning and significance of the names by which God is referred to in the Pentateuch (Torah, Five Books of Moses) is of great importance for understanding the text. The distinct meaning of the different names could not have been understood until recently. {1, 2}

Bible Versions (Making Changes)

In Genesis Chapter 5, the Septuagint and the Samaritan Pentateuch smoothed out the Masoretic chronology's listed life spans, each in a different way, and so smoothed out, obscured, clues needed for understanding the meaning of the text. {4}

Obscuring Meaning by Making Changes

Consider the names in Genesis Chapter 2 about rivers flowing out of Eden. Here the translators of the King James Bible apparently concluded that then current knowledge indicated that Cush and Asshur referred to Ethiopia and Assyria, even though these countries did not exist at the time of the events related in Chapter 2. By doing this they obscured the connection between chapters 2 and 10 of Genesis which confirms the meaning of the allegory of the rivers flowing out of Eden {1}, as follows:

	Name of	Hebrew	Named in Translation	
			Soncino Chumash	King James Bible
Gen 2: 13	Land	Cush		Ethiopia
Gen 2: 14	River	Hiddekel	Tigris	Hiddekel
	Land	Asshur		Assyria

Hidden Information in Pentateuch and Talmud

Where Pentateuch and Talmud contain hidden information, then this is pointed to, stated and confirmed, at the same time and in a number of different independent ways, to ensure the message is understood as it was intended to be understood.

In the Talmud, Jews did not openly write about Christian activists, Christian beliefs and Christians, they wrote about them in a roundabout way. A positive statement would be expressed using negatives or else turned upside down by stating its opposite. A good example is the hidden way in which the Talmud refers to Christians and early Christian beliefs in three different ways at the same time to make sure the meaning could not be misunderstood or misrepresented. {6, 8} <1>

Another example from the Talmud illustrates rather beautifully how opposites are used forcefully and convincingly to make a specific point which would have been unacceptable to the religious establishment if it had been openly stated. {7} <2>

Another example, in Genesis Chapter 5, is the hidden description of evil human behaviour before the flood. {4} <3>

And also, in Genesis Chapter 6, how verses 3 and 4 relate and confirm each other regarding the Nephilim. {9}

Use of Key Phrases for Linking Statements

A clear example of the use of key-phrases for linking statements comes from the travels of the patriarchs in Genesis. Three separate stories in different chapters form a connected statement. They are linked by the key phrase that in each case the patriarch is afraid of being killed by local men for the sake of his beautiful wife. That the linking is intentional is confirmed by a second key phrase, namely 'she is my sister'. {3} <4>

Another example, in the Gospels, connects the allegories of 'The Rich Young Man' and 'The Labourers in the Vineyard', the key phrase being 'But many that are first will be last, and the last first'. {6} <5>

And the Talmud records a key argument about whether the God-given Pentateuch or an establishment-favouring modification are to be taught and followed. Here also the statements are located in different volumes but connected by key phrases. {8} <6>

Politically Motivated Changes

Some changes have been and are politically motivated.

Take the argument in the Talmud about whether the God-given Pentateuch or an establishment-favouring modification are to be taught and followed. The argument clearly proves that it is the God-given Pentateuch which has to be followed. But Rabbinical Judaism (today's Judaism) ignores this and teaches the opposite, quoting only one statement out of context as if it were the concluding statement. {8}

A further example, from the Talmud, describes how the God-serving religious hierarchy was replaced by an establishment-serving religious hierarchy, and their antisocial changes to belief and practice. This is conclusively recorded in two different and separate ways which confirm each other. But Rabbinical Judaism (today's Judaism) does not teach this and so propagates a revisionist and antisocial version of Jewish belief and practice. {7} <7>

Another example comes from the Gospels. Matthew's gospel was the first to be written. It is closest to the events and so perhaps it is not surprising that it has always been the most popular and revered of the gospels. It was later followed by Mark's and this in turn was followed by Luke's gospel. The later authors were apparently aware of and knew the earlier gospels which seems confirmed by the successive changes which were made which changed the record of what Jesus taught and of the meaning of the stories and of the arguments. {6} <8>

Notes and References

Notes

<1> In {8} see what is recorded about R. Johanan b. Zakkai's disciple Joshua b. Hananiah.

<2> In {7}, under 'Shemaiah and Avtalyon', see '(1b) Identities and Purpose'. The verse begins with Naaman was a resident alien'.

<3> In {4} see 'Descendants of Seth (Behaviour of Human Beings'.

<4> In {3} see 'Sanctity of Marriage'

<5> See {6} about how this is recorded in different Gospels.

<6> In {8} see Figure 1 'Beth Hillel's Claims to Rule by Divine Right'

<7> In {7} see 'The Five Pairs (Zugot)' which includes Figure 2 'Names of the Pairs' and Figure 3 'Laying-on of Hands'.

<8> In {6} see 'Gospels'

References

{ 1} See chapter 6.1: Creation, Evolution and the Origin of Evil
Manfred Davidmann, 2000

{ 2} See chapter 6.6: Meaning and Significance of the Names of God in Genesis
Manfred Davidmann, 2000

{ 3} See chapter 6.3: Morality, Sexual Behaviour and Depravity
Manfred Davidmann, 2001

{ 4} See chapter 6.2: Pre-flood Evils and the Social Problems of Our Time
Manfred Davidmann, 2000

{ 5} See chapter 6.7: Meaning and Intent of Genesis: Essential Notes on Hebrew Grammar
Manfred Davidmann, 2000

{ 6}   ORIGIN OF CHRISTIANITY and JUDAISM
       Manfred Davidmann, 1994, 2006
       solhaam.org/

{ 7}   At the Time of Jesus, This is What Actually
       Happened in Israel: The Truth about Hillel and his
       Times
       Manfred Davidmann, 1978, 2007
       solhaam.org/

{ 8}   One Law for All: Freedom Now, Freedom for Ever
       Manfred Davidmann, 1978, 2007
       solhaam.org/

{ 9}   See chapter 6.4: Nephilim, Dominance and Liberty
       Manfred Davidmann, 2001

Chapter 7

About the Author

Manfred Davidmann is an internationally well-known and respected scientist and consultant, and author of a number of books and reports which have had considerable impact. His work usually breaks new ground and opens up new understanding and is written in meaningful and easily understood language. Outstanding is that his work is generally accepted as factual, objective and unbiased.

His works have made known and publicized the God-given human rights, social laws and social system, and the intense worldwide struggle to achieve them, to achieve freedom, liberty, independence and a good and secure life, here and now in this life.

His reports on motivation, for example, provide an objective, comprehensive and clear definition of 'motivation', of the factors which motivate and of what people are striving to achieve.

> "Motivated behaviour is purposeful, directed towards some end" says Manfred Davidmann. "The driving force is need. The direction is towards perceived reward and away from perceived punishment."

One works to achieve that which one needs and which one does not have. "Attaining goals leads to feelings of self-respect, strength and confidence", and "persistent lack of rewards leads to a view of society as being hostile and unrewarding".

Manfred Davidmann's first fundamental report on motivation, 'The Will to Work: What People Struggle to Achieve' (1981, 2006), includes a detailed step-by-step listing of what people are struggling to achieve, their needs and wants, their achievements and objectives. It is a unique analysis of the worldwide struggle for a better life at all levels of life and development, in all countries.

What we see in the working environment is each person, family or community struggling to advance at their own level of development.

How local and national governments are managing our affairs is of crucial importance to every citizen. Government has to make ends meet, has to bring about a rising standard of secure living, social security and an increasing quality of life for its citizens.

"There can be ups and downs but", says Manfred Davidmann, "failure to make ends meet is just as directly and surely the result of bad leadership and management as it is in any commercial enterprise." This is a severe criticism also of the kind of experts and consultants used, and of the way they are used. "The quality of one's experts and whether and how their expertise is used, and applied, are of decisive importance."

It was Manfred Davidmann who twenty years ago demolished the then-current economic myths about 'Price Inflation' and 'Wage Inflation', and about inflation and unemployment.

Fifteen years ago he coined the phrase 'Exporting Employment and Importing Unemployment', and pointed to, and warned about, the social and economic consequences of what is now often euphemistically called 'outsourcing' or 'globalisation'.

In his report **'Exporting and Importing of Employment and Unemployment'** (1996, 2002) he pointed out that imports were being priced at what the market will bear, or just under, and that if the enormous profit margins were left uncontrolled, these would then cause production to move from high-wage to low-wage countries. The consequence is a lowering of the standard of living in high-wage countries to that in low-wage countries, instead of a raising of the standard of living in low-wage countries to that in high wage countries.

"Unemployment has reached an unacceptable level" says Manfred Davidmann. It is a principle of economics that social costs have to be paid by those causing them. But manufacturers and suppliers tend to increase their profits by passing on to the community the social costs of their operations, costs such as disposal of packaging and waste, or of polluting.

"The social costs of unemployment have to be paid by the enterprise which caused the unemployment in the first place" says Manfred Davidmann. "Social costs need to be allowed for when taking decisions, need to be charged to the enterprise or organisation which is causing them. And this applies equally well to the social costs of redundancy and unemployment when transferring operations to countries with lower wages or fewer environmental safeguards."

In **'Democracy, Socialism and Communism: The Worldwide Struggle for a Better Life'** (2008) Manfred Davidmann outlined the battlefield in these terms:

Participative (democratic) organisation rests on the population electing representatives, on the basis of each person having one vote.

Representatives are responsible to, and accountable to, the population for putting into effect policies decided by the population.

What underlies participative organisation (democracy) is decision-taking by the people at the level of the people.

What needs to be stressed is that in a participative (democratic) organisation policies are decided by a well-informed population at the level of the population and that policies then become binding on management or government.

Representatives, governments or government officials do not have the authority or right to reduce or sign away the participative (democratic) rights of the electors, of the population.

The real struggle is not between political left and right, but is a struggle for participation, that is for the right of the population to be well-informed and to take the decisions which then become binding on management or government, as outlined by Manfred Davidmann in **'Multinational Summits and Agreements, Top-level Decision-taking and Democracy'** (2002).

In the report **"Family, Sex and the Individual"** (1998, 2011), Manfred Davidmann exposes the causes of what seems to be a progressive breaking down of family life and of social strength.

Clearly described and defined is the role of the family under modern conditions, and the differences between the behaviour of human beings and that of the primitive animals from which human beings evolved. He illustrated the underlying basis of teamwork within the family, stating the various roles and responsibilities and functional relationships of its members for effective teamwork within the family.

He was the first to clearly describe and show, eight years ago, the effects of increasing life spans on the family, on its members and on their responsibilities.

We now live much longer and the time spent full-time at home looking after the family places women at a disadvantage when returning to work outside the family after the children have been brought up. So women need to be supported when returning to work.

And Manfred Davidmann showed that the family compensates women for the life-long effects of their contribution towards the upbringing of the children. It is the role of the spouse, of the husband, to continue to provide for the family. A life-long contribution from him which means she does not lose out for the rest of her life because she stayed at home to look after the children, the husband's input into the family balancing her input of bringing up the children and looking after the family's members.

The report also investigates the impact of casual sexual relations and its effects on individuals, family and community, on the social strength of individuals and communities.

And the report examines and relates dominance and confrontation within the family to that in the working environment and considers oppression and exploitation within and outside the family.

Human rights are based on controlling primitive dominating behaviour, on concern, care and affection for our young and our families, for people and for our communities. Human rights express themselves in co-operation and teamwork between men and women to achieve a good life of high quality.

It is in democracies that a high standard of living has been achieved. In democracies people can struggle openly for a better life but we see that what has been gained has to be defended and extended.

This report is an unprecedented and comprehensive overview, states new insights, proves basic underlying causes. (See chapter 5)

Manfred Davidmann's groundbreaking discoveries about Judaism, Christianity and Islam, published over twenty-five years, are acknowledged as major advances. And in his report "**Judaism, Christianity and Islam**" (2004), we see for the first time the complete sequence of consecutive events.

Manfred Davidmann has shown that underlying Judaism, Christianity and Islam are the Pentateuch's benevolent and egalitarian social laws and social system which include laws protecting the people by restraining the behaviour of their rulers. Those in positions of trust, responsibility or authority must not oppress people and the laws forbid personal gain from the misuse of wealth or position.

He not only proves the meaning and intent of Genesis, the first volume of the Pentateuch, but also exposes the mistranslations and political misrepresentations of the past. For example he established the meaning of the names of God which had been 'lost'.

What Manfred Davidmann has done with his works on the Pentateuch and the Bible, on religion and church-state relations, is to expose and correct the misinterpretations and mistranslations of the past. His works are major breakthroughs, constituting essential information for understanding the meaning and significance of the Pentateuch and the Bible.

For example, in "**Meaning and Significance of the Names of God in Genesis**" (2000), Manfred Davidmann proved the meaning and significance of the different names of God which had been lost.

In "**Meaning and Intent of Genesis: Essential Notes on Hebrew Grammar,**" (2000) he stated the fundamental rules which were ignored at time of translation because required background knowledge was not available, with consequent mistranslations.

And in "**Bible Translations, Versions, Codes and Hidden Information in Bible and Talmud**" (2001), he showed how changes made in the past obscured the intended meaning.

Further, the Pentateuch records and details the Social Cause-and-Effect Relationship, a fundamental scientific law which is stated as such and which was discovered there by Manfred Davidmann. In his report '**Struggle for Freedom: The Social Cause-and-Effect Relationship**' (1978, 2002) he shows that this states that the consequences of keeping or not keeping the social laws are inescapable, that what happens to one is in the end the inevitable result of one's own behavior. It is stated to enable people to benefit from knowing the effects of their behavior.

Ignorance of these rules of behavior is no excuse and the relationship applies to all. History and social science confirm it, the prophets knew and understood it and predicted accordingly. Jesus confirmed it; the Koran records Prophet Mohammed repeatedly confirming the Pentateuch, referring to it both as a guide and as a warning.

Whole communities prosper or suffer as a consequence of their collective behavior. Manfred Davidmann says, "The consequences of our behavior cannot be avoided but we can change the course of events by changing our behavior."

And so his report "**The God-given Human Rights, Social Laws and Social System**" (2003) is a comprehensive statement of the human rights and obligations which underlie freedom, liberty, independence and well-being.

Directly relevant to today's social and economic problems, these rights and obligations determine the quality of life in areas such as social and economic security, social responsibility and accountability, ownership and decision-making, government and management, humane behaviour, teamwork and trustful cooperation.

Genesis and Evolution

Manfred Davidmann's report **'The Meaning of Genesis: Creation, Evolution and the Origin of Evil'** (2000) proves that there is no conflict or contradiction between Darwin's theory of evolution by natural selection and what is written in Genesis. Conflicts have arisen because some parts of Genesis have been mistranslated or misinterpreted.

The 'Creationism' hypothesis apparently assumes that the resulting erroneous text correctly states God's deeds. Following the publication of Manfred Davidmann's report, and of the publicity it generated, the 'Creationism' hypothesis was abandoned as untenable. But a similar hypothesis was then put forward called 'Intelligent Design' which apparently assumes that the same erroneous text could correctly state the deeds of some other supernatural being.

What Manfred Davidmann proved in **'The Meaning of Genesis: Creation, Evolution and the Origin of Evil'** (2000) was that Genesis clearly states the evolution from reptilian to mammalian instincts, feelings and behaviour and the evolution and behaviour of human beings from humanoids (animals resembling humans) through Homo erectus (early man) to Homo sapiens (human beings, ourselves).

For example, the allegory telling about Adam and Eve in the Garden of Eden describes the evolution of Homo sapiens (human beings, ourselves) from Homo erectus. Genesis records that childbirth became more difficult as a result of the increased brain size (evolution of neocortex) which enabled Homo sapiens to know the difference between good and evil and to choose between them. Also stated is the necessary division of work between the male and the female, as equals in different roles, in protecting and bringing up their children, and much more.

ISLAM: Basis - Past - Present - Future

Knowing about Prophet Mohammed's struggle for recognition of his mission and message, is of vital importance if one wishes to understand what Mohammed taught and the Koran. Just what upset the elite so thoroughly and persistently that it caused him and his followers to be harshly opposed and actively persecuted?

The events and struggles which took place after Mohammed's death, and how the Koran and Islam came to be, shaped Muslim belief and practice, formed Sunnism and Shiism, underlie today's conflicts and confrontations within Islam.

In his book 'ISLAM: Basis - Past - Present - Future', (2003, 2010) Manfred Davidmann assembles, evaluates and objectively records the events of the formative years which shaped Islam. He enables one to understand how Islam came to be and its present beliefs and practices, conflicts and confrontations.

Comprehensiveness of information, and depth of analysis, can be judged by the book's chapter headings:

Prophet Mohammed's Struggle for a Better Life for All (2003)

Text, Language, Dialect and Interpretation of the Koran (2003)

The Divine Right to Rule (2003)

Compiling the Koran: Hadiths (Traditions) State the Underlying Reality (2003)

Caliph Uthman's Rearrangement of the 'as revealed' Koran's Chapters (2003)

Prophet Mohammed's Word of Allah and the Voice of the Ruling Elite (2003)

Muslims and Jews (2003)

Church and State, Government and Religion

Judaism, Christianity and Islam (2004)

Religion, Government and Education (2004)

The book, and the earlier individual research reports which are included in it, contains not only Manfred Davidmann's clear and factual compilations about what actually happened after Mohammed's death, but also his comprehensive and detailed findings, definitions and conclusions about the 'Text, Language, Dialect and Interpretation of the Koran' (2003), about how the Koran was compiled and about its contents. Published 2003, guided to some extent by some of the Koran's 'abbreviated letters'.

General Management (Middle, Senior and Top Level)

As said already, Manfred Davidmann is an internationally well-known and respected scientist and consultant, and author of a number of books and reports which have had considerable impact. His work usually breaks new ground and opens up new understanding and is written in meaningful and easily understood language. Outstanding is that his work is generally accepted as factual, objective and unbiased.

He brings to his tasks a rare combination of practical experience, knowledge and understanding backed by years spent training middle and top-level managers. Expert knowledge is expressed in clear and meaningful language.

What Manfred Davidmann has done in his work on the general management of enterprises and communities is to lay the foundation for, and develop, what truly can be called 'management science'. He developed and defined the scope and content of General Management, in these reports:
Directing and Managing Change
Organising
Style of Management and Leadership
Motivation
Work and Pay, Incomes and Differentials:
Employer, Employee and Community

'**Directing and Managing Change**' (1979, 2006) includes
adapting to change, deciding what needs to be done;
planning ahead, getting results, evaluating progress and performance;
and appraisal interviews and target-setting meetings.

'**Organising**' (1981, 2006) is a comprehensive review showing how to arrange matters so that people can work together successfully and well. It is about achieving effective co-operation and teamwork, particularly in large organisations where many experts have to work together in teams to enable aims and objectives to be achieved.

The most confused and intractable organisational problems tend to be about functional relationships and coordinating. Concerning these, the report's descriptions, definitions, specifications and examples, are outstanding.

Manfred Davidmann's report '**Style of Management and Leadership**' (1981, 2006) is a landmark in management and community science and methodology. The term 'Participation', meaning by this 'participation in decision-taking', was first coined, and defined, by Manfred Davidmann when he published his analysis and recommendations about the style of management, in 1981.

It was Manfred Davidmann who formulated, clearly stated and then published his principle that the real political struggle was not between political 'left' and 'right', but was for participation in decision-taking, for the right to take the decisions.

Manfred Davidmann's concept of participative government and management, of participation in decision-taking, has become a household word, in daily use when referring to government and management styles, worldwide. His concepts are applied all the way from village government and community projects to national policies and elections, are applied by cooperatives, companies and global corporations alike.

Clearly defined and described in this report is the whole scale of style of management and organising, from fully authoritarian to fully participative. It applies to community organisations, commercial enterprises, political parties, whole countries. The social assumptions underlying each of the styles are given, as are problems they create, the symptoms by which they can be recognised, and the ways people work together or against each other within them.

The extent to which authority is balanced between top and bottom, and the corresponding style of management, are also discussed. This report pulls the diverse world-wide events in labour relations and in government/people confrontation into a meaningful, clear and highly significant picture of interrelated events fitting into a consistent pattern.

In '**Motivation Summary**' (1982, 1998), Manfred Davidmann summarises different motivation theories, draws on his earlier work including evidence from his U.K. study, and utilises material used by him for lecturing to degree-level students and for training experienced middle and senior managers.

Manfred Davidmann's report '**Work and Pay, Incomes and Differentials: Employer, Employee and Community**' (1981, 2007) is a concise all-embracing review and analysis of the whole subject, in clear and easily understood language. What makes this report so special is that it covers incomes and differentials from the point of view of the owner or employer, from that of the individual and his family and from that of the community, discussing their interests and requirements.

When talking about pay, incomes and differentials we are dealing with matters which are at the centre of confrontation and conflict and around which rage controversy and strife. We are dealing with matters which determine how one man stands in relation to another, with something which depends on negotiation and bargaining between those who employ and those who are employed. The result is that almost all one sees about pay and differentials is biased towards one side or the other and both points of view are then equally misleading.

But Manfred Davidmann here provides the underlying knowledge and understanding for scientific determination and prediction of rates of pay, remuneration and differentials, of remuneration scales and of national patterns of pay and differentials.

These correlations and methods represent a major breakthrough and rates of pay, incomes and differentials can be assessed with a high degree of reliability. Now pay bargaining can include agreeing basic guide-lines of the kind described here as governing pay increases.

Illustrated are National Remuneration Scales which record the remuneration pattern for a group or profession and the position of every individual in it, showing also how income depends on age and degree of success. Illustrated also is the National Remuneration Pattern which is a precise pictorial record of the differentials within a country, from top to bottom, from young to old. Both are used to assess changes in pay, remuneration and differentials for individuals, groups and professions.

However, it is easier to tell the rich to share their wealth with the poor than to persuade them to actually do so. And companies, corporations and governments, owners, managers, experts and politicians, too often work for personal gain instead of serving employees, customers or citizens, exploiting instead of serving their community.

Just consider the following examples of corporate and individual antisocial practices.

One of the most controversial operations of multinationals, transfer pricing, has been clearly described and defined by Manfred Davidmann in his report 'Multinational Operations: Transfer Pricing and Taxation' (1991, 2006).

The report showed that multinational companies were minimising their liability for corporation tax by transfer pricing, that is by making book entries which transfer profits to the country with the lowest corporation tax.

Say a multinational has increased its profits in such ways. As the government's expenses have not changed it must make up this shortfall elsewhere. From its other tax payers, say from its citizens. So its citizens pay more tax, the government can now spend the same amount as before, the multinational's profits have increased.

This tax avoidance is legal and governments have not legislated to prevent this practice.

The multinational, and this means the owners and directors of the multinational, are thus in effect taxing the country's citizens, its population, in this way increasing the multinational's profits and thus their own incomes and wealth.

A matter far removed from earning reasonable profits from providing needed quality goods and services at reasonable prices in open competition with other corporations.

And in "Inflation, Balance of Payments and Currency Exchange Rates" (1981, 2006), Manfred Davidmann explores how national and international accounts and accounting reflect the quality of management in national and local government, reflect multinational operations such as devaluation pricing, profits maximisation, transfer pricing, importing from low-wage countries, transferring work to low-wage countries. And he reviews different ways of balancing income and expenditure, causes of inflation, and tax avoidance.

In this report Manfred Davidmann reviews a country's ways out of a payments crisis and details the consequences of increasing interest rates, greater borrowing, selling assets or printing more money.

To give just a few examples, he:

> Shows how rising interest rates follow from balance of payments deficits.

> Shows how interest rates determine share prices and thus the extent to which pension funds are in surplus or underfunded.

> Shows how inflation affects currency exchange rates, trade and competing abroad.

Clear and meaningful language is backed by easily understood illustrations. And easy-to-follow diagrams illustrate the relationships.

Manfred Davidmann

ISLAM: Basis – Past – Present– Future

Knowing about Prophet Mohammed's struggle for recognition of his mission and message, is of vital importance if one wishes to understand what Mo-hammed taught and the Koran. Just what upset the elite so thoroughly and persistently that it caused him and his followers to be harshly opposed and actively persecuted?

The events and struggles which took place after Mohammed's death, and how the Koran and Islam came to be, shaped Muslim belief and practice, formed Sunnism and Shiism, underlie today's conflicts and confrontations within Islam.

In this book Manfred Davidmann assembles, evaluates and objectively re-cords the events of the formative years which shaped Islam. He enables one to understand how Islam came to be and its present beliefs and practices, conflicts and confrontations. Comprehensiveness of information, and depth of analysis, can be judged by the book's chapter headings:

>   Prophet Mohammed's Struggle for a Better Life for All
>
>   Text, Language, Dialect and Interpretation of the Koran
>
>   The Divine Right to Rule
>
>   Compiling the Koran: Hadiths (Traditions) State the Underlying Reality
>
>   Caliph Uthman's Rearrangement of the 'as revealed' Koran's Chapters
>
>   Prophet Mohammed's Word of Allah and the Voice of the Ruling Elite
>
>   Muslims and Jews
>
>   Church and State, Government and Religion
>
> >   Judaism, Christianity and Islam
> >
> >   Religion, Government and Education

Manfred Davidmann is an internationally well-known and respected scientist and consultant, and author of a number of books and reports which have had considerable impact. His work usually breaks new ground and opens up new understanding and is written in meaningful and easily understood language. Outstanding is that his work is generally accepted as factual, objective and unbiased.